Academic Language
for
English Language Learners
and Struggling Readers

How to Help Students Succeed
Across Content Areas

Yvonne S. Freeman & David E. Freeman

Foreword by Robert J. Marzano

HEINEMANN
Portsmouth, NH

Heinemann
361 Hanover Street
Portsmouth, NH 03801–3912
www.heinemann.com

Offices and agents throughout the world

Library of Congress Cataloging-in-Publication Data
Freeman, Yvonne S.
    Academic language for English language learners and struggling readers : how to help students succeed across content areas / Yvonne S. Freeman and David E. Freeman ; foreword by Robert J. Marzano.
        p. cm.
    Includes bibliographical references and index.
    ISBN-13: 978-0-325-01136-3
    ISBN-10: 0-325-01136-2
    1. English language—Study and teaching—Foreign speakers.   2. Limited English proficient students—Education—United States.   3. Language arts—Correlation with content subjects—United States.   4. Reading—Remedial teaching—United States.   I. Freeman, David E.   II. Title.

PE1128.A2F743 2008
428.2′4—dc22   2008037399

Editor: Lisa Luedeke
Production: Vicki Kasabian
Cover design: Jenny Jensen Greenleaf
Cover photograph: Julie Farias
Typesetter: House of Equations, Inc.
Manufacturing: Valerie Cooper

Printed in the United States of America on acid-free paper
    14 15 16   RRD   4 5

We dedicate this book to two teachers who have made a difference in their students' lives

To our daughter,
Mary Soto, a secondary teacher of English and ESL for more than ten years. In this book we used several examples from her classes because they exemplify a caring and knowledgeable teacher helping her students to develop academic language. It is a joy for us as parents to see the principles we have written about over several years demonstrated in her professional work.

To Rusty DeRuiter,
whose poem opens this book. In it, Rusty reflects the struggles of a caring, talented teacher faced with older students who lacked the academic language they needed to succeed, many of whom had given up on themselves. Rusty always looked for new ways to instill a love of reading and writing in all his students. When Rusty died unexpectedly in 2006, he left a legacy of former students who knew he cared enough to teach them the academic language they needed to succeed.

Contents

Foreword

Middle school and high school teachers face difficult challenges on a daily basis. The amount of content in the curriculum increases yearly, as does the pressure to help students pass high-stakes tests and move on to the next grade—or to graduate. With content and testing demands, teaching would be difficult enough if every student was well prepared.

The reality, however, is that many students are not well prepared for the mounting demands of secondary education. They lack background knowledge. They struggle to read content-area textbooks. They cannot write reports, summaries, and other kinds of academic papers in a manner that meets the expectations for their age and grade levels. For most secondary content teachers, these challenges represent new territory. They are well versed in their subject areas but were not trained to teach the basic reading and writing skills many of their students need.

Further complicating the situation, many secondary students—even some born in the United States—have limited English proficiency. Some native English speakers began school speaking another language, learned to speak and understand English, but cannot read and write it well. Other struggling students entered school speaking a nonstandard variety of English; they can communicate orally with little trouble, but find academic reading and writing beyond their immediate reach.

Add to all this the fact that because the issues associated with teaching these students are relatively new to American schools, few professional books in the marketplace provide strategies for simultaneously teaching secondary-level content-area knowledge and developing the literacy skills of students who aren't well prepared for academics. Yvonne and David Freeman's *Academic Language for English Language Learners and Struggling Readers: How to Help Students Succeed Across Content Areas* fills this need. Written specifically for secondary content-area teachers, it explains who these struggling students are and the specific support they need to succeed academically.

The Freemans distinguish among three types of English language learners (ELLs). Some are newly arrived in the United States but were well prepared in the schools of their homelands. They often succeed in school but face the challenge of learning English quickly enough to pass standardized exams. Others come with limited academic knowledge and limited literacy in their native language. These students must learn to read and write in English and develop content-area knowledge in it. Still others, the long-term English learners, have been in the United States for some time. Consequently, their conversational English is often quite good but they lack academic English.

In addition to the three types of ELLs, some struggling secondary students speak nonstandard English. For many of them, reading content-area textbooks and composing academic papers present big problems. Indeed, these students, referred to as standard English learners (SELs), show many of the very same characteristics as long-term English learners. With their classification system for students as a backdrop, the Freemans discuss what each type of student needs in order to read and write effectively in the different content areas.

The Freemans make an important distinction between two types of language: conversational language and academic language. A wide gulf often separates conversational and academic English. The differences, which extend well beyond mere vocabulary and into syntax, text organization, and register, help explain why an adolescent can speak English very well but might have trouble composing academic texts.

Academic Language for English Language Learners and Struggling Readers breaks academic language down into smaller and more discrete levels of organization, beginning with the text level and proceeding through the paragraph, the sentence, and finally to the word. Shedding light on the structure of academic genres, the text level, the Freemans show how genres commonly required in the different content areas can be made more accessible. The genres are then examined at the paragraph and sentence levels, to see how students can be given a chance to appropriate academic language in richer and richer ways. Students often write paragraphs that are not coherent or cohesive, and their sentences are either short and simple or convoluted and tangled. This book explains how to guide students toward writing well-organized paragraphs and complex sentences.

Reading and writing for school is difficult because many students lack academic vocabulary. The Freemans provide a thorough discussion of the nature and function of academic vocabulary leading to specific suggestions for increasing it through a combination of extensive reading, learning strategies, and the direct teaching of key content-area words.

The Freemans outline specific supports that can give English learners and struggling students ways to overcome the obstacles encountered with content-area textbooks. They also provide useful suggestions for supplementing textbooks, creating new avenues for students to take toward deeper subject-area understanding. They further provide classroom examples that demonstrate the kinds of instructional activities that motivate students and engage them in content-area reading and writing.

Academic Language for English Language Learners and Struggling Readers explains the particulars of an area of key importance to most every teacher: how to balance the dual objectives of content standards and academic language development. Students need to learn both, and teachers must have a well-written, differentiated plan to achieve these goals and help students learn to express content knowledge. Content and language objectives help teachers intentionally develop both content and language, and the Freemans provide specific examples of both types of objectives.

Putting all this well-researched information together into effective teaching is the crux of the matter, of course. The Freemans advocate organizing curriculum around integrated thematic units that keep the focus on teaching both language and content. All secondary students benefit from this sound approach, but the types of students on whom this book is focused should gain even more from it than their well-prepared peers. The Freemans' ideas for planning curriculum offer a highly effective framework for instructional design that allows teachers to differentiate their instruction to meet the needs of ELLs and struggling students while continuing to support the other students in their classes.

Teaching secondary students in the content areas is hard enough under the best of circumstances. When students are not well prepared academically and also lack academic literacy skills, the challenge can seem overwhelming. Fortunately, *Academic Language for English Language Learners and Struggling Readers* can help secondary content-area teachers provide these students with the academic support they very desperately need.

Robert J. Marzano
Centennial, Colorado

Acknowledgments

We wish to acknowledge the many people who encouraged and supported us in writing this book. Without their help, the book would never have become a reality.

First, we would like to thank all our friends at Heinemann. It is such a pleasure to work with this dedicated group of professionals. We want to give special thanks to Maura Sullivan, the editoral director at Heinemann. It was her encouragement that helped us finish this book, a book we found more difficult than others to complete. Maura also does a wonderful job of suggesting titles and promoting our books. Her expertise has made all our books better, and her friendship means a great deal to us.

Our editor, Lisa Luedeke, read the manuscript carefully and gave us very helpful suggestions. She helped us to rethink and rewrite some sections and some whole chapters. The result is a book that more clearly expresses the ideas we wish to convey. In addition to offering her helpful comments, Lisa encouraged us to keep writing.

The final book looks both appealing and professional thanks to the skills of our production editor, Vicki Kasabian. We are especially pleased with the new look of the cover. We very much appreciate the extra care she always takes with the details of our books.

We have worked with Beth Tripp on several books. The writing in the book looks much improved thanks to her copyediting skills. Beth always catches writing errors and makes good suggestions for improving our writing style. It is a pleasure to work with such a competent copy editor.

Leigh Peake, the former vice president and editorial director at Heinemann, supported and encouraged us in all our writing. Under her leadership, Heinemann consistently produced high-quality books for us. Thanks, too, to the rest of the team at Heinemann—Stephanie Turner, who helped prepare the manuscript, and Eric Chalek, who, among other things, helps with writing the back cover and advertising copy. The final book reflects the efforts of all the team at Heinemann.

We wish to acknowledge as well the many teachers and students who have helped shape our ideas about academic language. Francisco, whose story we tell, shows that with the right motivation from people in and outside of school, any student can succeed. William Roach shared the challenges that administrators face in trying to understand students who struggle academically. Student samples in the book illustrate important points about academic language. Our own students, including our current doctoral students, have helped us think more carefully about the different aspects of academic language. As we have discussed books and articles with them and then responded to their writing, we have gained a deeper understanding of what is involved in developing high levels of academic language proficiency. All these individuals have helped us to convey our ideas more clearly as we write about how teachers can support academic language development for English language learners and struggling readers.

Introduction

I Don't Know What to Do
Rusty DeRuiter

I don't know what to do.
So many angry faces
Who have heard all the teacher
Promises before.
For too many years
They have been put down.
Too many teachers
Who have given up.
Who have not understood.
And now it is big time.
High School.
Time to show and shine,
To be cool with *compañeros*,
To be tough.

It's tough to start school,
Especially when you are
Angry with life.
Having to ask for money
From parents who don't have it,
Wanting the right shoes,
And shirts and pants.
Needing to make your mark early.

Fathers and mothers
Come home late
With peach fuzz and grape juice
Deep into their fingernails,
With the smell of sweat
And the pain of swollen
Feet and hands,
And cuts from shoulder
To fingertips.
The fields are mean.

And the parents dream
Of success for their children.
"You need to work hard, *mi'ijo*,
To get the education I never had."
It is the parents' heart cry.
But they don't understand
The classroom pain of not knowing.
Of not knowing the big words.
Of not understanding what
The teacher says in class.
And of not asking
Because you are
Expected to know.
Because this is high school.
And the look you get
When you ask for help
Just one more time.
Mom and Dad know
The pain of the fields: But
They do not know
The pain of school.

Pretty soon you don't ask.
You learn to smile.
And day by day the wall
Grows taller.
Walls of words and sentences
And paragraphs and pages.
You learn to look busy,
To be always looking for the answer.
You learn to use María's knowledge.
To sit close to her,
At the right angle,
So you can see her paper
And the teacher can't see you.
Tricks.
Tricks of being a student
Without being a student.
Shine 'em on
And yet the pain is there.
Times of embarrassment when
It doesn't work out right,
When your *compañeros*
Are reminded of what you can't do.

In the quiet wood-paneled room,
Protected by night's blackness
And the familiarity of my big chair,
The unwanted tears slowly well up
And fall gently on my bare chest.
The anger, the fear,
And the deep sorrow
Fill my mind and my heart.
I know not what to do.

This powerful poem was written by Rusty DeRuiter, an experienced intermediate school teacher who, at the time of writing this poem, had just begun teaching developmental reading to struggling high school students. He wrote this poem late one night as he tried to understand both his students and his own frustration with teaching them.

Rusty was asked to teach these students because of his success with intermediate school students in his rural, agricultural district and because district officials did not know what to do with the growing numbers of students who were dropping out of school. Most of Rusty's students were of Mexican descent. They had started school speaking Spanish, now understood and spoke English well, but could not read or write at grade level.

At the time of the writing of this poem, Rusty already held a master of arts in reading and was working on his Bilingual Cross-Cultural Specialist Credential. He returned to graduate school because he wanted to understand his students better. Rusty was ahead of his time. Academic language was not yet being widely talked about at conferences or written about in journal articles and books. Still, Rusty's poem shows that he understood his students' need for being able to understand, read, and write the academic language of school.

Across the country, teachers are faced with classrooms filled with large numbers of students who struggle with the academic demands of school. Like Rusty, other teachers want to know how to help these students. With the current nationwide emphasis on standardized tests, exit exams, and other high-stakes assessments, attention has been given to students who lack the language of school. Many of these students are English language learners (ELLs) and struggling readers. Reports from educational agencies and literacy educators have begun to focus on the need for helping these students develop academic language, and *academic language* has become a kind of buzzword at conferences and inservice presentations. However, just what academic language is and what it entails have often been vague or limited to a discussion of vocabulary.

While many educators are concerned about their students' lack of academic language, few could define academic language, identify which students have it and which do not, or give specific ideas about how to help students develop academic language. In this book we attempt to bring together information from researchers, teacher educators, linguists, and practitioners in order to clarify some of the confusions about academic language and provide suggestions for how to help ELLs and struggling readers succeed in school. In the seven chapters of this book, we talk about the students who need academic language, what it is, when and where it is used, the problems that textbooks cause, the different aspects of academic language, how to write objectives to teach academic language, and how to engage students in effective instruction to build academic language proficiency.

We begin in Chapter 1 by describing real students and their academic struggles. We show the many challenges they face and the factors that influence their academic performance. Many of these students are English language learners, but an even larger number are no longer identified as ELLs and, in fact, have been in our schools for years. These long-term English learners (LTELs) usually speak English well but struggle with reading and writing. Other struggling students we describe are standard English learners (SELs). These students are native speakers of English who speak a variety of the language that differs from standard spoken English. Some SELs along with some students who come to school speaking standard English are below grade level in their ability to read and write academic texts. All of these students need academic language, and it is important that educators understand these different groups, their needs, their similarities, and their differences.

In Chapter 2, we review the differences between academic and conversational language proficiency. We report the research that shows how long it takes ELLs to acquire each type of language proficiency. Many ELLs have developed conversational English. In fact, they are quite good at talking in class and at trying to distract teachers from the reading and writing assignments that they find difficult. These students are not simply lazy or unmotivated. Their evasion of work is often a cover-up for their fear of being found out: they do not understand the academic texts they are expected to read and cannot express their ideas in academic writing.

For students who enter school speaking a language other than English, providing support for the development of academic concepts in their first languages while they are learning English is the best option. This approach provides students with the common underlying proficiency (CUP) that Cummins (1981) explains gives them something to draw upon when learning English. In other words, what an ELL knows in his first language transfers to English. Unfortunately, few students come to schools with a strong base in their first languages. Students with adequate formal schooling make up the smallest portion of English learners in most schools.

It is critical, then, that educators come to understand academic language and what it involves. In Chapter 3 we explain that there are different academic registers. When teachers understand these registers, they can better plan instruction to help students develop the academic language of the different content areas. In this chapter we also discuss the differences between oral and written academic language. Students need to develop both oral and written grammatical and communicative competence in English in order to succeed in school.

Students acquire competence in English through membership in social and cultural groups. All people acquire the ability to communicate appropriately within their own cultural groups. Gee (2008) refers to the way of speaking within our own context of culture as our primary discourse. We also acquire secondary discourses, and the discourse of school is one of them. Students must learn how to think, act, believe, speak, read, and write in a way that is expected in school. Some students come to school with backgrounds that facilitate the acquisition of school discourse, but many do not. ELLs, LTELs, and SELs have not acquired this discourse for a variety of reasons. In order to help students acquire school discourse, or the academic registers of school, educators should first understand the complexity of academic language.

We discuss academic language at the text level in Chapter 4. We begin by describing the characteristics of academic texts. We discuss the problems with textbooks and the challenges they present to students. After describing the problems with textbooks, we suggest ways to help students cope with the textbooks they are assigned in their content classes.

In Chapter 4 we also discuss the importance of involving students in informational reading early and of providing them with a variety of expository texts. We explain why middle school and secondary students are not engaged readers and discuss an engagement model of instruction. Through several examples, we show how teachers have helped ELLs and LTELs become more engaged in reading and suggest ways to organize and encourage reading in school.

At the text level, it is important to help students understand that there are different genres within each subject area. They need to be able to read and write the different genres and interpret the intent of each genre.

In Chapter 5 we consider academic language at the paragraph and sentence levels. Students need to learn ways to connect sentences to create coherent and cohesive paragraphs. At the sentence level, teachers must help students understand how to construct complex and compound sentences and how to use signal words. Knowing how and when to combine sentences appropriately does not come naturally to students, and they need different supports to learn how to do it.

Because vocabulary development is so important and has received so much attention in schools, we devote Chapter 6 to a discussion of academic language at the word level. Students have to learn content-specific words in the different content areas, those key words for the content being studied. However, students also need to learn general academic words that are used across content areas. Within math, *multiply* and *fraction* are content-specific words. Words such as *analyze* and *prove* are general academic words found in science, literature, economics, and social studies. Often teachers do not emphasize the general academic words because they assume students know them.

In Chapter 6 we also discuss the importance of writing both content and language objectives. Content teachers who support students struggling with academic language realize that in order for their students to succeed, they should be able to understand and use the academic language of their subject area. Each time they teach a lesson, the teachers ask themselves, "What language do my students need to be able to understand, talk, read, and write about this concept?" In other words, students need to learn not only the content but also the language of the content. Educators can help students with the language of their content area by writing language objectives as they plan. Including content and language objectives in lesson planning helps teachers make lessons comprehensible for students who have trouble understanding academic tasks.

We begin our final chapter by discussing the scarcity of appropriate instruction for struggling readers and writers and the need for challenging curriculum for students who do not speak English well. We list recommendations from key studies. Teachers whose curriculum encourages identity, engagement, and motivation are most likely to reach all their students, including ELLs and struggling readers. Teachers can encourage identity, engagement, and motivation by teaching both language and content, organizing around themes, and including culturally relevant books.

Our final classroom example shows how Mary, a high school teacher, engages struggling high school students in meaningful literacy activities, how she motivates them to participate actively in classroom activities, and how she encourages them to identify with what they read and write.

Academic language is a complex topic. Throughout this book, we provide specific examples from different content areas to help readers understand what it is and how to support its development. We encourage educators to get to know their students so that they will understand their students and their students' needs. When teachers organize their curriculum in ways that support the development of both content knowledge and academic language, they provide their students with what they need for academic success. We invite you to consider the ELLs, LTELs, SELs, and native English-speaking struggling readers you work with and, then, as you read this book, to carefully plan your instruction in ways that will support the development of academic language.

Academic Language
for
English Language Learners
and Struggling Readers

1

Understanding Who Needs Academic Language

Monday morning's administrative meeting fueled a heated discussion of who the English Languages Learners (ELLs) at Wayland High School were. One administrator stated that they were all the students in the English as a Second Language (ESL) program, another administrator insisted they were ESL students and the students classified as Limited English Proficient (LEP), a third administrator argued that regardless of their official classification, all of the students whose first language, natural language, was not English were ELLs. "It does not matter how long a student has been attending school in the United States, they are still ELLs," he argued.

What ignited this debate in a normally tranquil administrative meeting? A decision had to be made as to what needed to be done to help native Spanish speakers, many of whom have communicative competence in English, what Cummins calls BICS (Basic Interpersonal Communicative Skills), but not academic English competence, what

Cummins calls CALP (Cognitive Academic Language Proficiency), be more successful in their core content-area courses.

This quote comes from a paper written by William, a doctoral candidate studying curriculum and instruction with an emphasis in bilingual studies at our university in South Texas. He is an administrator in a district in the border area where the university is located. The discussion the administrators were having was not insignificant. The most recent demographic data for the district's schools, much like that of most of the schools along the Texas-Mexico border, showed a 97.6 percent Hispanic population with 23 percent officially identified as limited in English and 64 percent classified as at risk (PEIMS 2006).

Demographic Trends

The administrators' concerns at Wayland High School are real and are the same concerns educators across the country are discussing. There are too many students in our schools who are struggling academically and often fail high-stakes standardized tests. A large number of these struggling students started school speaking a language other than English and are the children of first- or second-generation immigrants. Reports show that one in five children in K–12 schools has at least one parent who was born outside the United States, and it is expected that that number will soon rise to one in four. This population of ELLs is dispersing, and they are now not only in the five most highly populated states of California, New York, Texas Florida, Illinois, and New Jersey but moving into states such as Nevada, Nebraska, and North Carolina. These states have experienced increases as high as 205 percent (Capps et al. 2005).

Many of the newcomer children are appearing in secondary and middle schools, and, in fact, one in three foreign-born immigrants is found in grades 6 through 12. In these middle and high schools, there are fewer resources allocated for English learners than there typically are in elementary schools. In addition, fewer educators at secondary schools are prepared to provide the language and literacy instruction these students need (Cohen, Deterding, and Clewell 2005).

These are not the only considerations that educators must take into account when planning for new immigrants. Schools, especially urban schools, are seeing growing poverty among immigrant children. For example, 2002 data shows that 47 percent of foreign-born students in grades 6 through 12 were from low-income families and 60 percent of all LEP children in schools were from homes with high poverty rates (Capps et al. 2005).

Although these demographics on recent immigrants are alarming, perhaps an even greater concern for educators is another, less obvious population of ELLs: long-term English learners. These students have been in school for seven or more years and may even be the children of second- or third-generation immigrants. More than half of the students identified as LEP in secondary schools are LTELs born in this country (Batalova, Fix, and Murray 2007; Fix 2005). The fact that this large number of students is still classified as limited English proficient at the secondary level indicates that these students are not being well served by our schools.

In the spring of 2008, we presented a webinar on types of English learners and effective approaches for working with them to more than six hundred educators across the country (see Freeman and Freeman 2008). We described three types of learners: newly arrived with adequate formal schooling, newly arrived with limited or interrupted formal schooling, and long-term English learners. During the webinar, we took a poll asking participants which of the three types of learners were most common in their schools. Only 3 percent of the participants reported that most of their ELLs were recent arrivals with adequate schooling, 38 percent had a majority of newly arrived students with limited or interrupted schooling, and 58 percent had more long-term English learners than other types.

The results of the poll for long-term English learners further confirms that many secondary ELLs have been in U.S. schools for a number of years without developing academic English. Schools are not providing the instruction these students need. Programs have not developed the first languages of the long-term learners. They speak English quite well but do not have the underlying base in their first languages to transfer the knowledge they need for academic success. The general public and, in fact, most educators believe that more English equals more English, when the truth is the opposite. More first-language knowledge equals more English, as we discuss in more detail in Chapter 2.

A last complicating factor confirmed by national data is that most ELLs are in schools with many other students like them. The result is that the ELLs are economically, ethnically, and linguistically isolated from mainstream students. These "high LEP schools are disproportionately failing to meet state standards"; they are "more heavily urban and larger than schools with few or no LEP students," and "their principals and teaching staffs are less experienced" (Fix and Capps 2005, 3). In Texas, a state "whose standardized, high-stakes accountability system became the model for the nation's most comprehensive federal education policy" (McNeil, Coppola, and Radigan 2008, 1), more than 135,000 young people drop out yearly. A recent study of over 271,000 students in a large, urban district in Texas revealed dropouts are actually caused by an accountability system with high-stakes tests, and those most affected are "our most vulnerable youth, the poor, the English language learners, and African American and Latino children" (2). All these facts and figures signal alarming trends. It is apparent that schools, especially middle and high schools, face seemingly insurmountable challenges.

ELLs are not the only struggling learners whose challenges are related to language. There are also native English speakers whose dialects are nonstandard, students whose home languages differ in structure and form from standard academic English. These standard English learners may live in the rural areas of Maine or Oklahoma or may live in cities with parents who learned English as a second language themselves. While ELLs are the key focus of this book, we also acknowledge this group and suggest that these students also need support with the academic language of school.

The focus of this book is on describing academic English and explaining how teachers can support ELLs and struggling readers as they develop academic English. Goldenberg explains that academic English is

> a term that refers to more abstract, complex, and challenging language that will eventually permit you to participate successfully in mainstream classroom instruction. Academic English involves such things as relating an event or a series of events to someone who was not present, being able to make comparisons between alternatives and justify a choice, knowing different forms and inflections of words and their appropriate use, and possessing and using content-specific vocabulary and modes of expression in different academic disciplines such as mathematics and social studies. (Goldenberg 2008, 2)

Getting to Know the Students

The administrators at Wayland High School were on the right track because they all recognized that they needed to identify their English language learners in order to begin to meet students' needs. As the administrators realized, a simple LEP designation is probably not enough to identify which students need academic support. In order to succeed in course work and to pass standardized tests, ELLs need to be able to read academic texts, discuss them, and write academic papers.

Schools need to identify the types of ELLs they serve and know the needs these students have. Let's consider four students who are representative of two types of English learners who lack academic language skills and struggle in schools, long-term English learners and students who arrive in our schools with limited formal schooling. By looking at the specific characteristics of these two types of ELLs, it is easier to decide what kinds of instruction will help these students succeed.

Long-Term English Learner: Teresa

Teresa has been in schools in the United States since kindergarten and speaks English well; yet, according to her seventh-grade language arts teacher, she arrived in junior high school without being able to write paragraphs in English. She lives in a city in the Central Valley of California, where she attends a large inner-city school. Teresa's mother works in a laundry, and her father works for a farmer on the outskirts of the city. Neither parent had more than an elementary school education in Mexico, and although they both attended adult ESL classes on and off, they do not speak, read, or write English well. Teresa serves as their language broker. She translates when her parents go to the doctor, do business with different agencies, and attend school conferences.

When she was younger, her parents were migrant workers. From May to October, Teresa traveled with the family to Washington and Oregon, where she worked to help support the family and did not attend school at all. Because school officials told her parents how important it was for Teresa and her siblings to stay in school all year long, her parents decided not to travel any more and chose to settle in their present location because they have relatives living there.

Teresa is the oldest of four children and has many responsibilities at home, including cooking and cleaning, because her parents work long hours at their jobs. She also spends time with her extended family, and she often serves as a caretaker for her younger cousins as well as her siblings. Her family goes to Mexico each year in December, staying a month because of strong family ties there.

Teresa is an extremely quiet and shy student. The only time that she is vocal and outgoing is when she is playing soccer. In the classroom, Teresa is so shy that she talks only in groups of other Latinas, preferably her personal friends. During her schooling Teresa has been in and out of bilingual and ESL classes, but she has not developed grade-level literacy skills in Spanish or English. She also lacks content-area knowledge. Because she behaves well and turns in her assignments, she earns Bs and Cs. However, Teresa doesn't really understand much of what she studies, and her scores are very low on standardized tests. It is questionable whether she will be able to succeed academically in high school.

Long-Term English Learner: Yan-Cheng Chang

Yan-Cheng Chang (known as Chang to his friends) has also been in schools in the United States since kindergarten and speaks English well. Chang's parents came to the United States from Taiwan before Chang was born. His father found a job in a Chinese restaurant in a semirural part of Texas where other relatives worked. His mother took care of him until he was old enough to go to school and then began to work in the restaurant as well. Chang's parents are unable to help him with his homework. Both parents work nights in the restaurant and speak only enough English to take orders and communicate with others at work. Interestingly, they can communicate in basic Spanish because so much Spanish is spoken in the area where they live and some coworkers are Spanish speakers.

At home the family speaks Taiwanese. Chang understands Taiwanese and speaks some, but he is more comfortable in English even though he entered school as a monolingual Taiwanese speaker. He also has conversational Spanish because so many of his classmates speak Spanish. All his schooling has been in English. During his elementary years Chang was a low to an average student, but when he reached junior high school, his struggle with academic work became more apparent.

Chang is outgoing and popular among his peers, but his high school teachers have told administrators that they doubt he will be able to pass the tenth-grade exit exam. He talks a lot in classes but avoids reading and writing whenever possible. It is clear to his teachers that he does not understand much of what he reads. His writing contains many errors in mechanics, and his organization is poor. He is a classic example of a student who has good conversational English but lacks academic English.

His teachers tried to give him extra homework, and he was put into an after-school tutoring program. Chang didn't seem to try very hard, and once he got into high school, he began to be seen as a student who didn't care and had no motivation. Chang's parents have been told he is doing poorly in his studies. They try to force him to study, but they don't understand when he tells them the work is too hard and he doesn't understand it. He wants to quit school as soon as possible and start working in a restaurant like his parents.

Analysis of Teresa and Chang

Teresa and Chang are both long-term English learners, students who have been in schools in the United States for seven or more years and speak English quite well. Some, like Chang, were born here. This group has grown to be the largest group of concern for educators. Although many are not officially designated as LEP, they do fit that definition under current federal law. According to the No Child Left Behind (NCLB) Act of 2001, LEP students have specific characteristics related to where they come from, their primary language, and their academic success.

NCLB (U.S. Congress 2002) defines an LEP student as someone between the ages of three and twenty-one "who was not born in the United States or whose native language is a language other than English or who comes from an environment where a language other than English has had a significant impact on the individual's level of English language proficiency" (section 25, [A] [B]). The definition includes migrant students who come from homes where English is not the dominant language. Perhaps most significantly, LEP students are defined by NCLB as students "whose difficulties in speaking, reading, writing, or understanding the English language may be sufficient to deny the individual (i) the ability to meet the State's proficient level of achievement on the State assessment" and "(ii) the ability to successfully achieve in classrooms where the language of instruction is English" (section 25, [D] i, ii).

Certainly, both Teresa and Chang fit this definition. They also fit the definition of Generation 1.5 students described by Harklau (2003), who points out that Generation 1.5 students are a very diverse group with some common characteristics. These students come from homes where a language other than English is most frequently spoken. Generation 1.5 students may have attended school here for several years and may even have been born in this country. They are "equipped with the social skills in English" and "appear in conversation to be native English speakers"; "however, they are usually less skilled in the academic language associated with school success" (1). As Harklau explains, Generation 1.5 students are likely to struggle with the academic language needed in school, language that is not simply the typical language of social interactions.

Harklau's description of Generation 1.5 students helps us understand Teresa and Chang. Both come from homes where a language other than English is spoken. They have spent many years in this country. Their conversational English is nativelike. Yet they both struggle academically and are in danger of failing high-stakes tests. Their teachers realize they have trouble reading and writing but do not understand the reasons for this. Teresa responds to her academic difficulties by remaining silent in school except with her friends, while Chang is social but seems to be resisting school and is in danger of becoming a dropout. There are many students in U.S. schools who have characteristics similar to those of Teresa and Chang. It is important that administrators and teachers recognize this type of ELL so that they can plan how best to help them.

A second type of ELL that educators must understand how to help is the newcomer who arrives in school with limited formal schooling. Limited formal schooling (LFS) students are older immigrants who, for a variety of reasons, received little to no education in their home countries. A look at two examples will help to flesh out the characteristics of this type of ELL.

Limited Formal Schooling Student: Ismael

Ismael first came to the United States at age fourteen. Only a few days after arriving, he enrolled in a large rural ninth-grade school located on the border between Mexico and the United States. His mother had decided to leave her rural village because of constant mistreatment from Ismael's father. She and her son found asylum with relatives who lived in the area.

From the beginning Ismael seemed resistant to school. The teacher of his newcomer class believed it was because he was aware of how hopeless his academic situation was. Ismael knew he could not speak English and was behind many of his peers in academic Spanish. In Mexico, he had attended school only sporadically. The nearest rural school closed frequently because there were no teachers. When there was school, he seldom did homework because his home situation was chaotic. As a result, his reading and writing skills in Spanish were the equivalent of about a second or third grader, and his academic content knowledge was equally limited.

In his new school, his ESL teacher, who spoke Spanish, used many different strategies to try to engage her students, but Ismael sat at his desk and did nothing for several weeks. One day his teacher offered an activity she hadn't tried before. She told him he could write a letter in Spanish to anyone he wanted to. Ismael spent two class periods writing a romantic letter to a girlfriend using his limited skills in writing in Spanish. After that breakthrough, Ismael began to participate more. When he went to high school the next year, his ESL teacher from the previous year also moved there. She saw that he was beginning to gain a little bit of English. However, he was so far behind, there seemed little hope of his ever being able to pass the state test for tenth graders.

Limited Formal Schooling Student: Halima

Halima, a Somali Bantu refugee, came to the United States at sixteen. Before coming to the United States, she and her family, which included her parents and six other siblings, spent more than ten years in refugee camps in Kenya. At first they were at Dadaab, a refugee camp of more than 100,000 Somalis living in extremely crowded and difficult conditions.

The last two years before coming to the United States, Halima and her family were moved to Kakuma, an even poorer refugee camp where girls did not attend school often because they did not have proper clothes to wear. Being a Somali refugee was difficult, but being a Bantu meant Halima and her family suffered discrimination even among fellow Somalis. Because of the hardships the Somali Bantu have suffered and because there was no other country to take them in, the United States offered them asylum in 2003.

Halima's family immigrated to the Minneapolis–St. Paul area, home to the largest number of Somali refugees in the United States. Although Halima had attended a two-week orientation in the refugee camp, nothing prepared her for life in the big city. Almost overnight the family moved from sleeping on the ground, huddled together in a space smaller than most bathrooms, to living in a three-bedroom apartment with modern-day gadgets and television.

School posed even more challenges. All the children in the family needed to learn English, but the older ones, like Halima, lacked not only English but also the content knowledge expected at their grade levels. Although refugees like Halima bring many experiences with them, those are not the experiences that help them understand the school system and the academic expectations the system has for them.

Halima works hard and has learned an amazing amount of English in her first year in school. However, she realizes that she is significantly behind her native English-speaking peers. She also sees that the drills with sounds and basic English are not really helping her with the academic work she needs to understand. While she is grateful for the opportunity to go to school, she has begun to wonder if her dreams of becoming a doctor someday are unrealistic.

Analysis of Ismael and Halima

Ismael and Halima represent recent arrivals with limited or interrupted formal schooling. Limited formal schooling (LFS) students come to school in this country with limited academic knowledge and limited English proficiency. Students like Ismael and Halima struggle with reading and writing in English. Most students with limited formal schooling are significantly below grade level in reading and writing in their native language. In addition, they lack basic concepts in the different subject areas. LFS students are usually at least two years below grade level in areas that are not heavily language dependent, such as performing math computations.

Students like Ismael and Halima are faced with the complex task of developing conversational English, becoming literate in English, and gaining the academic knowledge and skills they need to compete with native English speakers. Because they do not have academic English or the academic background to draw upon in their native languages, they often struggle with course work in English and receive low scores on standardized tests. Many also lack an understanding of how schools are organized and how students are expected to act in schools.

Standard English Learners

In this book we particularly want to address the academic language needs of ELLs. However, as mentioned earlier, we also want to acknowledge another group of students, many of whom lack adequate levels of academic language. These students are struggling readers who speak English as their native language. They are referred to as standard English learners because although they understand Standard English, they do not speak it. They "are those students for whom Standard English is not native and whose home language differs in structure and form from standard academic English" (Los Angeles Unified School District 2002, 2). Students labeled as SELs come from various groups including African Americans, Native Americans, Mexican Americans, and Hawaiian Americans.

Students from these groups have traditionally been marginalized from schooling, and it is questionable whether it is their language differences or other influences that result in their poor academic performance. Ogbu and Matute-Bianchi (1986) have explained how certain groups often do poorly in school for reasons in addition to language differences. It is important to understand these factors when evaluating the academic language needs of both standard English learners and long-term English learners and also to understand how these students differ from limited formal schooling students.

Ogbu's Classification of Immigrant and Involuntary Minority Students

Ogbu (1991) distinguished between two types of minority students: immigrant and involuntary. Many limited formal schooling students have the characteristics of immigrant minorities. On the other hand, many long-term English learners and standard English learners have the characteristics of involuntary minorities.

Immigrant minorities • Immigrant minority groups are not generally influenced by the attitudes and values of the mainstream society because they measure their success by the standards of their homeland. New students from Somalia or rural Mexico, for example, might be living in poverty by U.S. standards, but their condition in the United States is probably much better than what it was in Africa or the Mexican countryside.

In addition, as Ogbu pointed out, the cultural differences between immigrant minorities and the mainstream are primary differences that existed before the cultures came into contact. These differences are specific and easy to identify. They include such things as language, food, customs, and clothing. So, for example, Francisco, an immigrant student from El Salvador, happily eats *pupusas*, thick tortillas that are stuffed and grilled, at home but realizes he won't find those for sale at school.

In his research Ogbu found that immigrant minorities could alternate their behavior between home and school. For example, at home Halima and her family cook, eat, and interact much like they did in Africa. At school, however, the children work very hard to fit into their new culture. They dress in Western-style clothes, study hard-to-learn English, and are anxious to learn as much as possible about the culture and customs of their new country.

Sikh students from India often take on some aspects of Western dress in school and speak English there. At school, they can dress and act in ways that would not be appropriate at home. At home, they have to dress, speak, and act according to their cultural norms. However, alternating behavior between home and school is not something immigrant minorities find difficult. They assume that they must do this to succeed in the school world, and they conform to maintain cultural traditions and values at home. In addition, some immigrant minorities are motivated by the belief that they can go back to their homeland someday and use the skills and academic degrees they earn in the United States.

Most members of immigrant minority groups are highly motivated to adapt to the U.S. culture because they believe that it will enable them to succeed. However, two points should be noted. First, since the time that Ogbu conducted his research, many more older immigrant minority students have arrived in the United States. Second, many of these students have interrupted or limited formal schooling. While younger immigrant minorities may succeed academically because of factors such as high levels of motivation and the ability to alternate behavior between home and school, older immigrants, such as Ismael and Halima, face a formidable challenge. They have a great deal to learn in a short time. Although they are highly motivated, they often need extra help to achieve academic success, and they may need more time than traditional school systems allow.

Involuntary minorities • The other category of students Ogbu identified, involuntary minorities, includes groups like African Americans, Mexican Americans, and Native Americans. Many of them have lived in the United States for generations. These are minority groups who either were in the United States before it became a country, were brought as slaves, or lived in regions, such as the Southwest, where wars resulted in border shifts. Since many members of these groups have lived in this country for generations, they are highly influenced by majority-group attitudes and values and measure success by mainstream standards. They cannot export skills or academic degrees to a distant homeland.

According to Ogbu, involuntary minorities are characterized by secondary cultural differences. These are differences that developed after the cultures came into contact, and they are more a matter of style than content. They might include different ways of walking, talking, or dressing designed to signal identity in a particular social group. For example, they may wear gang colors and dress in styles that other members of their gang wear. Not all involuntary minorities are gang members but few are part of the mainstream school culture. Since the differences are intended to indicate distinctions between the minority group and members of mainstream culture, involuntary minorities generally do not alternate behavior. They act the same way at school and outside school.

In many cases, involuntary minorities develop a folk theory for success that puts a low value on education. Successful members of involuntary minority groups generally move away from the area where they grew up, so they don't serve as positive role models for other group members. Often, involuntary minorities, then, do not put a high value on education and see few, if any, examples of success related to education. Not surprisingly, involuntary minorities have higher rates of school failure than immigrant minorities. Many LTELs and SELs have the characteristics of involuntary minorities. A look at one example of an SEL who is also an involuntary minority might help educators better understand the challenges these students and their teachers face.

Standard English Learner: Victor

Victor is a seventeen-year-old now serving a two-year prison sentence for robbery. Victor's mother is a Mexican American who was born here. She understands Spanish but speaks only English. She dropped out of high school at seventeen to marry Victor's father, who left her shortly after Victor was born. She later married a man from El Salvador. He came to the United States in his teens but never finished high school. He has been here for more than thirty years and speaks English but is more comfortable in Spanish. He has not had a strong influence on Victor.

When Victor began school he could understand some Spanish but spoke mainly English. During his elementary years, he was an average student at the neighborhood school and seemed to be progressing fairly well. However, when Victor went from elementary school to middle school, he was separated from his elementary school friends. At the large inner-city middle school, he was threatened by older boys, and they encouraged him to join a gang. His mother realized that separation from his friends was a problem and tried to get Victor transferred, but school officials refused her request.

Unfortunately, Victor seemed to lose interest in school. He didn't do his homework and complained that the work was either too difficult for him or boring. His grades at the end of his seventh-grade year were all Ds and Fs. Victor's friends at school did not study and encouraged him to go out with them after school. Victor's parents seemed to be losing their authority over him, and when he was at home there was a great deal of fighting between the parents and their son about his schoolwork, the gang clothing he was wearing, his friends, and his lack of respect.

Victor's mother turned to her husband's El Salvadoran family for advice and help. One cousin had graduated from college and was a teacher. He tried to encourage Victor to work hard in school, join a sports team, and make the right kinds of friends. He talked to Victor about the importance of the family and of showing respect and working hard. However, Victor did not feel comfortable at family events. His Spanish was limited, and he could not really understand the importance the family put on family loyalty, respect, and hard work.

When Victor got to high school, the situation became worse. One high school counselor told Victor's mother that he was not college material and that he should perhaps get a job and forget about school. Victor complained that his classes were irrelevant and too difficult. He began to skip school and was eventually arrested when he and other gang members were caught robbing a sporting goods store.

Victor is a classic example of an SEL who is an involuntary minority. His parents wanted him to succeed but did not really know how to help him. His stepfather did not spend much time with him, and Victor did not form a strong connection with his stepfather's side of the family. He joined the gang to have somewhere to belong. Victor had serious academic needs in junior high and high school, but his situation was complex. His academic needs might have been met if he had been better understood. Victor developed conversational fluency in English, but he lacked the academic language he needed to succeed in school.

Standard English Learner: Jason

We do not want to give the impression that only SELs from historically marginalized ethnic groups and ELLs struggle with the academic tasks of school. Jason is not from one of the groups listed previously, but he lacked the academic language needed to succeed in schools.

Jason was born in Oklahoma and attended elementary school there in a small town. He never knew his father, and because his mother was an alcoholic, he was moved into foster homes until his maternal grandmother was given custody. She moved to a city in central California with Jason where they lived in a trailer park.

Jason went from a small rural school to a large middle school of almost two thousand students. Students and teachers alike noticed his accent, and he sensed they looked down on him because of it. His language arts teacher was shocked at Jason's lack of writing and reading skills and had him tested for learning disabilities. Based on the test results, Jason was labeled as dyslexic. School officials reasoned that because Jason could not do the reading and writing required in regular classes, he should spend part of his school day in the resource room.

Despite his academic problems, Jason was outgoing and made friends easily. In high school, he got involved with backstage work for the school drama group and found a girlfriend among the drama students. It was hard for Jason to be in resource classes part of the day because the rest of his friends were not in special classes and did quite well academically. He looked at the kind of work those students could do and felt hopeless. He couldn't read content-area textbooks and had no idea where to start when he was given reading assignments. He had to ask for help from his girlfriend to properly fill out a job application.

Jason accumulated enough credits to graduate from high school. At the time he attended, the school did not require an exit exam. After high school, he took classes at the local junior college but got discouraged when he failed the remedial writing class for the third time. He studied to become a truck driver and now has a license and works driving trucks across the country. It is not a job he likes, but he does not see any alternatives. Jason is a good example of an SEL who never developed the academic language proficiency needed for school success.

Academic Language Proficiency for Struggling Adolescent Students

Our review of the lives of only a few struggling adolescent learners shows that they exhibit different characteristics and that a number of factors contribute to their school success or failure. This review helps show why the administrators at Wayland High School had difficulty deciding who their English learners were and how to help them. Although there are different types of ELLs, it is clear that all these students need to be able to access academic texts and to understand and analyze what they read. Beers, who has conducted research on adolescent struggling readers, comments:

> There is no one answer to understanding why an adolescent struggles with reading. For there to be only one answer, there would have to be only one cause, and for there to be one cause, all students would have to be alike, learn alike, have had the same experiences. (2003, 7)

Type of Learner	Conversational Language		Academic Language	
	English	L1	English	L1
Long-term English learner (LTEL) *Teresa and Chang*	×	×		
Newly arrived with limited formal schooling (LFS) *Ismael and Halima*		×		
Standard English learner (SEL) from historically marginalized group *Victor*	×	(English is L1)		
Standard English learner not typically considered from marginalized group *Jason*	×	(English is L1)		

figure 1.1 Language Proficiency of Different Kinds of Students

The students we have described are certainly not all alike, and they have had very different experiences. Some of them have developed conversational English, but all of them lack the academic English proficiency they need to succeed in school. Figure 1.1, adapted from Freeman and Freeman (2002), shows the conversational and academic language proficiency of the different types of learners we have described here.

As Figure 1.1 illustrates, newly arrived students with limited formal schooling lack both conversational fluency and academic English proficiency. The other three groups have all developed conversational fluency in English, but all three also lack academic language proficiency. In the following chapter, we discuss the distinction between conversational fluency and academic language proficiency in more detail, drawing on the extensive writing of Cummins (1981, 2001, 2008).

English Learners with Adequate Formal Schooling

Before we analyze factors that influence school success for ELLs further, it is important to describe one other type of ELL. We have discussed ELLs who arrive with limited formal schooling and long-term English learners. These two types of students do not usually do well academically. However, there is another group of ELLs, those who arrive with adequate formal schooling, who often do succeed. While the focus of this book is not on these students, it is important to understand who these students are and why they do well in school in English.

When newcomers come to this country with adequate formal schooling, they have several advantages over other ELLs. In the first place, they understand how schools work and the expectations of teachers and others at school. While the systems may be different, students with adequate formal schooling have enough experiences in school to adapt fairly quickly. More importantly, these students read and write in their first languages and sometimes in other languages as well.

Two short examples help us understand this type of student. Juan Carlos came to the United States from El Salvador at age seventeen. His father was an important military official there, and the family had enough money to send the children to private school. In addition, the parents traveled to the United States and Europe with the children. Juan Carlos' English was limited to basic conversational English taught in school, but he had a strong background in all the academic subjects in Spanish. After two years in the United States and long hours of study, he graduated from high school with honors and went on to a university, where he eventually earned a master's degree in engineering.

Avi came to the United States from Israel. His family is from Argentina originally, and when he first arrived in Israel as a young boy, he spoke only Spanish. When he came to the United States in junior high school, he spoke, read, and wrote in Spanish and Hebrew. Although he did not speak English, he could read and write some English, as he had studied English formally as a subject in school. Although Avi struggled with understanding and speaking English at first, within less than two years, he was doing well academically and could converse with his peers with almost no accent. Figure 1.2 shows the kinds of language proficiency Juan Carlos and Avi had when they arrived in the United States.

As the chart in Figure 1.2 shows, both had strong academic preparation when they arrived in the U.S. The knowledge these two students had in the languages they brought to school served them well as they studied academic subjects in English in this country. They had academic language proficiency in one or more languages. The knowledge and skills they had gained in their previous schooling transferred to their learning in English. As educators plan instruction for ELLs it is important that they distinguish between those with adequate formal schooling and the other groups. Although all students need effective instruction to succeed, students who lack academic language proficiency in their first language or in English need additional, long-term support if they are to gain adequate levels of academic English and subject matter knowledge.

Type of Learner	Conversational Language		Academic Language	
Newly arrived with adequate formal schooling	*English*	*L1*	*English*	*L1*
Juan Carlos	some	×		×
Avi		× (Spanish/ Hebrew)	some	× (Spanish/ Hebrew)

figure 1.2 Language Proficiency for Students with Adequate Formal Schooling

ELLs and SELs: A Comparison

Many SELs as well as ELLs with limited formal schooling and LTELs struggle to develop academic language proficiency. Even though all the students in these three groups face a challenge, there are differences among them that suggest that they may need different kinds of support. The chart in Figure 1.3 summarizes the characteristics and needs of students from each of the groups that we have discussed. The chart also incorporates ideas from Short and Fitzsimmons (2007).

The chart shows the typical schooling history for each type of student. The early years for SELs often do not give school officials too much to be concerned about. SELs speak English and appear to be progressing at the same level as their peers. However, once they reach the intermediate grades, where there is more emphasis on the reading of content textbooks and the writing of essays, many begin to struggle.

While SELs understand English, their reading and writing skills are below grade-level expectations. Like Jason, they speak a nonstandard variety of English, and educators with limited background in linguistics may regard this as the cause of their academic problems. However, the real issue is not the variety of English they speak so much as their struggles with comprehending, discussing, and writing academic texts. Because they experience little academic success, SELs may become troublemakers at school and, at times, outside of school.

Long-term English learners experience some of the same academic struggles as SELs. When they begin school, they speak limited or no English. Sometimes they get some first-language support in early grades, but even those who receive bilingual education usually are transitioned to English after only a year or two because

	Standard English Learners	Long-Term English Language Learners	Limited Formal Schooling ELLs
Categorization from Ogbu	can be involuntary minorities	can be involuntary minorities	usually fits new immigrants
Previous schooling	studied all in English; after early grades, began to struggle academically	may have studied in bilingual or ESL programs; after early grades, began to struggle academically in English	little to no schooling in any language
School designations	often labeled as struggling readers or learning disabled; often perceived as not trying	often labeled as struggling readers or learning disabled; often perceived as not trying	may be labeled; often remain in newcomer or ESL programs
Learning orientation	often placed in lower track or remedial classes with rote learning and little active engagement	often placed in lower track or remedial classes with rote learning and little active engagement	if there was schooling, it was often traditional with an emphasis on rote learning
Reading abilities	read and write below grade level in English; may decode well but read with little comprehension	read and write below grade level; may decode well in English but read with little comprehension; do not read L1 well	read and write below grade level; decoding does not lead to comprehension as they do not understand much English

figure 1.3 Comparison of SELs, LTELs, and LFS Students

they appear to speak English well enough to handle the academic curriculum. However, after one or two years of first language instruction, students have not developed high enough levels of academic language and content knowledge in the first language to transfer that knowledge to English.

Many LTELs get no first-language instruction, and while they may be placed in an ESL program, the instruction often focuses on helping them develop conversational fluency in English. Often, LTELs receive inconsistent supports for their lack of English proficiency. Some may have bilingual education one year, ESL the next, no special services the next, and then some ESL again the following year.

	Standard English Learners	Long-Term English Language Learners	Limited Formal Schooling ELLs
Oral English	speak a nonstandard dialect of Engish (e.g., Black English, Tex-Mex, Downeast Maine)	often speak a non-standard dialect of English	speak little or no English
Written English	avoid writing in English and writing is below grade level	avoid writing in English and writing is below grade level	usually are unable to write more than labels and/or short sentences
Background knowledge brought to schooling	usually have background for references that are specific to U.S. culture and history	usually have some background for references that are specific to U.S. culture and history	lack background of U.S. culture and history; lack background of school culture
School content background knowledge	have studied content in schools but may not have understood or retained basic information for a variety of reasons	have studied content in schools but may not have understood early schooling in English or retained basic information	often have little to no content knowledge that is assumed for grade level

figure 1.3 *Continued*

Despite the different kinds of supports for ELLs in the early years, almost all of them develop conversational English. Many also maintain conversational ability in the first language but are not able to read or write it well. The conversational English the students gain is deceptive, because they do not have the academic language needed to understand classroom instruction or to read and write well in English. As a result, these students are often labeled as unmotivated and the perception is they are not trying. Because they find school difficult, long-term English learners sometimes become discipline problems and eventually drop out of school.

The third group of students shown in Figure 1.3 enters school in the intermediate or secondary grades with limited or no schooling. These students face a huge challenge. They must learn English and catch up in all the content areas. The older the students are, the more daunting this task is for both the students and the teachers. It takes from four to nine years to acquire the academic English proficiency needed for school success (Cummins 1984, 2008; Collier 1989), and when it is necessary to also learn all the subject area content that was taught in earlier grades, both the students and their teachers become overwhelmed. Certainly, this group of students lacks the reading, writing, and academic skills to achieve grade-level norms on state exams in one to two years, as NCLB requires.

Challenges Facing Teachers of ELLs and SELs

Educators working with ELLs and SELs face many challenges. Although these students may speak conversational English, they have not developed the academic English or content knowledge needed for school success. They are usually from families living at low socioeconomic levels. They also experience ethnic and linguistic isolation. In addition, schools are faced with growing numbers of immigrant students in areas that have not had ELLs before. Many teachers at the intermediate and secondary levels have not been adequately prepared to work with students who lack grade-level reading and writing skills.

Administrators like those at Wayland High School are concerned that their older ELLs are not succeeding in schools. They realize that they are not meeting the needs of these students. Their situation is not unique. A news release by the Associated Press based on data collected by John Hopkins University shows that, for a very large number of high schools, only 60 percent of the students who start high school as freshmen graduate four years later. Many of the students who drop out cannot pass the reading and math exams required by current law (Balfanz and Legters 2004; Zuckerbrod 2007).

The focus of this book is to help educators work effectively with underprepared students. We mentioned a key concern at the beginning of this chapter, and we return to this point again:

> *Fifty-seven percent of LEP adolescents nationwide are U.S. born.* Up to 27 percent of all LEP adolescents are members of the second generation, and 30 percent are third generation, meaning that many students educated exclusively in U.S. schools still cannot speak English well. (Batalova, Fix, and Murrary 2007, 13)

We know, then, that many students are not succeeding in schools. Most of those students are SELs and ELLs who are long-term English learners or limited formal schooling students. These students need a great deal of support. Schools need to provide instruction that will enable them to read academic texts, think critically, solve problems, and respond to what they learn orally and in writing. The 2003

Program for International Student Assessment (PISA) measured how prepared young adults, approaching the end of compulsory schooling, were for the challenges of today's "knowledge societies" (Brozo, Shiel, and Topping 2007–2008, 305). To be considered well prepared, students must perform different kinds of reading tasks, including

- Retrieving information by locating one or more pieces of discrete information in a text and forming a broad general understanding
- Developing an interpretation by constructing meaning and drawing inferences using information from one or more parts of the text
- Reflecting on the content and structure of texts by relating the text to one's own experiences, knowledge, and ideas and critically evaluating ideas (306)

Academic tasks such as these are quite complex and require that students manipulate texts and understand them well. It is these kinds of activities that the students we described earlier—Teresa, Chang, Ismael, Halima, Victor, and Jason—struggled with in school.

We hope to show you how to help students perform well in their academic tasks. Throughout the text, we provide examples of how teachers can help their students develop the academic language they need for the content they are learning. When teachers understand academic language, they are better prepared to meet the needs of the diverse struggling students in their classrooms.

Applications

1. Read over the section at the beginning of the chapter titled "Demographic Trends." Which of these trends best fits your local school situation? Which do you think needs the most attention and why?

2. Prepare a series of short-answer questions for a class of middle or high school students with at least some ELLs. Feel free to add to or modify these questions:
   - What language or languages did you speak and/or understand when you began school?
   - What language or languages do you and your parents speak at home?
   - What language or languages do you speak with your siblings and extended family?
   - How do you feel about reading and writing in school?
   - What is your easiest subject in school? What subject is most difficult? Why?

From the answers to the questions, identify how the students do or do not fit into the category of long-term English learners. Bring your questions and results to class or your study group and be prepared to discuss your findings.

3. Are there refugee children in your local schools? Where do they come from? What information does the district provide about these students? Can you easily get the kind of information provided in this chapter for Ismael and Halima? Be prepared to discuss what you have learned. Do you have suggestions for the district?

4. Review the section of the chapter on Ogbu's classification of immigrant and involuntary minorities. Find a student who you believe would represent each group and interview each student. Ask the students the same questions as in application 2 and any other questions that seem relevant. Bring your questions and results to class or your study group and be prepared to discuss them.

5. Look at Figure 1.3, which compares SELs, LTELs, and LFS students. Discuss with a partner why it is important for educators to understand the characteristics of each. Think of a student who fits into one of these categories and explain to a partner why he or she fits.

6. Review the section of the chapter titled "Challenges Facing Teachers of ELLs and SELs." What are the kinds of reading and writing tasks that well-prepared students in "knowledge societies" must perform? List the tasks. Are schools you know doing a good job of helping prepare students? How? If not, what could be done differently? Bring your answers to class or your study group to discuss.

7. Interview five middle and/or high school teachers. Ask them what they know about the ELLs in their classes. Do they seem to be aware of the differences among ELLs? Do they know if the students speak, read, and write their first languages? What do they think is helpful to ELLs when they teach? What kind of support do they think the students need? Be prepared to discuss their answers.

2

Distinguishing Between Academic and Conversational Language

Dolores came to the United States from El Salvador when she was fourteen. In El Salvador she had attended a rural school through the sixth grade. In the United States she attended classes at a newcomer center for two weeks and then, based on her age, was transferred to a large urban high school. Her schedule included two periods of ESL, a sheltered biology class, physical education, algebra, and history.

At the time we worked with Dolores, she was a seventeen-year-old senior. She had accumulated enough units to graduate. As a senior she still had two periods of ESL. Since her ESL classes counted toward English credit, Dolores never took a regular English class. Although she had passed all her classes, she had not yet passed the basic skills tests in reading, math, or writing required for graduation.

Based on the typology of students described in Chapter 1, Dolores was a newly arrived student with limited formal schooling. Her mother had come to the United

States when Dolores was quite young, leaving her in the care of relatives. In the United States her mother remarried and now had seven children by her second husband. When she first arrived, Dolores lived with this family, but she had conflicts with them. She resented her mother for leaving her behind for so long. She didn't want to be in the United States and expressed a desire to return to El Salvador. Eventually, she left her mother's home to live with other relatives in the area.

Dolores could carry on conversations in English, but she struggled with academic subjects taught in English. We worked with her to try to help her improve her English writing. The first time she took the writing test, the topic was "Why do teenagers become troublemakers?" She was marked down on her exam for going off topic. When we discussed the test with her, she commented that she didn't know much about teenagers in the United States. In spite of the conflicts with her family, she was certainly not a troublemaker. She was a quiet young woman who wanted to complete high school and find a job. Since she didn't have much to say about why teenagers become troublemakers, it was not surprising that she had gone off topic.

Dolores' Essay

To begin our discussion of the differences between academic and conversational language, we present an example of a practice essay Dolores wrote as she worked with us. This time she chose the topic. It was one she knew more about. She titled the essay "Problems with Minorities." Figure 2.1 shows Dolores' essay as she wrote it. She left this note with her essay: "Okay, here is the essay you told me to write. I don't really know how to write. But I did my best. I hope you understand it. I write about minorities because it was more easy for me to tell. . . . I hope you don't get boring about my writing."

We weren't bored (and we hope we weren't boring) as we read Dolores' writing. We first noted that she made a good choice of topic. Students generally write better when they get to choose what they write about instead of responding to prompts. Dolores had quite a bit to say about problems with minorities, and this time she stayed on topic.

It is also clear from reading the essay that Dolores was trying to follow the organizational plan her teachers had taught her in class. In the introduction she states the topic and lists what she will do in the paper: she will explain why minorities can't attend universities and what needs to be done to enable them to attend. This sets up a good problem-solution structure that is an appropriate organizational plan for this type of academic paper.

PROBLEMS WITH MINORITIES.

There is a big problem with minorities. In this essay I will discuss and explain why students Latinos, Hmong and African Americans cann't attend Universities. Second I will write what I think needs to be done so that more, Hmong, Latinos and Africans can attend and graduate From Universities and college.

First reason that minorities cann't attend Universities and college, is because some of them are illegal aliens. sometimes is because they don't have the much money to pay, Universities.

The second reason that latinos, Hmong, and Africans cann't attend Universities is because their is to many descrimination. people are raices, sometimes teachers. They low grades. Their to many reasons that they can't attend universities. Many students said that if they give them alist one chance a

figure 2.1a Dolores' Essay

opportunity to show teachers and others, that they are good, they would taste them.

If they would taste latinos, Hmong and Africans, they would know that they know more, them they now. Minorities would show their family that they are good and valient. There will be so many changes for them. Two mayor changes for them it would be that minorities would became intelligent. Also they would have good money and work.

A second change that I hope will occur is that people will realize that importance of every people life. They would realize that all people has the right to decide by their own future. To have a better life.

In conclusion we know that minorities dossen't attend universities for many reasons. They are "illegal, aliens". Lower grades etc. For this situation they became "appathy". But many of us think that it could be a solution for this. If they,

figure 2.1b

could give them a opportunity
some people might be over—
crowded. But people migh realize
that all people live are ❤️ *valuable.*
That all have the right to
decide by their own.

figure 2.1c

In the second paragraph, Dolores gives two reasons minorities can't attend universities: they lack legal papers, and they lack money. Each of these reasons is simply stated in a sentence with no supporting details or examples. Thus, it appears that Dolores is following a pattern but is not fleshing out the details to support the reasons she lists.

The third paragraph begins with "The second reason." Dolores has already given two reasons, but now she turns to a third one: discrimination. She explains that teachers give minorities low grades because the teachers and others are racist. Students aren't given a chance to prove themselves. It appears that she has translated the Spanish word *probar* as *taste* rather than using a second meaning, *prove*. She could also be confusing *taste* and *test*. Although Dolores develops this third reason more fully, she does not provide any concrete examples or data to support her claims about racism.

Having explained why minorities don't attend universities, Dolores turns to her second point, what needs to be done to solve the problem. She argues that if minorities were tested, they would prove themselves. This would lead to changes. Minorities would become more intelligent, earn more money, and find work. This would cause other people to realize that everyone has the right to decide her own future and have a better life.

Dolores concludes the essay by reiterating the reasons that minorities don't attend universities and observing that this leads to apathy. She states that minorities should be given a chance to succeed, even though this might lead to overcrowding at universities. She ends by expressing the hope that people will realize that everyone is valuable and everyone has a right to make his own decisions.

In her essay, Dolores expresses her feelings clearly. She has something she wants to say, and her voice comes through. She follows an organizational plan she has been taught. The paper has an introduction, a body, and a conclusion. Nevertheless, this essay would not make the grade on an exit exam. The paragraphs are not developed. Dolores makes claims without supporting them. She provides no evidence in the form of data or specific examples to back up what she says. In addition, there are serious problems with her vocabulary, grammar, and mechanics. Even though Dolores could communicate her ideas to a reader through writing when we began working with her, she had not yet developed academic language proficiency.

Dolores' essay is typical of the writing produced by students with limited formal schooling. Her choice of words, sentence structure, and mechanics reflect her level of language development. Her essay also has characteristics of those written by long-term English learners and SELs who are struggling readers. These students might not insert a word like *taste* when they mean *prove* or *test*, but they might base arguments on personal opinion with no supporting evidence, and their sentence structure and mechanics might be much like Dolores'.

This essay contains elements of conversational language and lacks many of the features of academic language expected from a high school senior. Throughout this book we refer to Dolores' essay to illustrate differences between conversational and academic language.

Cummins' Theoretical Framework

Ask almost any teacher who has worked with English language learners to name a researcher who has written about the difference between academic and conversational language, and the response will be "Cummins." The teacher will probably be able to go on and explain about BICS (basic interpersonal communicative skills) and CALP (cognitive academic language proficiency). Cummins' work has been widely disseminated. He has written and spoken a great deal on this topic. Cummins explains that he developed the distinction between BICS and CALP "in order to draw educators' attention to the timelines and challenges that second language learners encounter as they attempt to catch up with their peers in academic aspects of the school language" (2008, 71).

In making the distinction between conversational and academic language, Cummins drew on work by Skutnabb-Kangas and Toukomaa (1976), who had studied Finnish immigrant children in Sweden. These children appeared to be fluent in both Finnish and Swedish, but their academic performance was below both grade and age expectations. Cummins hypothesized that there were two components of language proficiency, one that reflected the ability to carry on conversations on everyday topics and another that was needed to comprehend, talk, read, and write about school subjects. This helps explain why the Finnish children could carry on conversations in Swedish but did poorly on school assignments in Swedish.

Cummins conducted research in Canada to test the hypothesis that conversational and academic language are two distinct components of language proficiency. In one key study (Cummins 1984) he examined four hundred teacher referral forms and psychological assessments of ELLs from a large school system. These forms showed that teachers and school psychologists determined that many of the students had no problems in speaking and understanding English. In other words, these students had conversational fluency in English. However, they performed poorly on academic tasks in their classes and on cognitive ability tests. These activities require students to demonstrate academic language proficiency. The Canadian immigrants showed a pattern of language development similar to that shown by the Finnish children in Sweden.

The Canadian teachers and school psychologists assumed that the students' oral language interactions in class demonstrated their English proficiency. As a result, they attributed the students' academic difficulties to cognitive rather than linguistic factors and placed many of the students in special education classes. Cummins argued that these students did not have learning problems. They had developed conversational fluency, BICS, but had not yet developed academic language proficiency, CALP. Cummins defines academic language proficiency as "the extent to which an individual has command of the oral and written academic registers of schooling" (2000, 67). In other words, academic language is the specific language needed to understand and contribute to classroom talk and to read and write texts for school.

Cummins' purpose in distinguishing between the two types of language proficiency was to account for the fact that students who could carry on conversations in English had still not developed the kind of English they needed to do well in school tasks. He does not suggest that academic language is superior in some way to conversational language, just that they are different. As Baker points out:

> School-based academic/cognitive language does not represent universal higher-order cognitive skills nor all forms of literacy practice. Different sociocultural contexts have different expectations and perceived patterns of appropriateness in language and thinking such that a school is only one specific context for "higher order" language production. (2006, 176)

Students who have developed BICS but not CALP do not lack higher-order thinking ability. They simply lack the language needed to succeed in school.

Linguistic Studies That Support the BICS–CALP Distinction

Linguistic studies support the BICS–CALP distinction. Linguists have examined different corpora, very large collections of data with words from different sources. For example, one corpus could be based on recordings of conversations while another could be taken from academic textbooks. One such study was conducted by Corson (1997), who analyzed English vocabulary. He examined two different collections of words for his study. When Corson examined the Birmingham corpus, which lists words that ESL students, children and adults, need for daily communication, he found that only two of the 150 most frequent words, *very* and *because*, have Latin or Greek roots. The rest are drawn from Anglo-Saxon vocabulary. The vocabulary of everyday English comes primarily from Anglo-Saxon words. These are short words like *bread* and *house*. This is the vocabulary that makes up most of the conversational language that ELLs acquire.

In contrast, academic texts contain a high number of words with Greek and Latin roots, such as *transportation* and *sympathy*. Corson also examined the 150 most frequent words in the University Word List. This list, which includes words ESL students need to read academic texts, includes two words with Germanic roots and four others that entered English from French. The rest have Greek and Latin origins. English vocabulary, then, can be divided into two types, words with Anglo-Saxon origins used in everyday conversation and words from Latin and Greek sources that occur frequently in academic texts. (The University Word List has been refined and updated by Averil Coxhead. The result is the Academic Word List. It is available for downloading at http://language.massey.ac.nz/staff/awl/).

It is important to note that certain kinds of early reading for young children also contain academic language. Corson reports on a study that found that "even children's books contained 50 percent more rare words [from Graeco-Latin sources] than either adult prime-time television or the conversations of university graduates." In addition, Corson found that "popular magazines had three times as many rare words as television and informal conversation" (1997, 764).

Corson's study provides support for Cummins' claim that there is a difference between the language people use in daily conversation and the language required to read, write, and discuss academic texts. ELLs are exposed to conversational language to a much greater extent than to academic language, so it is not surprising that they acquire conversational fluency before acquiring academic language proficiency. Their access to academic language comes primarily from reading and writing academic texts, yet many ELLs and struggling readers spend very little time engaged in this kind of reading and writing.

The acquisition of academic vocabulary is complex. Looking again at Dolores' essay, we find some academic vocabulary, like *discuss, explain, attend,* and *discrimination.* She also uses the word *appathy* (as she spells it). This was a vocabulary word Dolores had recently been taught. However, like many ELLs and struggling readers, she had learned the basic meaning of the word, but not the different forms it can take. She writes in her essay, "For this situation they become appathy." She hadn't yet learned that the adjective form is *apathetic.* Dolores was beginning to acquire some of the language she needed for academic writing, but she still had much to learn. She needed to learn different forms of words like *apathy* and a larger number of academic words so that she could vary her vocabulary as she wrote. Extensive reading would help her do this.

A second study that supports the BICS–CALP distinction was conducted by Biber (1986), who also used two different corpora. The first was a collection of five hundred written text samples of about two thousand words each. These included fiction such as detective stories as well as press reports, and academic papers. Biber also added text from professional letters. To read or write these kinds of texts, students would need academic language proficiency. On the other hand, the second corpus reflecting conversational language was based on recorded conversations, broadcasts, and public speeches. The spoken language database contained eighty-seven texts of about five thousand words each.

Interactive Versus Edited Texts

Biber analyzed these two sets of data to identify how they differed from one another. He found three differences. First, the spoken texts were more interactive and showed more personal involvement. The written texts, partly because writers have more time to work on a text, used a greater variety of vocabulary and were more carefully edited. These texts showed less personal involvement. They were more detached in style. For example, when students do a biology experiment, talk about it as they work, and report back orally, the language they use is more interactive, less formal, and less precise than the language these same students use when they write up the experiment for their teacher using the specific vocabulary and structure for the report that the teacher requires. Biber refers to this difference between spoken and written language as *interactive* versus *edited* text.

Abstract Versus Situated Content

A second difference between the two types of texts was that the written texts were more abstract while the spoken texts were more concrete. Biber refers to this difference as abstract versus situated content. Written texts achieve abstraction by the use of a number of features, such as nominalizations and passives. *Nominalization* is a process of turning a verb into a noun. For example, the verb *destroy* can be changed to the noun, *destruction.* Nominalization allows writers to pack more information into each sentence. At the same time, the sentences become more abstract because the person or thing doing the action is removed. In "The beetles destroyed the redwood trees" the actor, the beetles, is named. In "The destruction of the redwood trees is terrible" no actor is named, so the idea is conveyed in an abstract manner. In the same way, passives remove the actor. An active sentence, "The beetles destroyed the redwood trees," becomes more abstract when it is made passive, "The redwood trees were destroyed." The result is an abstract, or more formal style.

Spoken language, in contrast, is more concrete and situated. Speakers name the agents who carry out actions. They also indicate the time and place more specifically. Spoken language, as a result, is more situated in particular contexts. The language is also more informal. For example, when students discuss a field trip they took, they can use informal language to talk about specific events that occurred in particular places at certain times. Their language is situated and informal. If, however, they write about the field trip, they use a more abstract, formal style to report what happened and to make generalizations about what they learned.

Reported Versus Immediate Style

Biber labeled the third difference as *reported* versus *immediate* style. A reported style is characterized by language that tells about events that occurred in the past and in a different place. Writers usually use past tense and write about places that are not near a reader. In contrast, the immediate style of oral language uses present tense more often. Speakers talk about current events or events that have recently occurred and often talk about local events. When teachers read books to their students in class and students respond immediately either in groups or in the whole class, their language is less formal as they talk about their immediate response. On the other hand, when students write a report about that book, discussing plot, character, theme, and setting or comparing the book with something else they have read, this reported style is more structured and much more distant.

Thus, in his study of a large number of texts, Biber identified three differences between written and spoken language. These were not differences in vocabulary, but differences in syntactic and semantic features. The spoken texts were more interactive, situated, and immediate. The written texts were more edited, abstract, and reported. ELLs are required to read many texts with these latter characteristics. They are also expected to write texts that contain these features. Since students develop conversational fluency before they acquire academic language proficiency, they often include elements common to spoken language in their academic writing.

For example, Dolores writes, "In this essay I will discuss and explain why students Latinos, Hmong and African Americans cann't attend Universities." Here she uses some academic vocabulary including *essay, discuss, explain*, and *attend*. She also writes a complex sentence with an initial prepositional phrase and a subordinate clause. These show that she was beginning to acquire academic language proficiency. She also uses an organizational structure common to academic writing. Her introduction then shows evidence of an edited, abstract, and reported style.

However, her use of the first-person *I* is more interactive, situated, and immediate than might be expected in an academic essay, which might start with "This essay will provide discussion and explanation of. . . ." This shift would create a more formal, distanced style. In addition, near the end, Dolores inserts "I hope" into a sentence, again making the writing more personal and less objective and formal. Her last paragraph begins, "In conclusion, we know that minorities dossen't attend Universities For many reasons." Here she uses the first-person plural *we* rather than a more formal structure such as "There are many reasons that minorities don't attend universities." Even though Dolores was beginning to include some of the elements of academic language that Biber identified, when she wrote this essay, she still retained features of conversational language in her academic writing.

Cummins' Quadrants

Cummins (1981) used quadrants formed by two intersecting continua to help educators conceptualize the distinction between BICS and CALP. This diagram is shown in Figure 2.2.

Context-Embedded and Context-Reduced Language

The horizontal line on the diagram represents a continuum that extends from *context-embedded* language to *context-reduced* language. At the left end of the continuum, the language used is contextualized by either external or internal factors or both. Cummins does not use the term *decontextualized* for the other end of the continuum since all language occurs in some context. However, there is a range of internal and external contextual support. When there is more contextual support, ELLs do not need to rely so much on language, and they can interpret a

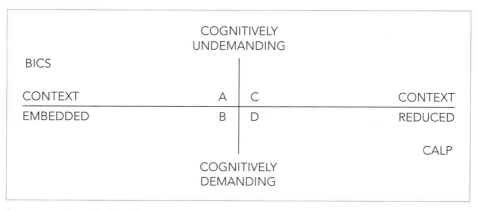

figure 2.2 Cummins' Quadrants

message with the help of nonlinguistic cues. However, when there is little contextual support, students have to rely more heavily on the language itself.

External context can take many forms. For example, the physical setting can provide clues as to the meaning of a message. If two people are standing under an awning to shelter themselves from the rain, and they are talking about the weather, the setting provides a great number of clues as to the meaning of the conversation. An ELL can pick up clues to meaning from the setting as well as the gestures and tone of voice the other person is using. A word like *umbrella* is not hard to understand if the other person opens her umbrella and says, "Open your umbrella so you won't get wet."

Early ESL instruction makes extensive use of gestures, visuals, and objects to make the English comprehensible. For example, many teachers use Total Physical Response (TPR) as an activity with beginners. In a TPR lesson the teacher gives a series of commands, such as "Stand up" or "Raise your left arm," and students follow the directions. If students are confused, they watch classmates or the teacher. After a short time they can follow most simple commands. In the process they learn some action verbs and other vocabulary, such as parts of the body. TPR is a good initial activity for ELLs because the physical actions provide an external context for the English language being used.

Internal context is provided by such things as background knowledge or previous experiences rather than things that are physical. To return to the weather example, all ELLs have had previous experience with different kinds of weather, including rain. They have background knowledge that enables them to make sense of a conversation about weather. This background knowledge provides internal context that makes it easy to understand talk about the weather.

All people bring different background knowledge to new language situations. Yvonne remembers a discussion that took place in Lithuania. She and David were to give a workshop to English teachers, and their interpreter, speaking in Lithuanian, was going over the setup for the workshop with the director of the school. There was an overhead projector, a flip chart, and a pointer in the room. Yvonne interrupted at one point and explained in English that they did not need a chart and pens, only an overhead projector. Both the interpreter and the director were surprised that Yvonne understood what was being discussed because Yvonne speaks no Lithuanian. Of course, there were some physical objects in the room that provided Yvonne with external context. But in addition, Yvonne used internal context to interpret what was being said. She had organized workshops so many times with school leaders that she had enough internal context from past experiences to understand the gist of the conversation. She had both the external and internal contexts she needed to make the language understandable.

A good way to understand the difference between context-embedded and context-reduced language is to consider the differences between face-to-face conversation and a phone conversation. Even though many contextual cues are present in a phone conversation, it is much harder to understand a phone call in a new language than to understand a face-to-face conversation. If an ELL is talking with a friend on the playground or on the phone, she has the same amount of background knowledge or internal context for the discussion. In both cases, tone of voice could help with meaning. However, many clues would be absent from the phone conversation. There would be no objects to point to. There would be no body language to indicate meaning. All a listener would have is a disembodied voice. The language of a phone conversation is not decontextualized, but it is much less context embedded than a face-to-face conversation.

Often discussions of context-embedded and context-reduced language focus on the listener or reader, the person receiving a message. Since teachers do most of the talking in a class, they are urged to use any means possible to embed their spoken language in a rich context. It is also recommended that ELLs be given materials to read that have text features such as pictures and charts to help provide a context for the language. However, the distinction between context-embedded and context-reduced language applies to speaking and writing as well as to listening and reading. It is easier for language learners to communicate in a new language if they can rely on the context to get their message across. ELLs might point to objects if they don't know the word. They can also use intonation for emphasis. These contextual supports allow them to communicate without relying too heavily on the new language. In the same way, teachers can encourage ELLs to add pictures or diagrams to their writing to be sure they are communicating in their new language.

Cognitively Demanding and Cognitively Undemanding Language

The vertical line on the diagram represents a continuum that extends from *cognitively undemanding* language to *cognitively demanding* language. Topics a student reads, writes, or talks about can range from cognitively undemanding to cognitively demanding. The conversation about the weather would not be too cognitively demanding in most cases. On the other hand, a conversation about how to repair a car might be quite demanding. The amount of demand depends to a great extent on the ELL's previous experience. Something a person has done many times takes less cognitive effort than a new task. Someone who repairs cars for a living would probably find a discussion about car repair quite cognitively undemanding, but for many other people it would take a great deal of mental energy to understand directions about how to fix a car or to give directions orally or in writing to a mechanic.

One difficulty new teachers often experience is that after they have explained a task to students, the students still seem confused, even if the teacher's explanation was clear. For example, if an inexperienced geometry teacher explains how to determine the radius of a circle, her explanation may be rather brief. She doesn't elaborate because the process is so familiar to her. She takes for granted that it will be equally easy for her students to understand. But, as many of us who teach realize, what seems easy to us may be very difficult for our students. The same task may place very different amounts of cognitive demand on two people, not because of the nature of the task itself, but because of differences in the experience and knowledge that the two people bring to the task.

Anyone who has tried to learn some new technology on the computer can understand this well. Recently, our university encouraged faculty to use a new program that can video and tape-record lectures, Powerpoint presentations, and classroom demonstrations and make them available later to students for review. When we were first shown this new technology, it seemed complicated and difficult to use. We had to turn on the microphone, find our PowerPoints, start the recording, and still teach! The technology people helping us kept telling us how easy the program was to use, but their brief explanations did not help.

After using the program several times, however, both of us could see that it was not so complicated. In fact, Yvonne then enthusiastically explained the program to another faculty member, whose comment after Yvonne's explanation was "Well, I guess I'll get it eventually. It certainly is complicated, however." At first the technology was cognitively demanding, but after experience with the program, it became cognitively undemanding to use.

Language Use and the Quadrants

Figure 2.3 illustrates the kinds of activities that fit into each of the four quadrants. Cummins defined BICS as oral or written communication that occurs when the language is context embedded and cognitively undemanding (Quadrant A). In Figure 2.3, the activities suggested for Quadrant A include interviewing a classmate and filling out a short form answering questions about the classmate's interests and hobbies. The teacher and students could also discuss the weather and read stories about the weather.

Quadrant C represents language that is not cognitively demanding but is context reduced. A telephone conversation, as we discussed earlier, is an example of this kind of language. A phone conversation about the school football game would not be cognitively demanding if speakers had knowledge of the game. However, because the conversation would not be face-to-face, the physical context, at least, would be reduced. The same would be true of an email. Listening

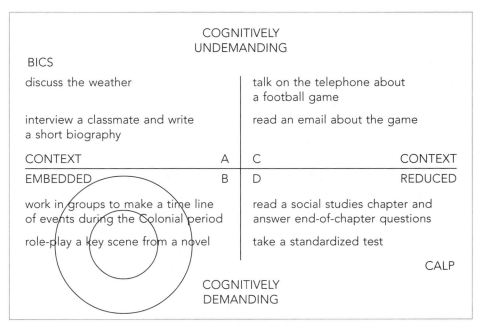

figure 2.3 Sample Activities for Cummins' Quadrants

to an ad on the radio would also be content reduced but probably not cognitively demanding.

In Quadrant D the language is both context reduced and cognitively demanding. A typical classroom example is an assignment to read a chapter in a history book and answer the questions at the end. A student would have to rely heavily on the language in the book to complete this assignment. To succeed, an ELL would need to have developed academic language proficiency; knowledge of conversational English would not be sufficient to do well on this sort of assignment.

One of the most difficult tasks for all types of students is taking standardized tests, which are both cognitively demanding and context reduced. Consider, for example, a standardized test of reading comprehension. Each reading passage is unrelated to the previous or following passage. If students do not have the background knowledge they need to understand the passage, and, in addition, do not have high enough levels of English language proficiency, they will struggle with the test. Additional activities that fall into quadrant D include listening to a lecture and writing a long essay.

Students need to be exposed to academic language in order to acquire it. Teachers should present cognitively demanding content in such a way that it is context embedded and understandable. Therefore, the target for teaching all students, and especially ELLs, should be Quadrant B. For example, rather than asking students to read a chapter and answer the questions at the end, a teacher might have students, including ELLs and struggling readers, work in small groups to create a time line of events described in a chapter and then present their time line to the class. The small-group work and the graphic representation of events on the time line would increase the contextual support so that ELLs and struggling readers could complete this cognitively demanding task.

An English teacher can make a novel more comprehensible by having students work together to identify characters, plot, and setting to prepare and present a role play of key scenes in the novel. This activity would belong in Quadrant B. Other activities that fit in quadrant B include using graphic organizers and having students make posters to show their understanding of key points in a science chapter.

Cummins emphasizes that the two dimensions that form the quadrants "cannot be specified in absolute terms because what is 'context-embedded' or 'cognitively-demanding' for one learner may not be so for another as a result of differences in internal attributes such as prior knowledge or interest" (2008, 74). Even though the distinction between conversational and academic language can not be specified in absolute terms, teachers can use the quadrants to help visualize the difference between the two components of language proficiency. The quadrants illustrate the importance of building students' background knowledge and of contextualizing classroom talk and activities so that ELLs can better comprehend instruction. An analysis of Dolores' writing using the two dimensions from the quadrants helps us understand the demands the task placed on her and the resources she could use as she wrote the essay.

Using the Dimensions to Evaluate Task Difficulty

Earlier we discussed the essay that Dolores, a student with limited formal schooling, wrote (see Figure 2.1). Our analysis places this essay in Quadrant D despite the fact that Dolores was provided with some contextual support. Dolore had learned a structure for organizing her essays, and she used her knowledge of essay structure as internal context to make this task more context embedded.

However, Dolores had limited experience with writing academic essays. She chose a topic she had formed opinions about. She wrote in her note to us, "I write about minorities because it was more easy for me to tell." Students should learn to choose and write about topics they care about, but they should also learn to support their assertions with examples and data rather then opinions. Dolores' ESL classes had not prepared her to do this, so she lacked the internal contextual support to write a convincing essay. At the same time, since this was a first draft she had not been given any external support in the form of feedback on her writing or suggestions to improve this essay.

Writing the essay was cognitively demanding for Dolores in two ways. She needed to conduct research on the topic. She could have surveyed other students or read articles about problems minorities face in academics. Then she could have used the information to support her assertions. This research would have been cognitively demanding.

In addition, Dolores had not learned to write paragraphs or sentences with the characteristics of academic language. Her essay is not edited, abstract, and reported. Instead, it is interactive, immediate, and situated. Probably the greatest cognitive demand for Dolores comes from spelling and punctuating her writing. It was extremely cognitively demanding for Dolores to focus on both the content of the essay and the form at the same time. For Dolores, writing an academic essay was context reduced and cognitively demanding and fits in Quadrant D. Students like Dolores need considerable support to complete the cognitively demanding academic writing tasks successfully. She needed scaffolded instruction that provided contextual support. With that kind of support this task would have fallen into Quadrant B, not Quadrant D.

Time to Develop Conversational and Academic Language

Although Dolores had developed enough English to write an essay in English, she needed much more experience reading and writing English to achieve grade-level writing competence. Cummins and others have conducted studies to determine how long it takes an English learner to acquire conversational fluency and how much additional time is needed to develop academic language proficiency.

In one study, Cummins (1981) examined data from school files in Canada to determine how long it took ELLs to reach grade-appropriate conversational fluency compared with how long it took them to reach grade-level norms in academic achievement. He found that it takes a new arrival to Canada about two years to develop sufficient oral English proficiency to converse easily with classmates but five to seven years to be able to perform at grade level on tasks in different academic subject areas. Cummins (2008) lists additional studies in the United States and in other countries that have confirmed these findings, including research by Collier (1989), Snow and Hoefnagel-Hohle (1978), and Hakuta, Butler, and Witt (2000).

Appropriate Program Placement

The schools Cummins studied placed ELLs in special education courses because administrators didn't recognize that it takes much longer to develop academic language proficiency than it does to develop conversational fluency. In much the same way, the failure to distinguish between the two components of language proficiency has led to the early exit of students from bilingual programs. Many early-exit programs in the United States transition ELLs into all-English instruction after about two years, at the point that the students have developed conversational fluency in English. Educators who do not understand that conversational fluency is not adequate for school success believe that students who speak and understand English should be learning in all-English settings. However, as we have explained, conversational fluency is not enough for these students to read and write English at grade level using the academic vocabulary and structures required. Since these students have not yet achieved academic language proficiency, they often struggle to pass standardized tests and do not do well in classes taught in English.

In a major study of different types of bilingual programs, Ramírez (1991) found that students in early-exit bilingual programs achieved at about the same rate as students who had not received any bilingual education. In contrast, students in late-exit programs, who continued to receive primary-language support for five or six years, achieved at higher rates when exited into all-English instruction. The explanation for these findings is that in late-exit programs, students develop academic language and concepts in their first languages that then transfer to English. Bilingual students in late-exit programs develop academic language in both their first languages and English.

The distinction between conversational and academic language and the importance of bilingual education are not well understood by the public in general. Casual observers note that ELLs who begin school speaking little or no English seem to pick up English quickly and can carry on conversations in English in one or two years. English-only legislation passed quite easily in California, Arizona, and Massachusetts because the public believed that more instructional time in English results in higher levels of English proficiency. The legislation passed because there was no understanding of how first-language academic development supports academic language development in English through transfer.

Common Underlying Proficiency

While English-only advocates believe in the logic that more English equals more English, there is an important theoretical construct that refutes this belief. Cummins (2000) has explained how first language academic knowledge supports academic success in a second language. His Common Underlying Proficiency (CUP) model holds that what we know in one language is accessible in a second language once we acquire a sufficient level of the second language. This he refers to as the interdependence principle:

> To the extent that instruction in L_x is effective in promoting proficiency in L_x transfer of this proficiency to L_y will occur provided there is adequate exposure to L_y (either in school or the environment) and adequate motivation to learn L_y. (29)

In other words, when students are taught in and develop academic and language proficiency in their first language, L_x, that proficiency will transfer to the second language, L_y, assuming they are given enough exposure to the second language and are motivated to learn it. Juan Carlos and Avi, the students we used in Chapter 1 as examples of students with adequate formal schooling, succeeded in school because they had developed academic competence in Spanish and Hebrew through their schooling in El Salvador and Israel. They both began school in English in their new country with grade-level skills in their first language. Students with a strong academic background can apply the knowledge they have in their first languages to what they are studying in English. These students have a huge advantage over students like Dolores, who enter school with limited formal schooling.

It is for this reason that second language acquisition experts promote bilingual education in schools. Students who begin school speaking a language other than English do better in school when some of their instruction is in their native language. If all their instruction is in English, they won't understand the teacher and will fall behind. As Krashen (1999) has pointed out, students in a bilingual class can learn academic content and develop the skills needed for problem solving and higher-order thinking in their first language while they become proficient in English.

When ELLs are faced with the task of carrying out academic tasks in English without adequate background knowledge in their first languages, their task is much more difficult. García (2002) points out that in order to acquire high levels of academic English proficiency, students need to be able to read and write academic texts. Native English speakers generally begin school with basic English proficiency. Teachers can build on this proficiency to help these students read stories and content texts. Bilingual students, in contrast, usually lack conversational English proficiency when they begin school. They can't understand or speak English if they come from a home where another language is usually spoken. By the time bilingual students develop conversational English proficiency, their native-English-speaking classmates have already begun to read and write school texts. Eventually, bilingual students learn to read and write in English, but they are behind native English speakers unless they have developed academic concepts in their first language, and as they move up the grades, the gap in achievement between bilingual students and native speakers increases.

García understands that conversational English is not enough for ELLs and that they need very deliberate instruction in English to develop academic English. He lists four ways for teachers to promote academic English development in their classrooms. These include

- providing students with ample exposure to academic English,
- being sure that students attend closely to the features of academic English,
- providing direct, explicit language instruction, and
- using multiple measures to assess the academic language development of English language learners.

These are excellent general guidelines for teachers to follow. If Dolores' teachers had provided this kind of instruction, she would have been better prepared for her writing exam. However, even with very good teaching, ELLs like Dolores and SELs who are struggling readers need time to develop the level of academic language needed to complete academic tasks and tests.

Conclusion

Cummins conducted research to show that there are two components of language proficiency. Conversational language is context embedded and cognitively undemanding. Academic language, on the other hand, is context reduced and cognitively demanding. Cummins' quadrants provide educators with a way to determine the language students must understand to succeed in school. Teachers need to ensure that language use in schools is cognitively demanding and context embedded so that students can learn both the academic language and the content they need. Teachers also need to be aware that most ELLs develop conversational proficiency in one or two years. However, it takes five to seven years for ELLs to acquire academic language proficiency.

English language learners not only need to develop conversational fluency but also need to learn the academic English that is valued in schools. As Dolores' essay demonstrates, this is a real challenge. Dolores had mastered some of the conventions of English writing. Nevertheless, she still had problems with spelling, punctuation, and grammar. She was learning to organize her writing and to present her ideas in a formal, objective, and authoritative academic style. These elements of her writing demonstrate her gradual development of academic language proficiency. However, some aspects of her writing reflect conversational language more than academic language. In the following chapters we explore academic language in more detail, and we suggest ways that teachers can help students like Dolores develop academic language proficiency.

Applications

1. We open the chapter with an essay by Dolores and discuss some of the strengths and some of the problems with the paper. Dolores' writing does not reflect academic language proficiency. Bring a piece of student writing that you think does not reflect academic language proficiency to class or to your study group. Discuss with a partner what the student does well and what concerns you have. If you could choose one area to work on with the student, what would it be?

2. Cummins distinguishes between BICS and CALP. Summarize in a couple of paragraphs what each of these acronyms refers to and be prepared to explain BICS and CALP in class or with your study group.

3. Corson (1997) explained that academic vocabulary comes from Graeco-Latin sources and that children's literature often contains those words. Pick out an illustrated children's book that you know is considered a piece of quality children's literature. Read through the book with a classmate. Pick out words in the book that have Graeco-Latin roots and are probably not words one would hear on television or read in a newspaper. Bring your list to class or your study group to share.

4. Biber (1986) explains that spoken texts contain language that is more interactive, situated, and immediate than the language of written texts, which is more edited, abstract, and reported. Listen on television to someone giving a speech. List several examples of how that speech shows evidence of being interactive, situated, and immediate. Now, look at a textbook. You may use this one. Pick out examples where the language of the book is more edited, abstract, and reported. Bring your results to share.

5. Research shows that it takes time to develop a second language. Based on Cummins' research, explain which of the following programs is most appropriate for ELLs: early exit, late exit, or English only. How would you respond to people who say that ELLs should be immersed in English early because it is the only way they are going to really learn English?

6. Using the diagram in Figure 2.4, list activities that are carried out in schools that fit each of the quadrants. Be sure you list effective instruction for ELLs in Quadrant B.

7. García (2002) proposes four ways that teachers can help students develop academic language in the classroom. Choose two of the suggestions and give specific examples of class activities that you have used or observed being used that fit those suggestions.

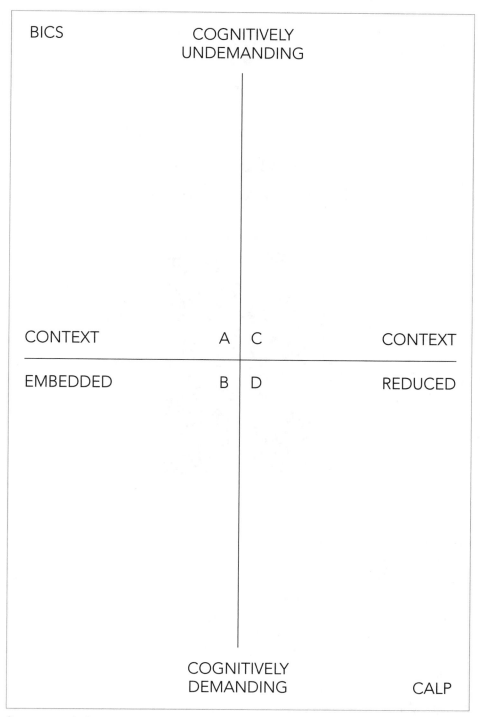

figure 2.4 Blank Cummins' Quadrants Form

3

Making Sense of the Academic
Registers of Schooling

José was born in Guadalajara, Mexico, and came to the United States when he was in first grade. José had no preschool or kindergarten in Mexico. In the United States his family first settled in a small rural community where José was placed in a bilingual classroom in first grade. In second grade, his family moved to another small community where there was no bilingual program. There he was placed in an all-English classroom and was pulled out for ESL support. In third grade, it was determined that José could speak English, and he received no further special services.

When José was in junior high, his family moved to a small city. He began to struggle with schoolwork and his yearly test scores were very low. During this period, José had a short involvement with gangs. However, his skills in playing soccer probably kept him from getting into serious trouble. He was recruited to play soccer, and his nickname on the soccer team was "El Conejo" (The Rabbit), an apt name for someone who can run fast.

At the end of his freshman year, José was a struggling reader and writer. Although José could communicate socially in English, he still lacked academic English. In his developmental reading class, his teacher found that José was good in discussion, but he would do almost anything to avoid any serious reading or writing. In ninth grade, he faced the reality of having little time to catch up before facing the tenth-grade high-stakes tests (Freeman and Freeman 2002).

José is typical of students in the long-term English learner category. He has been in the United States for all of his schooling. However, he has not had a consistent program that would allow him to develop age-appropriate academic concepts while learning English. As a result, he is below grade level in literacy skills and academic content knowledge. José is a classic example of a student Cummins identified as having conversational fluency but lacking academic language proficiency.

What Does Academic Language Involve?

Cummins defined academic language proficiency as "the extent to which an individual has command of the oral and written academic registers of schooling" (2000, 67). Cummins based the distinction between conversational fluency and academic language proficiency on research in which he examined school records of ELLs who had been referred for special education services. These students appeared to speak English well in social contexts. However, they struggled academically in their classes and scored low on tests. José, for example, speaks English without an accent, but he was placed in developmental reading in high school because of his academic performance in junior high school and his standardized test scores.

We begin this chapter by exploring in more detail what is meant by the *academic registers of schooling*. Then we look at how teachers can plan instruction to help students develop these registers. The academic registers of schooling are both oral and written, so we examine some of the differences between oral and written academic language. In order to control the academic registers of schooling, ELLs and SELs who are struggling readers need to develop both grammatical and communicative competence in English. We consider some of the complexities of both grammatical and communicative competence. We conclude by discussing how students acquire linguistic competence through membership in social groups.

Aspects of Context

Although academic language is context reduced, all language occurs in some context. Halliday and Hassan (1989) are systemic functional linguists. Systemic functional linguists are interested in how language functions in systematic ways in social contexts. They point out that there are two kinds of context. There is a context of culture and there is also a context of situation. In order to understand how language functions in different contexts, it is important to look at each of these.

Context of Culture

Each culture has certain ways of doing things. Halliday and Hassan (1989) refer to this as the context of culture. For example, children learn to eat with a fork and spoon, with chopsticks, or with their hands depending on the norm in their culture. Adults learn whether to drive on the left or the right side of the road. In school, children learn to raise their hands before asking a question in the United States and to stand when answering a question in some other countries. This knowledge is acquired as one interacts in a particular context of culture.

In fact, we are usually aware that there are cultural norms for most daily activities only when we enter another culture. Americans, who are used to standing in lines at banks, post offices, and stores, are often annoyed when they find themselves in settings where people crowd to the front. When she was living in Venezuela, Yvonne became very frustrated as she patiently waited her turn to order bread at the bakery. The store was busy, and people who entered after her walked straight up to the counter, put in their order, and got their bread. They all seemed to know just how to catch the eye of one of the workers and to get their order. Finally, a sympathetic man who noticed that Yvonne had been standing by the counter for some time came to her rescue and helped her put in her order (Freeman and Freeman 2001). Yvonne had difficulty communicating, not because she lacked the language, but because she was not familiar with the context of culture.

ELLs, especially those with limited formal schooling, are also often unfamiliar with the context of culture that exists in schools. They haven't learned classroom norms for asking or answering questions. They may not understand that it is important to work with others in group activities or that being silent in class is not always what teachers expect or want. Some students who have not been in schools before may not know that they should be quiet if the teacher is talking and that they should stay in their seats. In some cultures, it is appropriate to share what one knows, and it would be culturally unacceptable to withhold information that fellow students ask for. Teachers who do not understand different cultural norms may believe that immigrant students are cheating or misbehaving when, in fact, the students have simply not acquired the unstated rules for the context of culture in schools in their new country.

Context of Situation and Register

In addition to a context of culture, there is also a context of situation. Of course, each situation occurs within a particular culture, and any discussion of the context of situation must be understood to exist within a particular culture. In each situation, language is used slightly differently. Halliday and Hassan (1989) and other systemic functional linguists describe a context of situation in terms of three elements: field, tenor, and mode.

The *field* refers to the topic being talked or written about. The *tenor* is the relationship between the speaker and the listener or the reader and the writer. And the *mode* is the means of communication. Two modes we commonly use are speech and writing. Together the field, tenor, and mode constitute a language register. A register, then, is the way language is used in a particular context of situation within a particular culture. For the purposes of our discussion of academic language, we will consider academic registers to be the language used in schools.

An example might help explain register. When two teachers are discussing a new student as they eat lunch in the faculty room, they use a certain language register that is appropriate to that context of situation. The three components— field, tenor, and mode—help determine the language they use. The field, or topic, in this example is *new students*. The tenor, or relationship among those communicating, is *colleagues of equal status*. And the mode is *spoken*. The tenor would change if one of the teachers were new and the other very experienced. The mode would change if one teacher were writing a report on the new student for the student's file. Different language forms, such as vocabulary and syntax, would be used if any element of the context of situation—the field, the tenor, or the mode—changed.

The term *register* can be applied in different ways. We can refer generally to the registers of schooling, such as the math register and the social studies register. We can analyze each content area in general terms, or we can make a more detailed analysis of a specific lesson or part of a lesson using the same three components: field, tenor, and mode. For example, a math discussion among students working in a small group is different from a math test. Although the field remains the same, the tenor (student to student versus teacher or test to student) and the mode (oral versus written) are different. Since the registers are different, the kinds of language the participants use are also different.

Using Classroom Discourse to Build Academic Registers

The challenge for teachers of ELLs and SELs who are struggling readers is to help students learn the appropriate registers to use in their classes. Clearly, the language used in school settings is different from the language ELLs would use with their friends after school or with their parents at home. In different contexts of situation, people use different vocabulary and syntax to communicate. The registers used in content-area classrooms require a different vocabulary and syntax than those used in other contexts. Classroom language is what is generally referred to as academic language. Content-area teachers need to help students develop the appropriate language for their subject through carefully scaffolded instruction. However, many teachers simply focus on the content knowledge rather than attending to both the content and the academic language needed to comprehend and produce that content knowledge.

In many classrooms, teachers do most of the talking. Research in classroom discourse has confirmed that the typical exchange between a teacher and student follows a predictable pattern (Cazden 2001). The teacher asks a question. The student gives a short response. Then the teacher evaluates the response. This pattern, referred to as an IRE sequence (initiation, response, evaluation) is shown in the following example:

TEACHER: Who were the main characters?
STUDENT: Julia and Robert.
TEACHER: Good answer. Julia and Robert were the main characters.

This pattern predominates in schools, but it doesn't help ELLs or other students develop academic language. In the first place, the question only elicits a short response. Secondly, the teacher's next comment does not extend the discussion. Instead, the teacher evaluates the student response. In essence, this interchange becomes a sort of oral quiz. The purpose seems to be to find out if the students have done the reading. The teacher has asked a question to which she already knows the answer. The student simply demonstrates that he knows the answer. No new learning takes place.

This IRE pattern seldom occurs outside classroom settings. If a friend asked you a question to which she already knew the answer and then evaluated your response on the basis of whether it was right or wrong, you probably would be offended. Can you imagine the following conversation taking place in a coffee shop?

JILL: What is the name of the kind of doughnut you ordered?

MARÍA: It's a jelly doughnut.

JILL: That's right, you ordered a jelly doughnut.

Ways to Extend Student Talk

ELLs need to learn that the pattern of talk in classrooms is quite different from the patterns they have experienced in other settings. For ELLs to increase their proficiency in academic language, teachers need to ask more open-ended questions and then respond to students in ways that encourage them to extend their language and their thinking. Mohr and Mohr (2007) comment that even when ELLs make an appropriate response to a question that asks for simple recall, the teacher can confirm a correct response and also encourage the student to explain the response. They suggest using phrases such as "You're right! Can you tell me more?" or "Yes, that's good. What else do you know about that?" (444). In the previous example, the teacher might have responded, "Yes, Julia and Robert are the main characters. How did you figure that out?" Responses like this affirm students' answers and also push them to extend their language and their thinking. One feature of classroom academic registers is that students are considered more proficient if they can provide elaborated answers.

In some cases, students' answers are only partially correct. Mohr and Mohr suggest that teachers can affirm that students are on the right track while pushing them to add more or rethink their answers. For example, if a student had answered "Julia" to the previous question, the teacher might respond, "Yes, I agree that Julia is a main character. Do you or anyone else think there is a second main character?"

At times, students give answers that are not correct. Mohr and Mohr suggest that teachers should probe more to help students think through such answers by saying things like "Tell me more so I know what you are thinking," or "Do you think that Julia or Robert could be a main character?" As these examples show, even when they ask questions that require recall and that can be answered in one or two words, teachers can respond in ways that help students extend their language.

Bridging Conversational and Academic Registers

In addition to extending students' responses to questions, teachers can use classroom discussions to help students bridge conversational and academic language registers. In most cases, oral language corresponds to Cummins' conversational fluency because oral language is usually more context embedded and less cognitively demanding than written language. At the same time, characteristics of written language usually match more closely with academic language proficiency because it is generally less context embedded and more cognitively demanding. However, it is not difficult to find exceptions. Understanding a lecture requires a student to have developed some academic language proficiency, but reading a short message from a friend draws on conversational language proficiency.

Martin (1984, in Gibbons 2002) describes language use as ranging along a mode continuum. Some language is more spokenlike and some is more writtenlike. An oral lecture would have some features of written language, and a text message from a friend would have characteristics of oral language. Both of these might fall toward the middle of a spoken–written mode continuum. Effective instruction for ELLs involves moving them along the continuum from using language that is more spokenlike to language that is more writtenlike.

Gibbons (2002) provides an excellent model for teachers to use in her book *Scaffolding Language, Scaffolding Learning: Teaching Second Language Learners in the Mainstream Classroom*. She begins by asking her readers to consider the differences between the following four texts:

- Look, it's making them move. Those don't stick.
- We found out the pins stuck on the magnet.
- Our experiments showed that magnets attract some metals.
- Magnetic attraction occurs only between ferrous metals. (40)

The four texts represent four different registers. The first three were produced as students first worked in small groups on a science experiment with magnets, then reported to the class, and finally wrote up the results. The first text was spoken by a girl during group work. The second was part of her oral report to the class. The third text was part of her written report. The last text comes from a children's encyclopedia.

The language of each text changes with the context of situation. The field, magnetic attraction, is the same for all four texts. What changes are the tenor and the mode. In the first example, the girl is talking to classmates as they manipulate the magnets. The second is a report to the class. The mode is still oral, but the tenor changes from a child talking to a small group of children to a child talking to a large group that includes the teacher. The language of the third text changes because the mode is written. For the encyclopedia entry, the mode is also written, but the tenor has changed. The writer is now an expert speaking to an unspecified audience.

In analyzing the four texts, two things to note are that the reference becomes more explicit (the pronoun *them* is replaced by *pins*) as the distance between the speaker or writer and the audience increases, and the vocabulary becomes more technical (*stuck* is replaced by *attract*). These are features common to academic registers. Each text is appropriate for the context of situation. ELLs need to develop a range of registers so that they can vary their language to fit the task.

Gibbons (2002) describes how a teacher can scaffold instruction to help her students develop their academic language proficiency. In the previous example, the teacher involved her students in a small-group activity. She chose a science experiment. This was a hands-on activity in which language was contextualized by the use of the manipulatives. At the same time, it was cognitively demanding since the students were trying to understand principles of magnetic attraction. Students used everyday expressions to comment on what they observed or to ask questions. They didn't need to name the objects because all the group members could see them. They could point and use gestures to convey meaning.

Next, the teacher briefly introduced the key vocabulary, *attract* and *repel*. She explained that these were more scientific words the students could use to explain what happened as they moved the magnets. Students understood the words because the teacher connected the meanings to the activity the students had just been involved in. She also bridged from conversational to academic terms by saying things like, "You said that the magnet pushes away. Another way to say that is to say that the magnet repels" (45). She accompanied her explanation with gestures. She also limited the number of technical terms that she introduced.

The third stage was to guide the students as they gave their oral reports. Here the teacher worked in what Vygotsky (1962) defined as the zone of proximal development (ZPD). Vygotsky stated that learning takes place in social interaction. We learn when we receive instruction that is just beyond our current ability level. With the help of an adult or more capable peer, we can do things we can't do on our own. Over time, we can do the same things independently. The key is for the teacher to build on what the students say or do, scaffolding instruction to extend their language and their understanding of academic concepts.

As the students reported on the results of the science experiment to the whole class, the teacher provided words or concepts the students needed. She used the kinds of responses that Mohr and Mohr (2007) outlined. She affirmed their efforts and in some cases restated their language to include the scientific terms. For example, when one student said, "The two north poles are leaning together and the magnet on the bottom is repelling the magnet on top so that the magnet on the top is sort of . . . floating in the air," the teacher commented, "so these two magnets are *repelling* each other" (Gibbons 2002, 46). By emphasizing the key term *repelling*, the teacher helped all the students begin to acquire the term. Gibbons noted that the teacher contributed to the student talk during the reports, but the teacher always responded to what the students said, and the amount of teacher talk was about equal to the amount of student talk. This is different from typical classrooms, where teachers do most of the talking.

After the students reported to the whole group, the teacher asked them to write in their journals what they had learned. Since they had worked in the small groups and listened to the teacher's introduction of key terms and to the reports from each group, all the students were able to write an entry. This journal writing helped them bridge from oral to written language. The language changed because the mode changed. Later, the teacher reminded students to refer to their journal entries as they wrote more formal science reports.

The sequence that Gibbons describes, moving from small-group activities to teacher introduction of key terms, group reports, individual journal writing, and formal reports, is an excellent way to scaffold instruction for ELLs. At each stage they are supported. Throughout the sequence, the language is context embedded and cognitively demanding. All students can succeed because of the way the teacher structures the lesson.

Wells and Chang-Wells (1992) provide a number of similar examples of how teachers can help ELLs build academic language through collaborative classroom talk. They emphasize the importance of engaging students in group work during which they need to use talk to solve problems. For example, one group Wells and Chang-Wells described attempted to explain why objects seem to bend when they are placed in water. The students looked at a coin in a dish of water. With the teacher's help, they began to use terms like *refracting* and *reflecting* to describe how light appears to bend objects in the water. As they engaged in the activity, the students built their academic language proficiency and their knowledge of science. After working in small groups, students can write about what they have learned. The small-group work gives them concepts and vocabulary they can use in their writing.

Spoken Academic English

As Gibbons and Wells and Chang-Wells demonstrate, teachers can use classroom talk to help students bridge from conversational to academic language. By using talk effectively, teachers build on what students bring to school and help move students beyond what they already know and can do on their own. Such teachers work within their students' zones of proximal development. They scaffold instruction so that students develop the language and the concepts they need to succeed academically.

The scaffolded talk enables students to participate successfully in related reading and writing activities. Students need to develop both oral and written academic language registers. Recall that a register consists of three parts: field, tenor, and mode. Oral and written languages represent two different modes. When students report on their science experiments to the class, they use academic oral language. They include technical terms, such as *repel* or *refract*, and they are more explicit in their references since they are describing objects and actions their classmates cannot see.

These oral reports are in some ways more writtenlike than spokenlike, to use Martin's terms. Nevertheless, there are significant differences between the spoken and the written language modes. In his research, Biber (1986) used texts from broadcasts, public speeches, and conversations for his oral language sample. He found that these oral language texts had different features from the written text sources he examined. What would a researcher find who examined oral texts taken from academic contexts? Would these language samples be more spokenlike or more writtenlike?

An analysis of spoken academic English • Swales (2005) used data from a large corpus of language to analyze features of spoken academic English. The corpus that Swales used is the Michigan Corpus of Academic Spoken English. This database "is drawn from 152 speech events, including not only lectures, but also office hours, study group sessions, research group meetings, dissertation defenses and so on" (30). The question that Swales and other linguists working with this data investigated is "whether academic speech would be more like academic prose or more like conversation" (30).

Swales notes that academic writing has certain features. It consists primarily of declarative sentences. Sentences are, on average, long because they contain subordinate clauses. They are punctuated using colons and semicolons in addition to periods and commas. About 20 percent of the verbs are in passive form. Like Corson (1997), Swales notes that the technical vocabulary comes from Greek and Latin sources. The process of written text production is complex, with editing and revisions. In analyzing the Michigan corpus of academic speech, the researchers looked for similar features in the oral language. What they found, however, was that "lecture and discussion styles had most of the features—apart from some technical jargon—of ordinary conversation" (Swales 2005, 30). In other words, academic speech is more like everyday speech than like academic writing.

Swales gives several examples from his data to show that spoken academic English is more like speech than writing. For instance, English written language follows a syntactic pattern of subject, verb, and object. In the previous sentence, *language* is the simple subject, *follows* is the verb, and *pattern* is the object. In the Michigan data, the subject was omitted frequently. For example, the subject was left out 14 percent of the time when the verb was *depends*. If someone asks, "Going to the game?" speakers often begin their answer with *depends*, as in "Depends on the weather." Note that in this case, the question also lacks an overt subject. Even when speakers are discussing academic topics, the communication is face-to-face, so it is natural to leave out the subject.

Swales concludes his article by commenting, "I have attempted to show that the basic utterance in academic speech is fragmented and contains insertions, repetitions, and deletions that armchair grammarians [those that write grammar books] do not easily foresee" (2005, 34). In other words, even professors don't talk like a book.

The research by Swales and his colleagues shows that there are differences between oral and written academic language. When professors are giving lectures or students are meeting in a study group, their language has the features associated with face-to-face oral interactions even when the topic is academic.

Gibbons (2002) demonstrates how teachers can help students bridge from oral language to written academic language by having students work in small groups, then give oral reports to the class, do informal writing, such as journal entries, and then refine their writing in more formal reports. The key is to ensure that classroom instruction is context embedded and cognitively demanding so that with time ELLs and SELs who are struggling readers can learn to read and write texts that are cognitively demanding and context reduced.

It is also important for teachers to recognize that both oral and written language registers are complex and must be acquired in the process of solving problems, engaging in classroom discussions, and completing meaningful reading and writing assignments. The elements of oral and written language are too complex to teach directly. Instead, students acquire the registers of academic language as they use language in their classrooms.

The Complexities of Oral and Written Language Registers

Cummins (1994) and other researchers have shown that it takes from five to seven years to develop academic language proficiency. This is not surprising since oral and written communication are complex. Effective communication requires two kinds of competence. ELLs need to develop grammatical competence in English. They must acquire a high enough level of English phonology, syntax, semantics, and vocabulary to be able to communicate effectively. In addition, they must develop sociolinguistic competence, the ability to use language that fits the context.

Developing Grammatical Competence

Much teaching of English as a second language has focused on helping ELLs develop grammatical competence. However, grammatical competence has often been interpreted as learning the grammar of English using a traditional approach. Grammatical competence is more complex than understanding parts of speech or parts of a sentence. In her analysis of academic language Scarcella (2003) divides grammatical competence, which she refers to as the linguistic dimension of academic language, into five components: the phonological component, the lexical component, the grammatical component, the sociolinguistic component, and the discourse component.

The phonological component • In the first place, students with academic language proficiency can comprehend and produce the vocabulary used in schools. For example, an English teacher might use a word like *epitome* or a biology teacher might talk about *anemones*. ELLs may have trouble understanding these words because they are technical terms, and the pronunciation differs from the written form. They also may find it difficult to pronounce these words if they read aloud in class or give an oral report.

English phonology is also complicated because different forms of a word are pronounced differently. While ELLs might comprehend *medicine*, related words such as *medicinal* or *medication* might be difficult for them to comprehend or produce. The phonological component of academic language, then, has to do with oral language. ELLs often have difficulty understanding words or phrases teachers use as they lecture.

Teachers can provide support to help students develop the phonological component of academic language by accompanying lectures with written language, either in the form of handouts, key words written on the board, or PowerPoint presentations. If students can see as well as hear the words, they can more easily acquire both the meaning and the phonology of the new vocabulary. ELLs also need practice in producing this vocabulary as they discuss a topic in a heterogeneous small group with native English speakers. In addition, teachers can provide tapes of class texts so that students can listen to their textbooks being read as they follow along in their own books.

The lexical component • The lexical component refers to the vocabulary of academic English. The words used in academic speaking and writing are different from those used in everyday conversation. As Corson (1997) found, many everyday words come from Anglo-Saxon roots. These tend to be short words. Academic vocabulary, in contrast, often has Greek or Latin roots. Many of the words with Latin roots entered English through French during the period of the Norman conquest of England. Academic words are generally longer with more prefixes and suffixes. Brook (1998) provides several examples of words with related meanings. (We discuss her examples in more detail in Chapter 6.) French and Latin words are longer and used more often in writing than in speech. For example, *fear* comes from Anglo-Saxon, *terror* is from French, and *trepidation* comes from Latin. The Anglo-Saxon word is *holy*, the French borrowing is *sacred*, and *consecrated* comes from Latin. As these examples show, the French- and Latin-based words occur primarily in texts. For that reason, students acquire most of their academic vocabulary as they read academic texts.

The grammatical component • The grammatical component in Scarcella's (2003) model refers to sentence structure. Generally, sentences in academic writing and speech are longer and more complex than those in conversational language. Complex sentences carry more information by embedding ideas into dependent clauses. The challenge for a second-language learner is deciding how the ideas are related and which one or ones are more important.

Academic texts also frequently contain sentences written in the passive voice. In a sentence such as "The mixture was heated to a high temperature," the passive verb form, *was heated*, is complex. In addition, the grammatical subject of this sentence, *the mixture*, is not the logical subject. That is, in a passive sentence like this one, the subject of the sentence is not the one performing the action. The reader must supply a logical subject such as *the scientist* to comprehend the sentence, and this requires the use of background knowledge. The best way for students to develop the ability to comprehend sentences such as these is through engagement with academic texts. If students read extensively in different content areas, they acquire both the academic vocabulary and academic sentence structure.

In addition to extensive reading, ELLs benefit from some instruction. One good activity is to give students a series of related simple sentences. Working in groups, the students can combine these simple sentences into longer, complex sentences. Studies (see Weaver 2002) have shown that sentence-combining exercises like these improve student writing. Kilgallon and Kilgallon (2007) have written a useful student work text that includes sentence combining and other techniques students can use to produce more complex sentences. This book is a useful resource for teachers because it gives a variety of writing exercises to help students develop different grammatical structures.

The sociolinguistic component • The sociolinguistic component is the ability to use language for different functions, such as apologizing or introducing, and to read and write in different genres, such as science reports. We will discuss sociolinguistic competence in detail in the following section because of its complexity and importance.

The discourse component • According to Scarcella, the discourse component refers to the ability to structure connected ideas in a form appropriate for the subject area. It involves using logical connectors to transition from one idea to the next. Discourse can be either oral or written. In an oral report, for example, a student must organize ideas so that they follow logically. The best way for teachers to help students develop the discourse component of grammatical competence is through work on editing their writing to improve the organization and the links among the different parts. In Chapter 4 we examine the organization of academic texts in the different content areas in detail.

Developing Sociolinguistic Competence

In addition to grammatical competence, ELLs need to develop sociolinguistic, or communicative, competence. Hymes (1970) defines communicative competence as knowing when to say what to whom and under what circumstances. This is another way of saying that students need to develop the registers for different contexts of situation. They need to use language that is appropriate for the field (knowing what to say or write), the tenor (knowing to whom they are talking or writing and choosing language appropriate for that relationship), and the mode (under what conditions).

ELLs need both grammatical competence and sociolinguistic competence. Simply comprehending and producing sentences that are grammatically correct is not enough. Students also need to use language that is appropriate for the context of situation. In order to control the oral and written registers of schooling, ELLs need to acquire ways of talking and writing that are expected in school. They can do this only as they interact in school settings, since many aspects of language registers are too complex to be taught directly.

Gee (1988) explains that ELLs must learn to use language in ways that show their perspective on what they are saying. Whether they are using a conversational or academic register, speakers not only discuss subjects but also indicate which points are most important. In addition, speakers use language that signals their social identity. In academic language registers, speakers and writers attempt to establish themselves as authorities on a subject. The language they use establishes the tenor, the relationship between the speaker and the listener or the writer and the reader.

Perspective taking • One component of sociolinguistic competence is perspective taking. When we speak, we indicate how we view what we are saying, our perspective on the topic. The principal way that we show our perspective is by our intonation pattern. We stress certain words, and we group certain words together to convey subtle differences in meaning. That is, we use a particular prosodic structure to help a listener understand our intended message.

For example, consider the sentence "He only said he loved her." Many ELLs interpret this sentence as meaning that this was all he said. He didn't say anything else. And this could be the message if the stress fell on *only*. However, if the stress was shifted to *said*, most native English speakers would interpret this sentence as meaning that although he *said* he loved her, he didn't really mean it. The way the speaker's voice rises and falls changes the meaning. If the speaker stresses *only* and then lets his voice drop on *said*, he is signaling one meaning. If his voice rises on *said* and then falls, he sends a completely different message.

Gee (1988) points out that the prosody of an utterance (a word, phrase, sentence, or group of sentences) can signal several things. For example, a speaker can show how sure she is about what she is saying, what she is taking for granted as common knowledge, how what she is saying relates to previous segments of the conversation, and how formal or informal the conversation is. The subtle changes in prosody, such as stress and pitch, as well as the choice of words carry much of the meaning in a conversation. These aspects of a new language are acquired in the process of interacting with speakers of that language. No one can teach all of these subtleties.

When it comes to written language, ELLs can no longer rely on the meanings conveyed by pitch or tone in oral language. A writer could put some words in bold or italics or use exclamation marks to signal her perspective. For example a student could write an e-mail to a friend: That test was **really** hard! However, emphasizing with boldface type and inserting exclamation marks are not typical conventions used in academic writing. Punctuation helps show the syntactic structure of sentences, but it provides few clues as to pitch, tone, or how certain words in a sentence are grouped together. ELLs need extensive exposure to written language to understand how writers show the perspective they are taking on what they are saying. Successful academic writing is generally formal, objective, and authoritative.

Teachers can help students learn to interpret the perspective that writers of academic texts are taking on their subjects. For example, authors of social studies texts signal their point of view on their subjects in several ways, such as choosing certain facts to present. In the following chapter, we show how teachers can help students recognize point of view in social studies texts.

Solidarity and status • Gee (1988) explains that in addition to showing the perspective they are taking, speakers use language to signal social identities. We use language to establish who we are in relationship to the person we are speaking to. We use language differently when speaking to a peer than when speaking to someone we perceive to be of higher or lower status. Whenever we speak or write, we show in subtle ways something about our level of education and social status. The choices we make help establish the tenor of our communication.

Gee points out that in any conversational interchange, two conflicting forces are at work. On the one hand, speakers want to connect with listeners and be part of the group. That is, they use language in ways to show solidarity. On the other hand, speakers may want to indicate that they are of a higher status than their listeners. Think of the debates between presidential candidates. Candidates want to connect with their constituents. They often use *down-home* words and phrases. A politician in Texas, for instance, might sprinkle his speech with *you all* or even *y'all*. At the same time, if the politician is a presidential candidate, she would use language to signal a higher status than the common person. After all, people vote for someone they look up to, not someone who is just like them.

New teachers, especially teachers in secondary schools, often have trouble using the correct language to connect with their students while still maintaining their status as the teacher. They shift between everyday language, similar to that used by their students, and the more formal language of teaching in order to assert authority. A teacher might incorporate some slang expressions as she lectures. Nevertheless, teachers who talk too much like their students do risk losing their status. When they attempt to discipline students, they may have trouble. Often teachers shift back and forth between language that signals solidarity and language that indicates status.

Students also struggle with this conflict between solidarity and status. In giving an oral presentation in class, they may use informal pronunciation and vocabulary to show they are part of their peer group and, as a result, fail to establish the status necessary to deliver an effective academic oral report. Students also vary their language because the way they use language marks their relationship with other students and with the teacher. A student who is confident she knows the answer to a teacher's question must express that information in a way that avoids sending the message to her classmates that she is better than they are. For that reason, she might downplay her confidence. On the other hand, she wants to signal to the teacher that she really does know the answer. But she needs to do this without diminishing the authority of the teacher.

Often ELLs with high levels of grammatical competence have not attained similar levels of sociolinguistic competence. In classroom interchanges, they may come across in ways they don't intend, as timid, unsure, or perhaps as arrogant know-it-alls who are challenging the teacher's authority. Since teachers seldom correct these social aspects of language use, ELLs can acquire them only through extended opportunities to interact with native speakers in classroom settings.

Writers of academic texts choose forms of language to help establish themselves as authorities in their field. They assume a somewhat higher status than their readers. In the essay Dolores wrote that we discussed in Chapter 2, there was evidence that she was able to incorporate some of the features of academic writing, but other features were still lacking, and, as a result, she did not come across as an authority presenting information objectively. Writers like Dolores have trouble showing their higher status. They often use informal expressions and give opinions instead of using formal language and supporting their arguments with facts and specific examples. For example, writers of academic texts seldom use phrases like "In my opinion" as Delores did.

Yvonne has found that some of her graduate students have trouble writing their first papers with authority. Instead of making a point and then giving supporting information to prove their point, students use informal language and make statements such as "I truly believe that dual language is the best" or "Everyone knows that tests are bad for kids." While all writers try to connect with their readers and establish solidarity, the important thing in academic writing is to establish status as an authority. This is often difficult for students to accomplish.

Research on status and solidarity in classroom discourse • Linguists have studied classroom discourse in detail. Their findings are enlightening and demonstrate how teachers and students use language to establish status and solidarity. Lemke (1990), for example, has conducted extensive studies of the use of language in science classes. He presents a transcript (see Figure 3.1) that illustrates how teachers and students use language to convey knowledge and, at the same time, use language to establish social relationships in the classroom.

The excerpt shown in Figure 3.1 illustrates how a teacher attempts to maintain his status as the authority figure in his exchanges with a student who challenges him. The underlines indicate stress and the vertical lines show overlapping speech. The challenge is both to his authority to maintain discipline and to his authority as an expert in science. As the teacher begins to explain how the ground creates heat energy from light energy, Eric makes a side comment to a classmate. The teacher stops to ask if Eric has a question. He does this to discipline Eric, to remind him that he shouldn't be talking while the teacher is lecturing.

In most cases, a student called on in this way would just be quiet, but Eric takes the opportunity to ask a question. Usually, it is the teacher who asks questions, so Eric's move here puts him in charge of the conversation. When the teacher begins to answer, Eric jumps in with an objection that challenges the teacher's authority, noting that light is hot. The teacher points out that fluorescent bulbs are not hot, but another student, Anne, comments that the bulb has heat, an idea that Eric echoes. Here the students are using language to show solidarity with one another.

T: The <u>ground</u> is now creating <u>heat</u> energy | <u>from the light</u>
ERIC: | Well [aside]
T: —energy. Eric, you have a question?
ERIC: Yeah, how can it be the ground creates the heat energy, if the <u>sun</u> creates the heat energy?
T: <u>Well</u>, on the <u>sun</u>, and <u>in</u> the sun, the sun <u>is</u> creating a tremendous amount of heat energy. But it's sending most of its energy here as <u>light</u>. Traveling through space.
ERIC: But light is <u>hot</u>. Light is heat.
T: No! Some light is not hot at all. When I turned on these fluorescent lights today, I haven't roasted yet.
ANNE: The bulb has heat.
ERIC: Yeah, but when the | bulb is on you get—the bulb gets hot
T: | And essentially—
        most energy from the sun comes here in the form of light and <u>not</u> heat.
ERIC: So the ground can't be <u>creating</u> heat | because if the
T: | Well—
ERIC: ground wasn't dark, then it wouldn't absorb the light. And the light is heat so it's not <u>creating</u> it.
T: No, light is <u>not</u> heat. The light is light energy.
ERIC: Yeah, and <u>heat</u> is heat energy! [students laugh]

figure 3.1 Classroom Discourse (Lemke 1990)

At the same time, they are trying to understand the relationships between different kinds of energy.

The teacher interrupts Eric to take control of the discussion using a phrase he often uses to establish his authority, "And essentially." When Eric responds to the teacher's comments with an apt observation, the teacher tries to regain control by saying, "Well," but Eric continues to make his point. The teacher tries to take control once more by directly contradicting Eric, "No, light is *not* heat. The light is light energy," but Eric comments, "Yeah, and *heat* is heat energy," which causes the other students to laugh.

Lemke analyzes many different instances of classroom discourse like this one to show that teachers and students use language to do more than exchange information. The teacher and Eric use language to establish status and solidarity. Although aspects of oral language, such as marking status, are too complex to be taught, it is good for teachers to be aware of them. In particular, it is important for teachers to realize the ELLs may not understand these subtleties of their new language. During conversational exchanges in the classroom, ELLs who raise questions may not be challenging a teacher's authority. It is more likely that they simply haven't yet acquired the language proficiency they need to ask questions in a way that is appropriate for the social context. Of course, in many cases, ELLs do not act as Eric did. Even when they have questions or know the answer, they may hesitate to speak because they lack the grammatical competence to express themselves during rapid interchanges.

Primary and Secondary Discourses

ELLs need both grammatical and sociolinguistic competence to succeed in school. However, as Gee (2008) explains, effective communication requires more than linguistic and sociolinguistic knowledge. Any use of language occurs within a social context, and functioning effectively in a social setting requires additional knowledge. Gee refers to the practices of social groups, including the ways they use language, as Discourses (with a capital *D*). As he puts it, "Discourses are ways of behaving, interacting, valuing, thinking, believing, speaking, and often reading and writing, that are accepted as instantiations of particular identities (or 'types of people') by specific groups" (3). He goes on to argue that language can be understood only within a particular Discourse. Gee's notion of Discourse is similar to the functional linguists' concept of a register, the language used in a context of situation that exists within a context of culture. However, as a sociolinguist, Gee focuses on both the social aspects of context and on the linguistic aspects.

Gee gives many examples of how acceptance into a Discourse depends on more than linguistic knowledge. One such example is that of a biker who wants to join a motorcycle gang. Even if he walks into a biker bar and orders a beer, saying, "Give me a beer, will ya?" using the right words and the appropriate intonation, he will not be accepted into this group by other bikers if he rides up on the wrong kind of motorcycle wearing designer clothes and then dusts off the bar stool with a monogrammed handkerchief before sitting down. There are certain ways to behave, interact, value, think, and speak to be taken by other bikers as one of their group, to achieve the social identity of *biker*.

In the same way, students may be considered *struggling readers* or *gifted and talented* by their classmates and teachers depending on how they behave, interact, value, think, believe, speak, read, and write. The identity they develop in school depends on all these factors, not just on how they use language. As Cummins (2001) has argued, school is a place where students negotiate identities, and often bilingual students develop their identities based primarily on their lack of academic English proficiency rather than on the many positive attributes they may possess.

Everyone has a primary Discourse. As Gee writes, "nearly all human beings, except under extraordinary circumstances, acquire an initial Discourse within what-ever constitutes their primary socializing unit early in life" (2008, 156). This primary Discourse helps shape one's sense of self. It determines what is regarded as nor-mal, how normal people think, act, interact, and speak. Over time, all people add additional, or secondary, Discourses. These secondary Discourses might include the people at work, those in a book club, members of a church, and so on. In each setting, people act and speak differently.

School constitutes a secondary Discourse for everyone. Even native speakers of a language need to develop the school Discourse. They need to act in certain ways expected in schools, value certain things, think in certain ways, and also use language in ways that are considered appropriate in school. Becoming a member of the school Discourse is a real challenge for ELLs. Not only do they need to learn English, but they need to learn to use English in a particular way in a new context.

Gee (2008) argues that Discourses are largely acquired, not learned. To become an accepted member of a group, a person needs to have access to others who are already members and time to develop the different features characteristic of the group. The process is a kind of apprenticeship. The person must be motivated to join the group, and at least some of the members must be willing to accept the person and nurture her into full competency in the characteristic behaviors and beliefs of the group. For this reason, it is important for ELLs to be integrated at least some of the day with native English speakers. They need extended, positive experiences in school to develop an identity as successful students. If ELLs are isolated and interact only with other ELLs, they have no opportunities to acquire the Discourse of school. Further, if ELLs and struggling readers are tracked into low-level classes, they have no opportunity to interact with successful students and acquire their ways of behaving, interacting, valuing, thinking, speaking, reading, and writing. Valdés (2001) has documented how many middle school ELLs are isolated from native English speakers and given low-level tasks, such as coloring and cutting out pictures of vocabulary words.

Smith (1983) describes learning to read and write as joining the literacy club. People who want to read and write must be around other people who are willing to help them develop the skills, knowledge, and values needed to make sense of written texts. Joining a social group or joining the literacy club involves becoming a member of a particular Discourse.

In the process of taking on secondary Discourses, the primary Discourse may be changed or lost. Some bilingual children, for example, lose their first language and reject many of the cultural practices followed by their parents and grandparents. This is especially the case for many long-term English learners with the characteristics of involuntary minorities (Ogbu 1991). In Gee's (2008) terms, their primary Discourses die. Other students, particularly recent arrivals with the characteristics of immigrant minorities, move between their primary and secondary Discourses with little difficulty even when this means alternating between languages and cultures. Since it is only by joining the Discourse of school that ELLs gain control of the oral and written registers of schooling, the fact that recent arrivals can make the shift more easily than long-term English learners helps explain their higher success rate in school, especially if they come with adequate formal schooling.

A Head Start on Developing Academic Language

In some homes, parents prepare young children for school success by teaching some of the ways of talking and acting that are valued in schools. As Gee states, "Social groups that are deeply affiliated with formal schooling often incorporate into the socialization of their children practices that resonate with later school-based secondary Discourses" (2008 157). Many English-speaking parents teach their children the alphabet song and nursery rhymes, things they will hear in school. They also teach children to answer questions such as "Is this your nose?" and respond to commands such as "Point to your nose. Point to your ears." This prepares students to answer school-type questions and follow directions.

In addition, parents often teach their children how to tell the kinds of stories teachers expect during sharing time. These stories have a clear beginning, middle, and end. Parents also read to their children and teach them about books so their children can develop concepts of print. Gee calls these practices *early borrowing*. He says, "Early borrowing functions not primarily to give children certain skills, but, rather, to give them certain values, attitudes, motivations, ways of interacting, and perspectives, all of which are more important than mere skills for successful later entry into specific secondary Discourses" (2008, 158).

Students whose parents practice early borrowing have a head start at school. Heath (1983) conducted a study of three different communities in the Carolinas. One of these was Roadvillle, a white working-class community whose members had worked in the local textile mills for four generations. The second was Trackton, a black working-class community. The older generations had farmed, but the current members also worked in the textile mills. Children from both Roadville and Trackton attended school with mainstream whites and blacks, the townspeople.

Heath shows differences between the language registers that Roadville and Trackton children used. For example, Roadville children were taught to always tell the truth. Trackton children were encouraged to be imaginative and entertaining in their speech. Both of these patterns conflict with school-based Discourse. The Roadville children did not enjoy imaginative stories and had trouble writing creative stories. The Trackton children were able to tell very creative stories, but the stories did not follow the expected pattern of beginning, middle, and end. Instead, they consisted of a series of loosely related episodes that seemed to go on and on.

Roadville children were taught to speak only when spoken to, so they seldom volunteered in class. While they did behave, they were often seen as lacking initiative or motivation. At home, Trackton children learned how to break into a conversation and hold the floor by their creative use of language. This interactive style did not serve them well in school, where children are supposed to take turns and keep their responses short and to the point. Trackton children were often seen as undisciplined and rowdy.

Although none of the children in Heath's study were ELLs, the children from Roadville and Trackton were SELs. Since the Roadville and Trackton children's primary Discourses did not match the school Discourse, children from these communities experienced more difficulties in school than children from the town, whose parents prepared them for the ways of talking and acting that teachers in the school (who had themselves been townspeople) expected. The match or mismatch between students' primary Discourse and the school-based Discourse influences how quickly students develop the oral and written academic registers of schooling.

Certainly, many ELLs and SELs do not experience the early borrowing that Gee talks about and Heath describes in her discussion of the townspeople. In a review of the research about ELLs, García (2000) found that they are less likely to have early prereading supports (being read to aloud, using educational games and toys, inventing stories and rhymes) than native English-speaking children. We began this chapter discussing José, a new immigrant to this country when he entered first grade. José did not have any preschool or kindergarten experience in Mexico, and his parents did not know how to help him with schoolwork. There was a definite mismatch between his primary Discourse and the school-based Discourse. This mismatch extended beyond learning to speak English. José had to learn English and the Discourse of school. Although he did develop conversational language in English and could communicate with his peers and teachers, he struggled to develop the academic registers of schooling. What is perhaps most important for educators to understand is that no one around José, including his teachers, understood the complexities of the task José faced.

Conclusion

In this chapter we have looked more closely at the concept of academic language proficiency. Halliday and Hassan (1989) explain that a register is the language used in a certain context of situation. Cummins (2000) defines academic language proficiency as the extent to which students control the oral and written registers of schooling. Teachers can organize classroom activities to help students build oral and written academic language registers. For example, as Mohr and Mohr (2007) show, teachers can respond in ways that help students extend their language and their thinking. Gibbons (2002) explains how teachers can scaffold learning to help students bridge from conversational to academic language.

ELLs need to develop grammatical competence. Scarcella (2003) describes five components of grammatical competence. In addition, ELLs need to develop sociolinguistic competence. Gee (1988) discusses two aspects of sociolinguistic competence. He explains that speakers need to choose language that shows their perspective on what they are saying and choose language that marks their status or solidarity in relation to their listeners. ELLs often have difficulty in developing these subtle aspects of language. Both grammatical and communicative language proficiencies are complex and must be acquired in the context of meaningful use.

Gee (2008) argues that linguistic ability is only one component of sociolinguistic competence. All of us are born into a social group, and we acquire the norms for acting, thinking, valuing, and using the language of that social group. This is what

Gee refers to as our primary Discourse. We also acquire a number of secondary Discourses, and one of these is the school Discourse. Students must learn how to think, act, believe, speak, read, and write in a way that is expected in the school Discourse. School is a secondary Discourse for both native English speakers and ELLs. However, as Heath's research (1983) showed, some students start school with many of the attitudes and behaviors that are valued in school. In contrast, ELLs and SELs are exposed to the academic English registers only at school, so they need extended support to gain control of the academic oral and written registers of schooling.

Applications

1. We discuss the context of culture and the importance of understanding that different cultures have different norms. What are the cultural backgrounds of the ELLs in your schools? Interview a student from another culture and ask the student for examples of how things are done differently here than in the home culture. Specifically ask about how things are done differently in schools. Be prepared to share.

2. The context of situation is composed of three elements: field, tenor, and mode. In the week to come, observe three different events in schools. (For example, teachers giving directions to students, the principal's memo to the faculty, students talking in class, students working on a joint project). Describe each situation by including the field, tenor, and mode. How did these observations help you become more aware of the importance of context of situation?

3. Consciously reflect on your own teaching or observe another teacher in the next week. If possible, tape-record about ten minutes of the lesson. Notice how much time the teacher is talking and how much time the students are talking. Are the exchanges between the teacher and students following an IRE pattern, or is the teacher extending the conversation as suggested by Mohr and Mohr (2007)? Write an analysis of your findings to bring to class or your study group and be prepared to share.

4. Observe and record a group of students doing a project together and their reporting to the class. Pull out at least four statements that students make about the content they are working on for the project. Identify the field, tenor, and mode of the comments. Can you identify differences in register in those comments as suggested by Gibbons (2002)? Be prepared to discuss what you found out.

5. Scarcella (2003) discusses five components of the linguistic dimension of academic language: the phonological component, the lexical component, the grammatical component, the sociolinguistic component, and the discourse component. Define each and review the suggestions given in the book about how to help students develop each component. Add suggestions you have for each of the components.

6. In this chapter, we discussed the conflicts speakers experience between using language to express solidarity and using it to show status. Explain what is meant by showing solidarity and showing status. Observe some interchanges in school where you notice speakers showing solidarity or status. Take notes and bring them to class or your study group for discussion.

7. Gee (2008) discusses the idea of Discourse with a capital *D*. Explain Discourse in your own words. Then, list the secondary Discourse groups to which you belong. Also, describe the primary and a secondary Discourse group for some of your ELLs and SELs. Explain your conclusions. Be prepared to share your conclusions.

4

Coping with Academic Texts and Textbooks

We have seen the difficulties that Dolores had as she attempted to write using an academic style. She also struggled as she attempted to make sense of the thick textbooks she was expected to read in her different content classes. The following paragraph from a biology textbook (Biggs et al. 2004) is typical of the kind of writing that ELLs like Dolores and SELs who are struggling readers face daily:

> Like many of the organisms studied in this chapter, most flatworms, including planarians, are hermaphrodites. During sexual reproduction, individual planarians exchange sperm, which travel along special tubes to reach the eggs. Fertilization occurs internally. The zygotes are released in capsules into the water, where they hatch into tiny planarians. (707)

We begin this chapter by examining the characteristics of content-area texts. Next, we point out some of the problems with textbooks, like this biology textbook, that students like Dolores are expected to read. Teachers must find ways to help ELLs and SELs who struggle with reading cope with the challenges of reading academic texts. They can employ a variety of strategies to engage all their students in reading academic texts to build their academic language proficiency.

Characteristics of Content-Area Texts

The previous paragraph about planarians demonstrates certain characteristics of academic language at the text level. Fang (2008) identifies the unique features of expository language found in texts like this. The language is technical, abstract, dense, and authoritative. These features are typical of the academic texts students are given to read beginning in the intermediate grades and continuing on through middle and high school.

In the first place, expository texts contain many technical terms. In the first sentence of the paragraph from Dolores' biology book, we find words such as *organisms*, *planarians*, and *hermaphrodites*. These are specialized terms that students seldom hear or use in conversational exchanges or when they read stories. When students like Dolores try to read a text with a high number of unfamiliar, technical words, they often become frustrated and stop reading.

In addition, the language in the paragraph is abstract. Fang points out that one way writers create abstract texts is to use words like *reproduction* and *fertilization*. Both of these words are nouns. Yet the ideas they express would normally be conveyed by verbs. *Reproduce* and *fertilize* refer to actions. By adding a suffix, the writers have converted each word into a noun. The process of turning verbs or adjectives into nouns is called nominalization.

In English, nouns usually name the actors or participants in a sentence, and verbs express the actions. A more direct way to express the ideas in the paragraph would be to use the verb forms to express the actions: "Individual planarians reproduce when they exchange sperm. The sperm fertilize the eggs." When we talk, we usually use sentences like this in which the nouns name the actors and the verbs express the actions.

The process of nominalization makes the sentences more abstract. In the paragraph, both *reproduction* and *fertilization* have become processes. The sentences don't name the actors who are reproducing or fertilizing. By removing the actors, writers of academic texts make them more impersonal. Rather than discussing how planarians reproduce or how sperm fertilize eggs and presenting the ideas in concrete terms, the writers use the abstract ideas of *reproduction* and *fertilization* to discuss the processes.

A third feature of academic texts is that they are dense. Nominalization contributes to text density. Once writers have turned verbs into nouns, they can pack more information into each sentence. This increases the cognitive load and makes reading more difficult. Linguists measure the density of texts by calculating the number of content words (nouns, verbs, adjectives, and adverbs) in each clause that is not embedded in another clause.

Changing verbs or adjectives into nouns is one way that writers increase the density of academic texts. For example, once a word like *reproduce* is converted into a noun, other words can be added to modify the noun and create a complex nominal phrase. In the second sentence, for example, *reproduction* is modified by the adjective *sexual* and then further modified by the embedded clause "which travel along special tubes to reach the eggs." The result is a sentence with one non-embedded clause that has eleven content words (*sexual, reproduction, individual, planarians, exchange, sperm, travel, special, tubes, reach, eggs*) out of sixteen total words. This sentence is typical of the dense sentences that students have to unpack when they read content-area texts.

Academic texts are also more authoritative than oral or written narrative texts. Writers of academic texts create an authoritative tone in several ways. They use technical terms. Most of the sentences are statements, not questions or commands. Academic texts also use more passive sentences. The last sentence in the paragraph from the biology text, for example, is written in passive voice. The sentence begins, "The zygotes are released in capsules into the water." Finally, the subjects of sentences in academic texts either are very general (words like *scientists*) or are not directly named. In the passive sentence about zygotes, we are not told who or what releases the zygotes.

The combination of all these devices creates an authoritative tone. The writer is positioned as an expert who is stating technical information in a factual manner. As Fang puts it, "Taken together, these linguistic devices enable the author to present information accurately, objectively, and assertively" (2008, 481). Of course, every author has a point of view, so no text can be completely objective, and in some cases the information that is presented is not accurate. Also, information in textbooks is not usually complete. In social studies, for example, it is important for readers to realize that omissions of events and people in a textbook result in an inaccurate or biased view of history. Noboa (2006) has documented how Latinos are left out of textbooks in Texas, a state with a very large Latino population. As Daniels and Zemelman (2004) note, students must become critical readers, and they should consult multiple sources to get a more balanced view of any topic.

Inconsistencies in Textbook Language

In Chapter 2, we analyzed Dolores' essay and concluded that it did not contain the features Fang identifies as characteristic of academic texts. One reason that Dolores struggled with academic writing is that she had great difficulty reading her school textbooks. These books contained academic writing, but since Dolores had difficulty reading them, they didn't serve as good models for her writing.

Even if Dolores could read her math, history, or science books, she might have been confused by the variation in the style of these academic texts. Although most academic texts have the characteristics Fang identifies, the style of writing varies considerably, even within one textbook. Consider the following two paragraphs that appear on the same page in an integrated physics and chemistry text (McLaughlin et al. 2002) for high school students:

> If you are at the beach in the summertime, you might notice that the ocean seems much cooler than the air or sand. Even though energy from the Sun is falling on the air, sand, and water at the same rate, the temperature of the water has changed less than the temperature of the air or sand has.

> Compared with other common materials in Table 1, water has the highest specific heat, as shown in Figure 4. Because water can absorb heat without a large change in temperature, it is useful as a coolant. A coolant is a substance that is used to absorb heat. For example, water is used as the coolant in the cooling systems of automobile engines. As long as the water temperature is lower than the engine temperature, heat will flow from the engine to the water. Compared to other materials, water can absorb more heat from the engine before its temperature rises. Because it takes water longer to heat up compared with other materials, it also takes water longer to cool down. (161)

The first paragraph is written in a conversational style. The writers address the reader as "you" and use an everyday example to introduce an important science concept. The vocabulary is not technical. Although the sentences are long, they are not overly complex. In contrast, the second paragraph is written in a more academic style. The writers do not address the reader but instead present the facts. The writers refer to a table and a figure that appear on the page and that the reader is expected to consult and understand. There is more technical vocabulary here and the sentences have a more complex structure.

This variation in style is common in school textbooks. One problem posed by variation is that readers have to adjust their reading to match the changing styles.

A second problem is that these books do not provide clear models of how students should write. If Dolores wrote a science report following the style of the first paragraph, she would probably receive a lower grade than if she wrote following the style of the second paragraph. These are just two of the problems presented by textbooks for students like Dolores who are trying to develop academic language proficiency.

Problems with Textbooks

In middle school and high school classrooms, a textbook for each content area is nearly as inevitable as death or taxes. Most of these textbooks are thick compendiums that are purported to carry the accumulated wisdom of the experts in a field. The biology text we examined had 1,190 pages. Of course, since it was a teacher's edition, it contained extra pages with test preparation suggestions. Nevertheless, a student's edition of an integrated physics and chemistry book had 914 pages, and a world geography book ran 894 pages. Together the three books weighed a hefty 17 pounds, a heavy load both physically and mentally for teachers and students alike.

For ELLs and SELs who are struggling readers, textbooks like these are certainly intimidating. Even if they were written in a reader-friendly style, which is not the case, their bulk would make them seem overwhelming to students who lack confidence in their English-reading ability. These are certainly not inviting books that students want to curl up with in the evening.

Daniels and Zemelman (2004) list several problems with textbooks. In the first place, even though they are very long, textbooks are superficial. They attempt to cover so much content that they don't explore any area in depth. For example, it's quite a challenge for a writer to condense the important information about World War I into two or three pages.

As the biology passage we quote at the beginning of this chapter shows, a second problem is that textbooks are very hard to read. They are essentially reference books. Reading one of them is like trying to read an encyclopedia. Encyclopedias are fine for looking up information on a topic, but an encyclopedia entry would never extend for nearly a thousand pages, as most textbooks do. In addition, textbooks are dry. They often contain a series of facts. There are no narratives, no human stories that students can relate to. They are the essence of inconsiderate or unfriendly texts.

A third problem with textbooks that Daniels and Zemelman identify is that they are badly designed. Older textbooks contained page after page of print relieved only by an occasional black-and-white photograph or diagram. Today's textbooks are quite different. Every page has photos, charts, and diagrams presented in multiple colors. The font sizes are varied. Key words are bolded or italicized. Publishers seem to have attempted to replicate web pages in the pages of history books. However, as Daniels and Zemelman point out, "The problem is that these postmodern designs mostly don't work. Instead of inviting kids into the material, many of today's textbooks are a graphic maelstrom" (2004, 41). Students don't know where to focus or what information on a page is important. They are bombarded with so much visual information that they may be overwhelmed.

Textbooks are also authoritarian. Academic writers should establish an authoritative tone by using the devices we have described, but academic texts should not be authoritarian. No one person or book is the final authority, yet textbooks present information as though the authors have definitive knowledge and should not be questioned. Students need to learn to use multiple sources as they explore topics in depth, but textbooks give them a superficial overview.

Despite the authoritarian tone, a close examination of textbooks shows that they are often inaccurate. Daniels and Zemelman present several examples of errors in textbooks. It is not surprising that textbooks contain errors. New findings are published in different academic fields frequently, but textbooks may be updated only every five or six years. In addition, textbooks are written by teams of experts, and they cover a great many topics, so it is almost to be expected that there would be some errors. The problem with maintaining accuracy is compounded by the fact that editors of the textbooks are seldom knowledgeable about the topics, and they may not catch errors when they publish the books.

Another point that Daniels and Zemelman make is that textbooks are not written for students. In large states like California or Texas, committees set standards based on state testing requirements that the publishers must meet. These state committees screen textbooks and decide which ones should be placed on the official list for school adoption. Then, at the district or school level, other committees determine which books to purchase. Publishers, naturally, must market their texts for these decision makers rather than considering the students who will read the books.

Daniels and Zemelman's final concern is the cost, which ranges between fifty and seventy dollars per textbook. The price is not unreasonable given the size of the textbooks and the number of illustrations and color plates. However, if students take six subjects, that amounts to at least six hundred dollars in instructional materials for each student. Many schools face budget cuts, and since textbooks are considered an essential purchase, little money is left over for supplementary materials, such as magazines, trade books, or newspapers. Because of the high cost, schools may try to use the same textbooks for a number of years to save money, but then the information that students receive is out of date. This is a problem in all subject areas, but especially in fields like science in which new discoveries are made frequently.

Even though there are many problems with textbooks, content-area teachers generally rely on them. For new teachers, the textbook with its teacher's edition provides a guide for daily lesson plans. In many schools, teachers are expected or required to use the adopted textbook. Textbooks have become part of the culture of almost every secondary school. Even English teachers, who might be expected to use novels and short stories, usually rely on the anthology the school has bought. Despite their problems, textbooks dominate secondary classrooms.

Coping with Textbooks

If textbooks are fixtures in secondary classrooms, what can teachers do to help their students, especially their ELLs and SELs who struggle with reading, learn the content of their subject areas? One answer is to introduce informational texts in the lower grades. In addition, secondary teachers should supplement textbooks with informational texts that students can read, and they should teach students strategies for reading expository, academic texts. Students need to learn grade-level content. At the same time, they need exposure to texts they can read from the beginning. They also need scaffolded instruction that supports them in reading textbooks in the different subject areas.

Early Exposure to Informational Texts

Demographic data shows that the largest group of ELLs in the United States is long-term English learners. These are students who have attended schools in this country for at least seven years. Many of them have had all their education in the United States. The same is true for SELs who are struggling readers. Although these students have attended U.S. schools for several years, they have not received extensive exposure to informational books with academic language. They need to begin reading expository texts much earlier.

The genres most commonly used in schools shift as students move up the grades. Most of the texts that children in the lower elementary grades are exposed to fall into the category of personal genres. They read narratives, write and tell stories, or recount events that they were involved in. In a study she conducted in a first-grade classroom, Duke (2003) found that the average amount of time the children spent with informational texts was only 3.6 minutes per day. When she studied classrooms in low-socioeconomic-status districts, the kinds of classrooms most ELLs and struggling readers attend, the average dropped to just 1.4 minutes a day.

Duke lists several reasons for including more informational reading in the primary grades. First, informational text is the key to success in schools. From about fourth grade on, much of what students are given to read is informational. They read science, math, and history. Even in language arts, they are expected to analyze literature, not just write creative stories. In addition, most of the texts in standardized tests are informational. Second, most reading done outside school is informational. Much of what adults read at work is informational—directions, memos, reports, and so on. Duke also reports that a study conducted by Kamil and Lane (1998, in Duke 2003) concluded that an amazing 96 percent of the text on the Word Wide Web is expository.

A third reason to include more informational reading at the primary level is that many children prefer nonfiction. They like to read about animals, especially dinosaurs. They enjoy learning how to make things or finding out about different parts of the world. In fact, some students who appear to be reluctant readers when given only literature to read become eager readers when handed an informational text. A fourth reason for including more informational texts is that they often relate to children's interests and engage them in more extensive reading.

A fifth reason for using informational texts is that they help children build important background they need for science and social studies. They learn about animals and plants. They read about different geographical areas. They enjoy reading about real people from history. A final reason is that these texts include technical vocabulary that students need to comprehend their social studies, math, and science books in upper grades. They also include features such as charts, tables, time lines, and maps that are frequently found in school textbooks in the intermediate and secondary levels. As Duke argues, early exposure to informational texts would prepare students for the kinds of reading they are expected to do in later grades and after they leave school.

Engaging Students in Reading

A key to helping ELLs and SELs who are struggling readers succeed with academic texts is engaging them in extensive reading that includes informational books. This reading is crucial for helping students develop academic language. However, as students move from elementary school into middle school, many of them lose interest in reading. Even students who can read are not motivated to read. A number of factors contribute to this decline in motivation, including the fact that students are given fewer interesting informational books to read.

Guthrie and Davis (2003) conducted extensive research on struggling middle school readers. They found that these students are disengaged and unmotivated. They lack self-confidence and their motivation for reading is extrinsic. They read to receive a grade rather than for enjoyment or to obtain information they want to know. These students also demonstrate self-handicapping strategies. For example, they put off assignments until the last minute. Many struggling readers are also socially marginalized. They don't feel respected in school and don't try to develop positive relationships with classmates. Guthrie and Davis also found that middle school readers are sensitive to the social context. Their performance varies across classes. Students who appear to be disengaged, struggling readers in one class may look quite different in another class.

The characteristics of middle school readers can be linked to typical teaching practices in middle schools. At this level, teachers regard themselves as subject matter teachers, not reading teachers. They view their job as teaching history or math, not teaching students how to read. In addition, as we discussed earlier, the textbooks become much more formidable. Students are expected to give formal responses to the readings. For example, they answer questions at the end of the chapter or write summaries of their reading. Teachers want students to demonstrate that they understand the content, and they are less interested in the students' personal responses to the materials.

Further, students are given less choice in what they can read. In many elementary classes, students choose books from a wide selection. At the middle school level, all students read the same text. Also, teachers teach more students each day and spend less time getting to know individual students so classes are more impersonal. Finally, reading is less often connected to the world outside school. Students study science or geography, but lessons are not designed to help students apply the content knowledge to their lives. As a result of these different factors, many middle school and secondary students do not engage with reading.

An Engagement Model of Instruction

Guthrie and Davis (2003) have developed what they call an engagement model of instruction. They suggest that there are two pathways to motivation. First teachers can build on students' interests and connect this intrinsic motivation to reading. A student who is interested in losing weight, for example, would be motivated to read science articles about health and nutrition. Secondly, teachers can build stronger intrinsic motivation by encouraging students to interact with an adult or a peer who is highly motivated. If a teacher the student likes or a classmate shows a great interest in science, for instance, the student may also develop an interest in science.

The authors explain that "the most highly internalized level of motivational development is intrinsic motivation. At this point, readers will engage in literacy activities for their own sake, irrespective of whether they provide a reward or benefit" (71). Motivated students read for information or enjoyment. Students can become motivated and engaged readers in supportive classroom communities. When teachers follow effective instructional practices, they enable all their students to become engaged readers.

Guthrie and Davis have identified six practices that build motivation and promote reading engagement. As they comment, "This engagement can not be short term, lasting only a day or week, but must endure for many weeks and months in order to assure the acquisition of cognitive strategies that have not been learned in several years of previous schooling" (2003, 71). Classes with teachers who promote engagement are characterized by the following practices:

- knowledge goals
- real-world interactions
- many interesting texts
- support for student choice
- direct strategy instruction
- collaborative activities

Knowledge Goals

Many students are extrinsically motivated by performance goals. They read a chapter or write a paper to receive praise or a good test score. Guthrie and Davis explain that teachers should help students develop knowledge goals instead. Students with knowledge goals read to understand and communicate information about some academic content that matters to them. Knowledge goals are developed when teachers organize around themes and involve students in investigating big questions, such as How does global warming affect our lives? or How have computers changed society? The first step to engaged reading is to focus on meaningful content, not specifically on reading. Unless students read content they care about, they won't develop knowledge goals.

Real-World Interactions

As they involve students in investigating big questions, teachers can also find ways to connect reading to the world outside the classroom. For example, teachers can plan interesting science experiments on relevant topics or have students research a period of history and enact a scene from the period. These activities help make the reading real for students.

Daniels and Zemelman (2004) describe how a group of teachers at a school in Chicago involved their students in the study of fast food. The students read a variety of books on the topic, including *Fast Food Nation* (Schlosser 2001), which shows the dangers in the production and consumption of fast food. They also read magazine articles and Internet sources about fast food. Once students understood this topic in depth, they worked in groups to complete different projects.

For example, some students created a flier about the dangers of eating fast food and passed copies out in restaurants like McDonald's. Other students focused on cruelty to animals or the working conditions of immigrants in meatpacking plants. One girl wrote to her congressman about her concerns. Another group wrote a children's book about the dangers of fast food and read the book and discussed the issue with a first-grade class. Still others took photos of food served in the cafeteria or sold there and created a collage with arrows linking the foods to levels of the food pyramid, showing how almost all the foods contained fats, oils, sugars, or red meat. This project had a deep impact on the students. Many of them reflected on and changed their own eating habits. The students at this Chicago school were involved in what Guthrie and Davis call real-world interactions as they read and wrote.

Engagement and Motivation with ELLs: César Chávez Unit

Guthrie and Davis (2003) showed the importance of engagement for native English speakers. Meltzer and Hamann (2004) reviewed the research on academic literacy development for adolescents and extended this important research to adolescent ELLs. They point out, as we did in the first chapter, that ELLs and struggling readers come with different backgrounds and experiences, and it is critical that teachers connect curriculum to their lives and find ways to involve them meaningfully in literacy. Like Guthrie and Davis, Meltzer and Hamann concluded that engagement and motivation are keys to success for both native English speakers and ELLs. They list three promising practices to motivate and engage adolescents, including ELLs:

- making connections to students' lives
- creating a safe and responsive classroom
- having students interact with each other and with text (2004, 5)

Mary, whose class we describe in more detail in Chapter 7, used all three of these practices with a unit she taught on the Mexican American hero of migrant workers, César Chávez. Mary was teaching a class of newcomer ninth graders. All her students were recent arrivals from Mexico, and most had parents who worked in agriculture. In fact, many students worked in the fields themselves when they were not at school. Although all her students had heard of César Chávez, none of Mary's students knew why this important Mexican American was famous. They didn't know that he had headed the battle for the rights of farmworkers that eventually led to the formation of a national farmworkers union. To introduce the unit, Mary found several picture books to read to her class: *César Chávez: The Struggle for Justice* (Griswold del Castillo 2002), *Harvesting Hope: The Story of César Chávez* (Krull 2003), and *César Chávez: The Farm Workers' Friend* (Fleming 2004). She also had resources in Spanish telling about his life available in the classroom library, including *César Chávez: Líder laboral* (Morris 1994).

Mary read some of the books to the students, and the students read other books working in pairs. Then they brainstormed key events described in the books. The students worked in pairs to make large posters summarizing what they had learned. These elaborate posters included carefully drawn illustrations that represented key events in Chávez's life including important symbols such as the grapes that inspired the first march of oppressed workers to the California state capitol, the cruel short-handled hoe that Chávez made illegal for farmwork, and the farmworkers' black eagle symbol of *La Causa* (The Cause). The class also watched a video about his life. The district bilingual director, who had been a migrant child and had worked in the fields in California during the period when Chávez led many marches and strikes, came to the class and described the time that she had met César Chávez and the importance of the farmworkers' movement for her and her family.

With this background and drawing on a variety of resources, the students, with Mary's help, compiled poetry and excerpts from what they had read to produce a dramatic reading reflecting important events from Chávez's life. The script had parts for the boys, other parts for the girls, and some parts for the whole class. Directed by Mary, who has a background in theatre, the students practiced reading the script in class. (See photo at the beginning of this chapter.) Then they performed the reading for other classes and for district officials who were so impressed that they invited the class to attend a regional bilingual conference to present their readers theatre to a very large audience of teachers and administrators from around the area.

The conference was held at an ocean island resort about an hour's drive from Mary's school. Even though the ocean was only about fifty miles from their hometown, none of the students had ever been to the beach. They practiced their presentation each day, and their performance of the César Chávez reading was the hit of the conference. They received a standing ovation. After their presentation, the students spent a wonderful day at the beach. This experience was a highlight of the year for Mary's newcomers.

Through the various activities, Mary followed all of Meltzer and Hamann's (2004) promising practices. She made connections to her students' lives with the theme since all of them were aware of the difficulty of laboring in the fields and most had experienced this work. She established a safe and responsive classroom. As her students created their posters and worked on their dramatic reading, their creativity was valued and their voices were heard. Throughout the unit students interacted with each other and the different texts they read and helped to compose. Mary's students improved their written and oral English abilities and built their academic English proficiency as they engaged in activities that connected reading and writing to their lives and to the world beyond the classroom.

Authenticity • Real-world interactions lead to authentic reading and writing. According to Purcell-Gates, Duke, and Martineau (2007), authentic literacy activities meet two requirements. First, students must be "reading for information that one wants or needs to know or writing to provide information for someone who wants or needs it" (14). In addition, when literacy is authentic, the texts students read and write "must be like, or very much like, texts that are used by readers and writers outside of a learning-to-read-and-write context" (14). In other words, authentic activities are those in which students read to learn new information and share it using texts that are written to convey information or to entertain people rather than texts written to be used in school to teach students how to read and write.

The reading and writing activities that Mary's students and the students in Chicago engaged in meet both of the criteria for authenticity. The students read books, articles, and other sources to gain information about fast food or about the life of an important historical figure, and then they wrote, created fliers, developed projects, and performed readers theatre to convey this information to others.

Duke and her colleagues (2007) conducted research with younger students that demonstrates the importance of authentic reading and writing. For example, a second-grade class visited a local nature center as part of a science unit on pond life. The children enjoyed their visit because they could see many of the plants and animals they had been studying. A few days after the visit, the students received a letter from the director of the nature center. She wrote that she had enjoyed answering the many good questions the students had raised about pond life. She explained that other children who visit the center also had questions about the center and suggested that the students might develop a brochure with questions and answers about pond life to put in the center for other visitors to read. The students were excited. They became very involved in this project. As they conducted research and created the brochure, they engaged in many authentic reading and writing activities. This project helped them connect their reading to the world outside the classroom.

Purcell-Gates and her colleagues (2007) studied the effects of authentic activities on student learning. In a subsequent report of their extensive, large-scale experimental research, they concluded that "the degree to which children in second and third grade are involved in *authentic* literacy events with informational and procedural texts in science is impressively related to their degree of growth in their abilities to both comprehend and produce such texts" (41). They go on to add, "Whereas we cannot proclaim a causal effect for authenticity, these results do help to empirically support the theoretical claim that language forms are best learned in the context of authentic use" (41).

In addition, these researchers found that the benefits of authentic instruction applied equally to students at different socioeconomic levels. Children from low-income homes showed growth in literacy at the same rate as students from high-income backgrounds. This is an especially important finding, since many ELLs and SELs come from low-socioeconomic homes. With continued authentic instruction of the kind Duke and her colleagues (2007) describe, all students can learn to read and write academic texts, an essential step in developing academic language proficiency. The research on authenticity also supports the findings from Guthrie and Davis (2003) on the importance of real-world interactions that lead to authentic reading and writing for motivating students to become engaged readers.

Many Interesting Texts

In addition to helping students develop knowledge goals and involving them in real-world interactions, Guthrie and Davis (2003) describe four additional characteristics of classrooms that promote engagement. The first of these is to provide a rich variety of interesting books and other reading materials. Students won't become engaged readers unless they have access to books that they want to read. Students at the school in Chicago, for example, used their textbooks, but they also read many other books, magazine articles, newspaper reports, and Internet articles as they studied about fast food. Mary always has a bookshelf filled with magazines, novels of varied levels of difficulty, and picture books that would appeal to older learners, including books like the César Chávez books. In addition, she has novels available in Spanish as well as bilingual picture books.

Earlier, we reviewed several problems with textbooks. Effective teachers like Mary and the teachers in Chicago make a point of supplementing the required textbook with other texts on the topics the textbook covers. Many teachers develop text sets around the key concepts in their textbooks. A text set is a collection of books, magazines, articles on the Internet, and other resources connected to a topic. Text sets should include books and other materials at different levels of reading difficulty. If books around the theme are available in the languages of the ELLs in the class, these books can help support those students in their reading of English. Text sets are especially important for classes with ELLs and SELs who struggle with reading. By providing many different print resources that span different reading levels and are also in the native languages of the English learners, teachers ensure that all their students have access to the topic.

One effective strategy teachers can use is to divide students into groups and give each group an article or other short reading on the topic being studied. Teachers can choose readings that match the reading level of the students in the group. For example, in a history class studying the Civil War, a teacher might gather primary sources such as newspaper accounts from the period or letters soldiers wrote describing their experiences as well as biographical sketches of military leaders or stories about the war.

Working in their groups, the students read and discuss their texts. Once they understand their readings, all the students move to form new groups in a jigsaw activity. Each new group is composed of one student from each of the original groups. In these new groups, each student reports on the information he or she has learned. Then the teacher leads a whole-class discussion to consolidate key ideas. This jigsaw activity actively engages all the students with texts they can understand. By reading the texts in supportive groups, then reporting this information to peers in other groups, and finally discussing the articles as a whole class, all the students, including the ELLs and struggling readers, can learn important concepts and build academic language proficiency.

Support for Student Choice

In the jigsaw activity we described, students were given materials to read. Some school reading is assigned by the teacher. However, as Guthrie and Davis (2003) explain, it is important that students be able to choose at least some of what they read. Choice leads to greater motivation and engagement. Teachers who provide time for reading on a regular basis (often called sustained silent reading, or SSR) allow students to pick what they want to read from the classroom library. Krashen (2004b) has supported this idea of choice for some time by calling for free voluntary reading (FVR). He provides evidence from studies with native English speakers and students learning English and concludes "in-school free reading studies and 'out of school' self-reported free voluntary reading studies show that more reading results in better reading comprehension, writing style, vocabulary, spelling, and grammatical development" (17).

Research shows that SSR or FVR leads to improved reading ability and improved English proficiency. Many teachers, like the teachers in Chicago, give all their students some interesting books such as *Fast Food Nation* to read and then let them choose from other books and articles on the same subject. This practice provides students with choice and still ensures that what they read will help them build academic concepts and academic language.

Direct Strategy Instruction

Students need some direct instruction to be able to read their textbooks and other content materials. Guthrie and Davis note that "direct strategy instruction typically includes the processes of modeling, scaffolding, guided practice with feedback, and independent reading to gain fluency in the strategy" (2003, 76). This instruction is what ELLs and SELs who struggle with social studies, math, and science texts need. Without some direct instruction, these students have great difficulty reading content texts, even when the texts are interesting.

Daniels and Zemelman (2004) list several strategies that successful content-area teachers use to help their students as they read difficult texts. These strategies include connecting the reading to their lives or to other things they have read, visualizing what they are reading, actively questioning as they read, making inferences and predictions, evaluating the importance of different ideas, analyzing the way the text is written as well as the ideas being presented, recalling the information through retellings or summaries, and self-monitoring for comprehension. Two other direct instruction activities that are especially important for ELLs and SELs who struggle with reading are activating background knowledge and conducting think-alouds.

Activate background knowledge • It is important for teachers to activate or build the background students will need to read a content text. Often teachers assume that ELLs have knowledge that, in fact, they were never exposed to. Even though Mary's students had heard of César Chávez, none of them knew why he was famous. Some teachers might have assumed that Mexican students would know about an important Mexican American figure, but in Mexico, Mexican Americans are not usually studied, so Mary needed to help her students build the necessary background to comprehend what they would be reading about him. Without the appropriate background, text passages are very hard to understand.

Lee and Fradd describe how a science teacher drew on his Latino students' background knowledge to help them understand the Celsius and Fahrenheit scales on a thermometer. He began by asking them, "When you have a fever, what temperature does your mother look for? What number does she expect to see on the thermometer?" (1998, 18). Students' answers varied widely. Some said thirty-eight or forty while others answered with one hundred. When the students appeared confused, the teacher explained the two different scales. He commented, "Our thermometers are bilingual, just like you" (18). In this exchange, the teacher drew on the students' backgrounds in two ways. He used the fact that some students were familiar with Fahrenheit and others with Celsius to introduce the idea that different scales can show equivalent ways of representing information. At the same time, by comparing the thermometer's two scales with the students' own bilingualism, he made a personal connection that helped his students understand an important science concept.

We have used the following passage to help teachers understand the importance of background knowledge.

> With hocked gems financing him our hero defied all scornful laughter that tried to prevent his scheme. "Your eyes deceive you," he had said, "an egg not a table correctly typifies this unexplored planet." Now three sturdy sisters sought proof, forging along, sometimes through calm vastness, yet more often over turbulent peaks and valleys. Days became weeks as many doubters spread fearful rumors about the edge. At last, from nowhere, welcome winged creatures appeared, signifying momentous success. (Dooling and Lachman 1971, 217)

After they read the passage, we ask teachers questions such as "What does 'hocked gems' refer to?" "What does the writer mean by 'an egg not a table correctly typifies this unexplored planet'?" and "Can you name the three sturdy sisters?" Many readers are mystified and confused by the passage. Then we ask what a title for the passage might be. Usually, someone says, "Columbus' Voyage to America," and suddenly everyone understands. The passage makes complete sense once the teachers' background knowledge is activated. However, if we showed this passage to many ELLs, even a title wouldn't help. We would have to build their knowledge about Columbus, not just activate it. Building background knowledge is essential for helping ELLs understand content-area texts and develop academic language.

Think-alouds • Another effective way to help students develop strategies to understand content texts is for teachers to model the thinking processes of proficient readers through think-alouds. Teachers, like Mary, choose books to read aloud to their students. As they read, they stop to think out loud as they make predictions and connections or clear up confusions. Fisher, Frey, and Lapp (2008) studied the think-aloud strategies of twenty-five expert teachers from grades 3 through 8. They observed the teachers conducting think-alouds as they read carefully selected texts to their students. They clustered their observational data into four main categories: using think-alouds to improve their comprehension, to figure out vocabulary, to analyze text structures, and to understand the purpose of different text features. The teachers explained that they were thinking out loud to show the students what they do silently as they read.

Most often, the teachers modeled how they used strategies to comprehend texts. These included activating background, inferring, summarizing, predicting, clarifying, questioning, visualizing, monitoring, synthesizing, evaluating, and connecting. Many of these are the same strategies listed by Daniels and Zemelman (2004) mentioned earlier. Although the teachers modeled each of these strategies, they did not demonstrate them one at a time. Instead, they combined several strategies each time they thought aloud. When interviewed by Fisher and his colleagues, the teachers commented that they purposely mixed strategies. One teacher explained:

> I used to do it that way—focus on one comprehension strategy at a time. But I think that's a problem. I don't really read that way, and if I don't read that way, it's not really an authentic shared reading and think-aloud, right? (Fisher, Frey, and Lapp 2008, 551)

For example, during one think-aloud, a teacher made a connection to her past experience and also made a prediction about what would happen next.

Teachers also demonstrated how they used clues to determine the meaning of vocabulary. They differentiated between inside-the-word strategies, such as finding prefixes, suffixes, and bases or looking for cognates, and outside-the-word strategies, in which they looked for context clues. They also modeled how to use resources including peers, the dictionary, and the Internet to determine word meanings.

In addition, teachers modeled how they used information about text structures to help them comprehend the text. For example, one teacher noted how the author was using a compare-and-contrast structure to present ideas. She commented that she would use this structure to help her organize and remember the information she was reading. Another teacher pointed out that the text she was reading presented ideas in a sequence. The teachers' comments about text structure were designed to help students notice how texts were organized and to use that information to better understand and recall the information.

Finally, some of the think-alouds focused on text features, such as headings, captions, charts, and diagrams. For example, one teacher paused to discuss the highlighted words, and another commented that the headings helped her make predictions, find specific information later on, and organize her notes. Often, ELLs and SELs who are struggling readers ignore features of text. By thinking aloud, teachers can help students understand how to use text features to better comprehend what they read.

Think-alouds are an effective way for teachers to model how proficient readers think as they read. The teachers that Fisher and his colleagues observed used think-alouds to focus on different aspects of text and show students how they thought their way through difficult passages. They combined strategies in each think-aloud rather than demonstrating one at a time. This approach to strategy instruction is very effective.

Although think-alouds are a good way for teachers to model effective reading strategies, it is important to realize that as much as possible, these demonstrations should represent a natural process that good readers use. As the teacher quoted earlier said, "If I don't read that way, it's not an authentic shared reading and think-aloud, right?" Students can be encouraged and supported in using these same strategies as they work their way through challenging texts. However, strategies are designed to help students understand a text. They are not ends in themselves.

It is important, then, not to teach strategies in isolation. Jiménez, Handsfield, and Fisher (2008) observed classes in which teachers asked ELLs to use strategies just to demonstrate they could use them. For example, teachers required students to make a prediction or ask a question about the text, and they evaluated students on their ability to make predictions or ask questions. These teachers failed to make the crucial connection between the predictions or questions and greater text comprehension. In addition, students who already understand a text may already be using these strategies, and asking them to show how they can use a strategy simply diverts their attention from reading for pleasure or information. Further, students must be at a minimal level of reading and English ability to benefit from strategy instruction. If students can't decode most of the words in a text, they need a different text to read, not comprehension strategy instruction.

Collaboration Support

The last characteristic of classrooms that motivate students to engage with text, according to Guthrie and Davis (2003), is support for collaborative activities. While teachers may provide some whole-class instruction and some time for students to work individually, many activities should involve students in working in pairs or small groups. Collaborative group work is especially helpful for ELLs as well as SELs because they are often more willing to ask questions or make comments in small groups than in the whole class setting. In addition, it is important to remember that when ELLs are allowed to spend some time working in same-language groups, they can use their first language to understand academic concepts, and this concept knowledge then transfers to English.

The students who studied fast foods worked together in small teams as they investigated different aspects of fast food and developed projects to demonstrate their knowledge. Similarly, Mary's students worked in small groups and pairs as they created their elaborate posters and wrote and practiced their readers theatre about César Chávez. Group work motivates students, and teachers who regularly plan small-group activities create classrooms where their ELLs and SELs build academic language proficiency as they work with classmates.

The six practices that Guthrie and Davis outline all go together naturally. In effective classrooms teachers help students develop knowledge goals, they involve students in real-world interactions with text during authentic literacy experiences, they ensure that students have access to many different texts, they give students choice in what they study, read, and write, they provide strategy instruction, and they build supportive and collaborative classroom communities. In classes like this, students become engaged readers and writers.

Research by Guthrie highlights the importance of reading engagement. He reports: "For 9 year olds on the National Assessment of Educational Progress (NAEP) in 1998, the correlation between the indicators of engaged reading and reading comprehension achievement was higher than any demographic characteristic such as gender, income or ethnicity" (2004, 5).

What was remarkable was that highly engaged readers from low-income and low-education backgrounds outscored less engaged readers from higher-income and education backgrounds. Since many ELLs and SELs come from low-income, low-education backgrounds, this finding is significant. Coupled with the findings on authenticity by Purcell-Gates, Duke, and Martineau (2007), the NAEP study results suggest that with the right kind of instruction, ELLs and SELs can improve their academic language proficiency through reading engagement when texts and purposes for reading and writing are authentic.

Guthrie (2004) also reports nearly identical findings for fifteen-year-olds in an international study of thirty-two countries. These results were reported for the Programme for International Student Assessment (PISA). Guthrie concluded, "Globally, both within and across nations, the association of high engagement with high achievement and low engagement with low achievement was repeatedly observed" (5). Engaged readers choose to read books for pleasure and information. As they read, they build their academic language proficiency.

Challenges of Engaging Beginning ELLs in Academic Literacy

While engagement is a key to the development of academic language proficiency, ELLs need to reach a certain level of English proficiency and reading proficiency before they can read books with grade-level content. Although teachers should teach language and content from the beginning, the kinds of texts they select must match the students' ability levels, or else beginning ELLs may become frustrated. As the research by Cummins and others has demonstrated, it takes from five to seven years to develop academic language.

Ivey and Broaddus (2007) conducted research that reveals some of the modifications that need to be made when working with ELLs who are just beginning to learn English. The researchers studied an introductory eighth-grade ESL class. The students in this study were all newcomers from different parts of Latin America. The number of students in the study varied because some families left the area and others arrived. Fourteen students completed the entire year in this newcomer class. The teacher was an experienced ESL teacher, but she did not speak Spanish.

The students' reading proficiency was assessed in both English and Spanish using different instruments. The researchers also interviewed the students about their previous schooling experiences. Some students had higher levels of literacy than others, and some recalled studying content-area subjects in Spanish, but the researchers did not test the students' content knowledge. Based on the test results and interviews, the researchers concluded that, although the students varied in their schooling backgrounds, most of them had limited reading ability in Spanish and limited content knowledge. Ivey and Broaddus note, "All participants were at the initial stages of reading and writing in English. They were still developing knowledge of letter-sound correspondence, and they recognized few English words by sight" (2007, 522).

At first, most lessons were whole class and teacher directed. At the suggestion of the researchers, the teacher implemented more guided reading small-group time. Eventually, she developed a readers and writers workshop format with much more time for conferencing with individual students. Instruction could be individualized because there were usually three instructional assistants in the class, one of whom was a translator, as well as one or both of the researchers. Realistically, very few classrooms would have this many adults available to help students.

The researchers provided many interesting reading materials including informational texts for the students. Lessons consisted of time for self-selected reading followed by teacher-directed reading and writing activities. For example, after reading a book about reptiles, the students created a learning log of information and new vocabulary words. The researchers instituted language experience activities and found different scaffolds for student writing. Often, after the teacher read a book with a repetitive pattern, students wrote following that pattern.

Over time, the researchers refined the criteria for books they made available, suiting the books to the students' levels of English reading proficiency. They included books in English, bilingual books, and books in Spanish. The texts included emergent literacy content or concept books, wordplay books, wordless books, and picture books with repetitive patterns.

The team working with the students provided appropriate materials and a very high level of support. They were able to establish the foundation for later school success, but, as Ivey and Broaddus state, "For students in the study two, three, or even five years of extra support would not be sufficient for independently succeeding in regular classroom contexts that did not take linguistic differences into account" (2007, 541). The researchers found materials and strategies for engaging these beginning English readers in literacy activities. However, they were not able to engage the students with grade-appropriate content instruction in English. They conclude, "We would have found it difficult to provide these students with opportunities to learn the academic content included in the school's standard seventh- and eighth-grade language arts curriculum without the benefit of first language instruction" (543).

The students in this study made significant growth, but as Ivey and Broaddus' research shows, developing academic English, even under optimal conditions, takes considerable time, especially for older students at beginning levels of English literacy proficiency. These results suggest strongly that schools as well as those who write state and national testing mandates need to develop more realistic expectations about how quickly students can develop academic English.

Learning the Genres of Academic Disciplines

Earlier we discussed some of the aspects of the academic registers of schooling. At a general level, we can talk about the register of math or the register of science.

However, within each academic content area, students are asked to read and write different kinds of texts.

The different types of texts within an academic discipline are often referred to as genres. The term *genre* is most often used to describe types of text used in art and literature. For example, we might view an impressionist painting or read a novel, a play, or a poem. Each of these is structured differently, and each represents a different genre. Books about writing often discuss genres. Murray (1985), for example, makes several important points about genres. He comments that the particular form, or genre, of writing cannot be imposed from the outside. Instead, the form that writing takes depends on its function. Murray goes on to explain that the genre "may be considered a vehicle which carries meaning to the reader. Each genre has been designated for use—to tell a story, to persuade a listener—and has been continually redesigned by use. The writer can consider a genre by deciding which form will carry the writer's particular message to an individual reader" (25).

Systemic functional linguists have extended the term *genre* to include other kinds of texts, including the text types that are commonly used in schools. Each subject area has different text types. For instance, language arts has poems, and history has historical explanations. When students understand how these different text types or genres are organized and which features are associated with them, they can make better predictions as they read them, and they can produce writing that follows the pattern of the text type that is appropriate to an assignment. For example, if a teacher asks the students to write a science report, they should organize their writing and include features in ways expected of science reports and not in ways typical of a science explanation.

Schleppegrell (2004) describes several genres typically used in schools. She follows Martin's analysis (Martin 1989, in Schleppegrell 2004) by dividing the genres into three categories: personal, factual, and analytical. Figure 4.1 lists the genres in each category and some of the features associated with each genre.

Personal Genres

Personal genres report on personal experiences. They include recounts, accounts, and narratives. A recount retells a sequence of events. During sharing time in elementary school classes, students are often asked to recount what they did the previous day. Accounts link the series of events with reasons. Narratives report events using a problem-solution structure. Instead of simply retelling a series of events, the student tells about some complication that was resolved. This genre

Personal Genres *Present personal experiences*	Features	Examples
Recount: Retells a series of events drawing on personal experience.	personal pronouns past tense temporal (*later, when*) or additive (*and, also*) signal words and phrases	tells what writer did on vacation
Account: Relates a series of personal events. Links events with reasons.	personal pronouns past tense cause-effect signal words	tells why the writer got in trouble at school
Narrative: A story with a problem-solution structure. The teller is a character in the story.	includes more participants past tense or present tense adverbs of manner (*quickly*) cause-effect signal words and phrases	tells what writer did when he discovered there would be a test after lunch

Factual Genres *Present facts*	Features	Examples
Procedure: Lists steps for carrying out a task.	imperatives often written as a numbered list	how to dissect a frog
Procedural recount (used in science): Records what was done in an experiment.	past tense series of statements sequence signal words	tells the steps that were taken to dissect a frog
Historical recount (used in history): Retells events in a sequence.	past tense third person temporal signal words or phrases	tells the events leading up to the Civil War
Report: Presents information gathered on a topic.	present tense or past tense often classifies items or presents from general to specific descriptive words and phrases	the life of Thomas Jefferson the Atlantic salmon

Analytical Genres Analyze events or argue for certain interpretation of events	Features	Examples
Account: Relates a series of factual events. Links events with reasons.	past tense cause-effect signal words and phrases temporal or sequence signal words or phrases	reasons the French explored the New World the formation and path of a hurricane
Explanation: Interprets events, giving causes and consequences.	third person logical connections, not time connections past tense or present tense cause-effect signal words and phrases	reasons the French explored the New World and some outcomes of the exploration causes and consequences of a hurricane
Exposition: Argues for a particular interpretation by presenting different reasons.	past tense or present tense cause-effect signal words and phrases additive signal words and phrases contrastive signal words and phrases	two or more arguments showing that the French exploration of the New World benefited France two or more arguments that global warming is occurring

figure 4.1 Categories of Genres (adapted from Schleppergrell 2004)

is typically used to tell stories in which the student is one of the characters. For example, a child might tell about a time when she got lost in the mall, and a shop clerk took her to an office where they called her mother over the store's speaker system. In language arts classes at the middle school or secondary level, students learn the story grammar pattern that is typical of most narratives. The pattern includes elements such as a complication, rising action, a climax, and falling action.

Factual Genres

Factual genres present facts. They include procedures, recounts, and reports. Procedures relate a sequence of events. They are generally written in command form with no stated subject. Procedures are usually presented in numbered lists with items such as "Fill the beaker with water" and "Place the beaker on the Bunsen burner." Procedures could also be a series of directions for finding a location.

Recounts retell a series of events. In science, students may recount the steps in an experiment they conducted. In history, students may recount events from a particular period. Recounts use third person and past tense. They typically use sequence or temporal signal words to link events.

In contrast, reports are generally written in paragraphs using present tense for general information or past tense for information about past events or historical figures. Students can organize reports in different ways. They can classify the items or present them from general to specific. For example, in reporting on the life of Abraham Lincoln, a student could classify his life into his early years, years as a young adult, and later years and then discuss each period. On the other hand, a report on Abraham Lincoln could also begin with a general overview of his political accomplishments and then discuss specific events in his life that led up to his presidency and eventual assassination. General statements in reports should be backed up by specific facts. A student might report on some animal, telling where it lives, what it eats, and what enemies it has. Each of these general categories would be supported by detailed facts.

Reports often follow a comparison-contrast structure. In English class, students might compare and contrast characters in a novel. This same structure also applies in social studies, science, or math. For instance, students could compare and contrast two geographical regions, two types of animals, or two ways to solve a math problem. The comparison-contrast essay is used frequently in different academic fields. It is not a genre itself, but instead is a way students can organize and present information within both factual and analytical genres.

Analytical Genres

Analytical genres, the third category, analyze events or argue for certain interpretations of events. Writing in these genres usually follows a cause-effect pattern. Analytical genres include accounts, explanations, and expositions. An account relates a series of events linked by reasons. An account of the westward migration in the United States would include reasons that people moved from the East into the West. Instead of just recounting, "At first, most of the population was clustered along the East Coast, and then people migrated to the western territories," in an account, the writer would make the connections between events more explicit. For example, the passage might read, "At first most of the population was clustered along the East Coast. Lands opened in the West, so people left the crowded eastern cities and migrated to the western territories."

Explanations move beyond linking events with reasons. They offer an interpretation, looking at causes and consequences. An explanation of the westward migration would present a more unified description that reflected the writer's interpretation of why things happened in a certain sequence, including the factors that caused people to move and the effects of the migration on the region.

Expositions go one further step. They argue for a particular interpretation by presenting two or more arguments in favor of the interpretation. In the case of the westward migration, the writer might argue that the effects were positive for the United States for several reasons despite the negative consequences for Native Americans. An exposition in education might argue for an approach to teaching reading and base the argument on different empirical studies of children's reading acquisition.

Most writing in the early grades consists of the personal genres. Students give recounts, accounts, and narratives during sharing time. They tell or write stories about events they were involved in. Much of what they typically read is also narrative. The language of personal genres is more conversational than academic. As students move into the intermediate grades, more of their reading and writing is factual, although they continue to read and write stories. They begin writing procedures, recounts, and reports. They also read more informational texts. During this time, the language they use is predominantly academic. They are exposed to more academic texts, and they are expected to incorporate more features of academic texts in their writing.

Students in middle and secondary schools read and write analytical genres, including accounts, explanations, and expositions. They move from temporal (time) connectors to logical connectors with an emphasis on cause and effect. They learn to consider different interpretations of phenomena. At this stage, most of their reading, other than during their language arts class, is informational text and most of their writing is factual or analytical rather than narrative. By now, most of what they read and write requires an understanding of academic, rather than conversational, language.

Different content areas include somewhat different genres. In science, for example, the most commonly used genres are procedures, procedural recounts, reports, and explanations. Common genres in history are recounts, reports, accounts, explanations, and expositions. Language arts continues to include narratives and poetry but adds factual and analytical genres for interpreting literature. Students are less often expected to write during math classes. However, they are expected to read increasingly complex texts that include some explanations along with many figures and formulas.

One problem that ELLs and many struggling readers face is that teachers seldom teach these genres explicitly. Most academic content teachers have probably not thought consciously about how different genres in their field are organized, and they rarely take the time to show students how to read or write the different genres. In addition, textbooks seldom provide clear models of different genres. Science texts usually contain procedures, but beyond that, it is difficult to identify the genres, as they are often mixed together.

Read and Retell as a Tool for Understanding Genres

Brown and Cambourne (1987) have developed an effective way for students to improve in reading and writing different genres. This is a procedure they call *Read and Retell*. Students read extensively in one genre, such as social studies reports. Each day, the teacher selects a short example of the genre. He writes the title on the board. Then he tells the students to write one or two sentences about what a report with such a title might include. After they have written their predictions, he asks them to write down some words or phrases they might find in this report if their prediction from the title is right.

Students form groups of three or four. The students take turns reading their predictions to the group. Then, each student makes a comment on the written predictions of one other member of the group. Everyone else listens. At this point, the teacher passes out the excerpt, usually no more than a page, and everyone reads the text. The teacher may read it aloud first and then have the students read it over to themselves. Or the teacher may simply ask the students to read, depending on their level of English proficiency.

Read and Retell Procedure

1. Choose a short excerpt from a content-area text.

2. Write the title on the board or read the title to the students.

3. Students write one or two sentences predicting what the reading might be about.

4. Students list words that might be found in the reading.

5. Students form groups of three or four.

6. Each student reads his or her predictions to the group.

7. Each student comments on the predictions of one other group member.

8. The teacher passes out the excerpt.

9. The teacher reads the excerpt to the students.

10. Students read the excerpt by themselves.

11. Students do a written retelling without looking back at the excerpt.

12. Students find a partner and compare their retellings.

figure 4.2 Read and Retell Procedure (adapted from Brown and Cambourne 1987)

Next, students are asked to do a written retelling. They turn over the paper and write their retelling on the back without looking at the excerpt. They work quickly and don't worry about neatness or spelling. When students have had time to write their retellings, they find a partner and compare retellings. They ask each other questions such as, "What did I include or omit that is different from what you included or omitted? Why did you omit a certain part? Are there any parts that I got mixed up? Does it change the meaning of the story in a significant way? Did you paraphrase effectively? If you could take part of my retelling and put it in yours, what would you borrow?" Figure 4.2 summarizes the steps of the Read and Retell strategy.

Brown and Cambourne report that repeated use of the Read and Retell strategy improves students' reading and writing. They found that many of the words, phrases, and structures students used in their written retellings appeared later in the students' other written work. This process of focused reading and writing helps students gain greater understanding of the different academic genres.

Text Analysis as a Tool for Understanding Genres

In order to teach academic genres and help their students develop academic language proficiency, teachers need a clear understanding of how different kinds of texts are structured. Schleppegrell and her colleagues (Schleppegrell and Achugar 2003; Schleppegrell and Oliveira 2006) have worked with middle school and secondary teachers to help them understand how to analyze the texts they use to teach their subjects so that the teachers, in turn, can design lessons to help their students better understand their reading.

When Schleppegrell and Oliveira observed classes, they noted that the teachers did a number of things to help their ELLs and struggling readers understand the lessons. These teachers built background knowledge. They showed students how to survey a chapter and focus on the layout and visual features that would help them understand the text. The teachers also used cooperative learning, graphic organizers, and other good techniques for making the content comprehensible. However, the researchers noted that "when it came to actually reading text and getting meaning from print, teachers had few strategies to employ" (Schleppegrell and Oliveira 2006, 256).

Schleppegrell and Achugar worked with history teachers, showing them how to analyze selected texts. They state, "Even when teachers base their instruction on content-area goals, they still need strategies for dealing with language itself, as content is not separate from the language through which it is presented" (2003, 21). They examined the language of the text from three perspectives:

1. what it tells us about what is happening

2. what it tells us about the roles participants play and the points of view expressed

3. what it tells us about how information is organized in the text (22)

These three points correspond to the questions teachers generally ask about what happened, who was involved, where and when it happened, and why it happened.

The researchers helped the teachers understand how to teach their students to analyze a passage from a history text. For example, the researchers chose a short passage about the Missouri Compromise. Students started their analysis by listing the verbs in the passage. Since many students had difficulty identifying verbs, they were given a cloze version of the passage with the verbs deleted. First, they copied the verbs from the original passage into the blanks in the cloze. Then, working in pairs or small groups, they used a dictionary to look up the meanings of verbs they didn't know. This exercise helped them focus carefully on the verbs.

Verbs can be divided into four categories, depending on the kind of process they represent: action verbs (*run, jump, go*), thinking and feeling verbs (*suppose, like, enjoy*), saying verbs (*tell, report, claim*), and relating verbs (*was, have, included*). Students placed the verbs from the passage on a chart with four columns, one for each category.

Once students identified and categorized the verbs, the teacher led a discussion with questions such as "What are the events the historian has chosen to include in this passage?" To answer this question, students focused on the action verbs. Then the teacher asked, "What background does the historian provide?" To answer this question, students looked at the relating verbs. To answer "What does the historian comment on, and who is quoted or cited?" students looked for the information related to the thinking and feeling and the saying verbs. The teacher then asked what type of verb was most common. Since historians recount a series of events, action verbs are often most common. However, the other kinds of verbs each convey additional information about the background the writer provides and the point of view the writer takes.

After analyzing the verbs in the passage, students used similar techniques to identify the nouns and noun phrases. The nouns name the participants, who may be the agents who carry out the actions or the receivers of the actions. Through close analysis of the noun phrases, students gained a fuller understanding of who carried out the actions the historian was describing. In subsequent lessons, students analyzed the passage to determine whose point of view was being presented by looking at what the participants thought, felt, and said (the thinking/feeling and saying verbs). They also looked at the conjunctions and prepositional phrases to discover how the information was organized.

Schleppegrell and Achugar (2003) do not expect teachers to carry out this kind of close analysis with every text. However, they suggest that if teachers and students work through a key passage from each unit, students will develop the skills they need to more fully comprehend their content-area reading. Schleppegrell and Achugar write:

> Teachers find it difficult to scaffold language learners' reading of grade-level texts. We have suggested here that by analyzing the verbs that present the events in the text, the noun phrases that tell about the participants in those events, and the linguistic resources that indicate how the text is organized, teachers can help students learn academic English at the same time they learn history. (26)

Different genres would require a focus on different language elements, but the approach would be similar. By involving students in careful text analysis, teachers can build their academic language proficiency and their academic content knowledge.

Conclusion

The language of academic texts is technical, abstract, dense, and authoritative. These features allow writers to develop an authoritative style, but this style is also difficult for students to read. Textbooks present many problems, especially for ELLs and struggling readers. Students can better cope with their textbooks if they are exposed to informational texts in the early grades.

Engagement in reading is a key to academic success. Several challenges are involved in finding ways to engage beginning-level ELLs in reading content-area materials. Although academic texts share many features in common, they also vary. Students are expected to read and write a variety of genres in school. Two strategies for helping ELLs and SELs who struggle with reading to engage with texts that represent different academic genres are Read and Retell and text analysis. Both of these strategies scaffold academic language and enable students to build academic language proficiency.

Applications

1. Bring a content-area textbook to class or to your study group. In a group, read over the section of this chapter titled "Characteristics of Content-Area Texts." Together choose a passage from the textbook that you think students might have trouble reading and understanding. Analyze the passage. In your analysis, look for the features of academic writing: technical terms, abstract language, density, passive voice, and authoritative tone.

2. In a group, review the section of this chapter titled "Problems with Textbooks." Focus on the problems listed by Daniels and Zemelman (2004). Now look through the textbooks you have brought to class or your study group. Do the textbooks you are looking at have some of the problems suggested in the chapter? Make a list of the problems you find, and prepare to share them.

3. Observe and interview a middle or high school struggling reader. In the interview, ask the student to specifically answer questions about reading in school. Do the characteristics of your student fit the characteristics of struggling readers

suggested by Guthrie and Davis (2003)? You can ask the following questions and/or make up your own.

- How do you feel about books and reading?
- What do you want your teachers to know about you as a reader and a writer?
- Do you understand the textbooks or novels you read for class?
- Can you skim a textbook chapter and figure out the main ideas?
- How do you feel about what you write for class?

4. Guthrie and Davis (2003) suggest six practices that build motivation and promote reading engagement. Choose at least two of these and implement them in your classroom or with a small group of students. Keep records of what you did and the results to report back.

5. Students need to read and write different genres in school. In a group, describe to one another the characteristics of factual genres, including procedures and reports, and analytical genres, including accounts, explanations, and expositions. Which kinds of genres do you read and write as students? Which genres do students in middle and high school need to read and write? Give some specific examples.

6. Following the steps in the chapter (see Figure 4.2), carry out a Read and Retell activity with a reading that challenges students academically. Record what you did and be prepared to report back.

7. Schleppegrell and Achugar (2003) suggest text analysis for helping students understand academic text structure. Take a passage from a history textbook and categorize the verbs as Schleppegrell and Achugar suggest into action verbs, thinking and feeling verbs, saying verbs, and relating verbs. Sort the verbs into four columns. Then ask yourselves, "What are the events the historian has chosen to include in this passage?" "What background does the historian provide?" and "What does the historian comment on, and who is quoted or cited?" Do the answers correspond to the categories of verbs in your columns? Do you think this analysis helped you unpack the meaning of the passage? Why or why not?

5

Supporting Academic Writing at the Paragraph and Sentence Levels

Academic Writing at the Paragraph Level

In the last chapter we examined academic language at the text level by discussing problems with textbooks, ways to engage reluctant readers, and the importance of helping students read and write different genres within content areas. In this chapter we shift our attention to look closely at paragraphs and sentences. Academic language is complex, but when teachers understand the different levels of academic language, they can scaffold instruction and help all their students learn to read and write the academic language of school. We begin with an analysis of the second, third, and fourth paragraphs of Dolores' essay (see Figure 2.1) reproduced here as she wrote them.

First reason that minorities cann't attend Universities and college, is because some of them are illegal aliens. sometimes is because they don't have the much money to pay, Universities.

The second reason that latinos, Hmong, and Africans cann't attend Universities is because their is to many descrimination. People are raices, sometimes teachers. They low grades. Their to many reasons that they can't attend universities. Many students said that if they give them alist one chance a opportunity to show teachers and others, that they are good, they would taste them.

If they would taste latinos, Hmong and Africans, they would know that they know more them they now. Minorities would show their family that they are good and valient. There will be so many changes For them. Two mayor changes For them it would be that minorities would became intelligent. Also they would have good money and work.

In English, there is an expected structure for paragraphs in academic writing. Most paragraphs begin with a sentence that expresses the main idea, the topic sentence. The following sentences provide details to flesh out the idea. Usually paragraphs have four or five sentences, depending on sentence length and complexity. All the sentences should be connected to one another and to the topic sentence. Although it is clear that not all academic writing follows this pattern, it is a good starting point for ELLs and struggling students who are not sure of how to compose paragraphs. In writing this essay, Dolores would have benefited from instruction on paragraph structure. Her first paragraph begins with what could serve as a topic sentence. However, the idea that some students are illegal aliens is not expanded on. Instead, Dolores brings up a second reason, universities are expensive. These two sentences don't constitute a paragraph.

After she mentions these two points, she begins a second paragraph. She has already stated a second reason, but she appears to be trying to follow a pattern of one reason for each paragraph. This is probably the style her teacher taught the class. She does follow her topic sentences with two supporting sentences, or what should be two sentences. She connects the two with a comma rather than putting a period after *raices* [racist] and a capital on *Sometimes*. Students often use a comma splice to connect sentences. The following sentence, "Their to many reasons that they can't attend universities," doesn't fit because it doesn't expand the idea of discrimination. However, the last sentence does return to the topic. The next paragraph then builds on the idea introduced at the end of the last paragraph, that minorities need a chance, and expands that idea. These two paragraphs could be combined to make one good paragraph.

Although Dolores' writing contains errors in grammar and spelling, a teacher could help her develop paragraphs that state a topic and then develop it. All too often, we begin with the grammar and spelling in student writing. It is important for students to be asked to work on one or two types of errors in mechanics. However, it is equally important for students to learn how to construct coherent and cohesive paragraphs. For that reason, some instruction should be focused at the paragraph level to help students like Dolores organize their ideas and express them more clearly and forcefully.

Reading and Writing Cohesive Paragraphs

Dolores needs to write paragraphs in which the sentences all relate to a main topic. If she is writing about discrimination against minorities as being a reason that they don't succeed at universities, then the sentences should all be about discrimination. In addition to being coherent, that is, connected to the same topic, sentences in a paragraph should be cohesive. They should connect to one another in some logical fashion. Writers of academic texts use different devices to connect their ideas across the sentences in a paragraph.

Writing that is judged to be good academic writing contains different features that give it cohesion. Schleppegrell (2004) points out that writers connect ideas by using reference, conjunctions, and nominalization, among other strategies. Reference is established through the use of pronouns and words like *this*, *that*, *these*, and *those*, which are referred to as deictic words, that is, words that point to other parts of a text. Consider the following paragraph, taken from Guthrie and Davis:

> Struggling readers tend to be notably unmotivated. They are especially likely to have low confidence in their reading, which is termed *self-efficacy* in the research literature (Wigfield, Eccles, and Rodriguez, 1998). These students are likely to lack confidence in their ability to read or even to improve their reading skill. In addition to a lack of belief in their reading capability, struggling readers in middle school are more likely to be extrinsically motivated than intrinsically motivated. These students report that their incentive for reading consists of grades and meeting teachers' requirements. They are unlikely to read for their own enjoyment, seek satisfaction of their curiosity through books, or enjoy the challenge of a complex plot or intricate knowledge books. (2003, 60)

We have underlined the subject of each sentence in the paragraph. The subject of the first sentence is *struggling readers*. The next sentence starts with the pronoun, *they,* which refers to *struggling readers*. The third sentence begins with a deictic, *These students* to link again to *struggling readers*. The subjects of the next three sentences follow a similar connective pattern: *struggling readers, These students,* and *they*. The use of pronouns and deictics gives this paragraph cohesion. The subject of each sentence is linked to the subjects of the other sentences.

In some paragraphs, words like *this* and *these* stand alone. For example, consider these two sentences from Schleppegrell: "The author takes advantage of orthographic resources such as bolding, italics, and exclamation points to highlight terms and emphasize key points. This mimics the role of intonation in spoken language" (2004, 62). Here, *this* connects the ideas in the two sentences. *This* serves as a general pronoun that refers to all the ideas in the previous sentence.

Writers also use conjunctions and prepositional phrases, such as *however, nevertheless*, and *as a result*, to connect sentences and give texts cohesion. Often ELLs and students who struggle with reading and writing know only a limited number of these conjunctions. They may use a word like *because* every time they try to show cause and effect. Students need to develop a greater repertoire of conjunctions and begin to use more academic words and phrases, such as *consequently*. We return to this topic later in the chapter when we discuss signal words.

A third device writers use to connect sentences is nominalization. Earlier, we explained that nominalization is a process of turning verbs or adjectives into nouns. For example, the verb *procrastinate* can become *procrastination* by the addition of the suffix *ion*. The adjective *sincere* becomes the noun *sincerity* with the addition of *ity*. Sentences in academic writing are often connected by the process of nominalization. For example, consider the following two sentences: "The scientist *mixed* the two liquids. The resulting *mixture* gave off a strange odor." Here the nominalized form, *mixture*, links with *mixed* in the preceding sentence.

Patterns of Cohesion in Paragraphs: Constant, Derived, and Chained

Brown (2009) has described three ways that writers link sentences to create cohesive paragraphs. He begins by explaining that sentences can be divided into two parts, referred to as the topic and the comment. The topic is the beginning of the sentence or clause, and the comment is what follows. The comment "is the place where the writer develops the message of the sentence or clause, where the writer 'comments on' the Topic" (72). For example, in the first sentence from the paragraph by Guthrie and Davis, "Struggling readers tend to be notably unmotivated" (2003, 60), the topic is *struggling readers* and the comment is the remainder of the sentence. Writers can link sentences by connecting the topic of one sentence with either the topic or the content of the preceding sentence. Brown refers to the ways of connecting sentences in a paragraph as constant, derived, or chained. Writers may use just one of these patterns or, more commonly, combine all three.

Constant topic • The paragraph by Guthrie and Davis provides a good example of the first pattern: a constant topic. The topics are *struggling readers, they, these* *students, struggling readers, these students*, and *they*. The topic of each sentence is struggling readers. The authors vary their writing by using *they* and *these students*, but the topic is constant. By keeping a constant topic, a writer creates cohesion. Many students produce paragraphs in which the sentences do not seem to hang together. A good first step might be to teach them this constant topic pattern and have them practice using the pattern in their writing.

Derived topic • Another pattern that Brown (2009) identifies is a derived topic. This pattern is similar to the constant topic. However, instead of being identical, the topic of one sentence is related to or derived from the topic of the previous sentence. For example, if the topic of the first sentence was *plants*, a derived topic might be a type of plant, such as a *dandelion*. The following sentences illustrate this pattern: "Geometric shapes have different characteristics. A triangle has three sides. A parallelogram has four sides."

Chained topic • The third pattern Brown (2009) discusses is chaining. Chaining occurs when the comment of one sentence becomes the topic of the next sentence. For example, here are two chained sentences: "Struggling readers can become engaged readers with the right instruction. Engaged readers enjoy reading a variety of books." In this example, the comment of the first sentence, *engaged readers*, becomes the topic of the second sentence. This chaining process may be illustrated as follows:

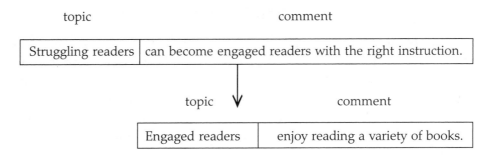

Brown describes three types of chaining. The first, which is shown in the previous example, is repetition. Key words from the comment of the first sentence are repeated as the topic of the second sentence. Too much repetition, of course, would become monotonous, so writers use two other ways to chain ideas. One of these is to substitute a word or phrase for the key words in the comment. For instance, the writer could have written the second sentence as "Students who love reading read a wide variety of books." In doing so, the writer substitutes *Students who love reading* for *Engaged readers*. The result is shown as follows:

Brown explains, "To substitute, you can use a synonym for one of the key words in the Comment, use a pronoun or summarize the main idea of the Comment" (2009, 93).

A third way to chain ideas is to use nominalization. Rather than repeating key words from the previous comment or substituting for those words, a writer can change an adjective or verb in the comment of the first sentence to a noun in the topic of the next sentence. To continue with our example, we could focus on the key words *engaged readers* and use the nominalized form *engagement* as the topic of the following sentence, thus creating a sentence such as "Engagement leads students to read a wide variety of books." This can be illustrated as follows:

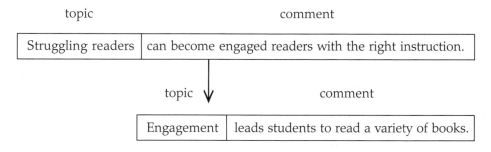

The following chart summarizes the three types of chaining:

Academic writing uses all these ways of connecting sentences to create cohesive paragraphs. Of the three, though, chaining using nominalization may be the most common since nominalization allows writers to pack more information into each sentence.

In the example we gave to demonstrate chaining, we used a simple sentence with just one clause. However, the three patterns we have described apply to complex sentences with more than one clause as well. For example, in the sentence "Engaged readers enjoy reading so they read a variety of books," the second clause uses a pronoun (*they*) to refer to the subject of the first clause (*engaged readers*). The pattern here is constant topic. The derived topic pattern could be shown with a sentence like "Engaged readers enjoy reading, and Mary's students read a variety of books." Here *Mary's students* is a subset of *engaged readers*. The third pattern, chained topic, is shown in this sentence: "Alexander Graham Bell invented the telephone, and this invention changed how people communicate." Here the verb *invented* from the first clause becomes the noun, *invention* in the second clause. As these examples show, writers can use the same devices to link either clauses in a sentence or sentences in a paragraph.

Consider the following paragraph taken from an integrated physics and chemistry textbook (McLaughlin, Thompson, and Zike 2002). It uses the patterns Brown describes to give it cohesion. We have reformatted it, listing each nonembedded clause separately.

1. Although <u>fossil fuels</u> are a useful source of energy for generating electricity and providing the power for transportation,

2. <u>their use</u> has some <u>undesirable side effects</u>.

3. When <u>petroleum products and coal</u> are burned,

4. <u>smoke</u> is given off that contains <u>small particles called particulates</u>.

5. <u>These particulates</u> cause breathing problems for some people.

6. <u>Burning fossil fuels</u> also releases <u>carbon dioxide</u>.

7. Figure 9 shows how the <u>carbon dioxide concentration</u> in the atmosphere has increased from 1960 to 1999.

8. <u>The increased concentration of carbon dioxide in the atmosphere</u> might cause Earth's surface temperature to increase. (296)

Clause 1 has the subject *fossil fuels*. Clause 2 uses *their* to refer to *fossil fuels*. In addition, *use* in 2 connects with *useful* in 1. The topic of clause 3, *petroleum products and coal*, is derived from *fossil fuels*, the topic of clause 1, since petroleum products and coal are types of fossil fuel. The topic of clause 4, *smoke*, is connected to the comment of 2, *undesirable side effects*. This is an example of chaining using the process of substitution.

The topic of 5, *These particulates*, is connected to the comment of 4. In this case, the chaining uses repetition. The topic of 6, *Burning fossil fuels*, connects to the previous *are burned*, the comment in clause 3, since *burning* is a nominalization. In addition, *fossil fuels* keeps the topic of clause 1. The topic of 7, *carbon dioxide concentration*, relates to the comment of 6 through chaining, and the topic of 8, *concentration of carbon dioxide*, is a variation of the topic of 7.

The analysis of this paragraph shows how the clauses are closely linked using many of the devices that Brown identifies. The paragraph has the characteristics of academic writing that we discussed in Chapter 4. It is technical, abstract, dense, and authoritative (Fang 2008). For example, the last sentence contains a complex subject, *The increased concentration of carbon dioxide in the atmosphere. Concentration* is a nominalized form. It is modified by the previous nominalized verb, *increased*, and by the following prepositional phrase, *in the atmosphere*. It is clear that ELLs and SELs who are struggling readers need scaffolded instruction to read and write texts like these.

Teaching Students to Write Cohesive Paragraphs

Brown (2009) suggests several activities to help students learn how to use the three patterns to give their paragraphs greater cohesion. First, the teacher explains what the topic of a clause is and has students practice finding the topics of a series of sentences. Then the teacher explains that the rest of a clause is called the comment. Students could divide clauses into the topic and comment.

Once students can identify the topic and comment of clauses, the teacher introduces the three patterns for paragraph cohesion. Students are then given pairs of sentences and asked to decide which of the three patterns they exemplify. They are also given paragraphs and asked to find places where there are no links between sentences. Once they have identified these places, they can write or rewrite a sentence to create a link.

Chaining is the most complex pattern for students to learn. Brown suggests giving them examples of sentence pairs with the three different kinds of chains (repetition, substitution, and nominalization) and asking them to identify the type used in each pair. Since nominalization is an important device for students to understand, Brown suggests giving them verbs and adjectives and asking them to add suffixes that convert them into nouns. For example, teachers could give students verbs like *ratify* and *discover* to change to nouns. Later, teachers can give students nominalized verbs such as *defiance* or *characterization* and ask them to provide the verb forms. These exercises would be especially difficult for ELLs with limited vocabulary in English. However, with support they could complete the exercises working in pairs or groups.

As a final step, teachers can give students pairs of sentences with the topic of the second sentence deleted, as shown below:

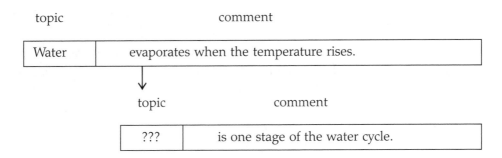

Teachers can provide prompts to help students fill in the blanks. For this example, the teacher could direct students to use nominalization to chain the two sentences. The goal is for students to begin to use these strategies to make their own writing more cohesive. Many struggling readers and writers have difficulty in writing paragraphs with connected sentences. By showing them how the writers of academic texts connect their sentences, teachers can guide their students to better writing. An understanding of these devices can also help students in their reading because they begin to see how the ideas in a passage are connected.

Academic Language at the Sentence Level

Even though research clearly demonstrates that ELLs need from five to seven years to catch up to native English-speaking peers on standardized tests, ELLs are required to take these tests after only a short time, usually after one year of instruction in English. As Short and Fitzsimmons (2007) note, ELLs face double the work of other students. They not only have to learn English but also have to learn content area subjects taught in English. Not surprisingly, ELLs score low on standardized tests given in English.

Wong-Fillmore and Snow (1999) have argued that the reason many ELLs struggle is that the tests are written in complex academic language. They analyzed prototype test questions from a state exam and concluded that competence in academic English was necessary to pass the test. The following question from a

Massachusetts Comprehensive Assessment System math exam for sixth graders is typical of the language they found:

> Students in Mr. Jacob's English class were giving speeches. Each student's speech was 7–10 minutes long. Which of the following is the best estimate for the total number of student speeches that could be given in a 2-hour class?
>
> A. 4   B. 8   C. 13   D. 19

The math knowledge required to answer this question seems appropriate for sixth graders. They should be able to convert 2 hours into minutes and then divide 7 and 10 into 120 to find the possible number of students who could give their speeches during the class. They do need to understand the math concept, *range*.

However, it is the English, not the math, on questions like this that led to the low scores for ELLs on this exam. The third sentence is the problem. It has a very complex structure. The subject noun phrase is *Which of the following*. ELLs may have trouble figuring out what this phrase refers to. To understand its meaning, they have to fill in the missing word, *answers*. This is an example of the kind of language used almost exclusively on tests, and unless students have taken many tests, they may not understand it.

The complement of the verb is also very complex. This long noun phrase, *the best estimate for the total number of student speeches that could be given in a 2-hour class*, contains a prepositional phrase that, in turn, contains a relative clause written in passive voice. The only technical math term in this word problem is *estimate*. The difficulty here is not the vocabulary; it is the structure of the sentence. This is the sort of academic language ELLs are expected to comprehend. In fact, many teachers of native English speakers have told us that issues like this are difficult for their struggling students, too.

Types of Clauses

In our discussion of paragraphs, we pointed out that sentences may be made up of several clauses. Complex sentences are typical of academic writing. ELLs and SELs who struggle with reading are expected to be able to read and write texts that contain these kinds of sentences. Here is a short passage typical of what is written in history texts:

> The early colonists struggled to become self-sufficient because they lacked familiarity with local conditions. Colonists who planted the

wrong crops or planted them at the wrong time could not survive in the new land.

These two sentences contain four clauses. Readers need to figure out how the ideas in these clauses are related and which are the main ideas. This is a formidable challenge for ELLs and struggling readers.

Teachers can help students with their reading and writing by showing them the different ways clauses are combined in English. While traditional approaches to teaching grammar are not effective for improving students' writing (Weaver 1996), a close examination of the language in students' textbooks or their own writing using a functional approach can give them insights into how sentences are structured.

Embedded clauses • In traditional grammar, clauses are categorized as independent or dependent. Independent clauses can stand alone as complete sentences while dependent clauses must be connected to an independent clause. In the first sentence of the history passage, for example, the first clause, *The early colonists struggled to become sufficient*, is independent because it could stand as a complete sentence by itself. The second clause, *because they lacked familiarity with local customs*, is dependent since it is not a complete sentence.

Functional linguists distinguish between two types of dependent clauses. Some dependent clauses are connected to the independent clause by a conjunction such as *because*. In the passage about the colonists, the second clause is of this type. Other dependent clauses are embedded within another clause. In the second sentence, the clause, *who planted the wrong crops or planted them at the wrong time*, is embedded inside the independent clause, *Colonists could not survive in the new land*.

A common function of an embedded clause is to provide more information about a noun that precedes it. In the previous example, the embedded clause tells the reader more about the colonists. The result is a complex noun phrase: Colonists *who planted the wrong crops or planted them at the wrong time*. Such complex nominal constructions are typical of academic writing.

Another way to modify nouns is to use a participle. A participle is a verb form that ends in *ing* and functions as an adjective. For example, in the noun phrase *the struggling student*, *struggling* is a participle that modifies *student*. A participial phrase is a phrase that begins with a participle. Participial phrases can also follow nouns, as in "the students *struggling with academic English*." Using participial phrases is one way to pack more information or description into a noun phrase. Although participial phrases can be used in any content area, they are most often found in literature (Weaver 2008). Embedded clauses and participial phrases result in sentences that are complex and lexically dense.

Lexical density • Earlier we explained that one characteristic of academic writing is density. Texts are dense when they contain a high percentage of content words (nouns, verbs, and adjectives). Linguists measure lexical density by the number of content words in each nonembedded clause. In the previous passage about the colonists, there are nineteen content words in the three nonembedded clauses, an average of more than 6.3 content words per clause. In contrast, according to Halliday (1998, in Schleppegrell 1994), spoken language contains about two content words per clause. The higher number of content words in academic writing is what gives it density. More ideas are packed into each clause.

Paratactic and hypotactic clauses • Clauses that are not embedded are related in one of two ways that linguists refer to as parataxis and hypotaxis. Paratactic clauses are equally important. The prefix, *para*, means *beside*. In other words a sentence with paratactic clauses puts two equally important clauses beside one another. Paratactic clauses are joined by coordinate conjunctions, such as *and*, *or*, and *but*, or are juxtaposed without a conjunction. For example, this sentence contains a paratactic clause with a conjunction: "The earliest colonists planted corn, but it failed to grow." This sentence contains one without a conjunction: "The earliest colonists planted corn; it failed to grow."

Hypotactic clauses are not equal. The prefix *hypo* means *under*, so the ideas in one clause are under or less important than those in the other clause. Hypotactic clauses are introduced by conjunctions such as *unless*, *if*, *since*, and *when*. In the first sentence about the colonists that we used earlier, "The early colonists struggled to become self-sufficient because they lacked familiarity with local conditions," the clause starting with *because* is hypotactic. The ideas in this clause are less important than those in the previous clause.

Combining Sentences to Reconstruct or Deconstruct Academic Texts

One way that teachers can help students understand the complex writing of academic texts is through sentence combining. Weaver (1996) cites research showing that sentence combining is an effective strategy for improving student writing. Weaver also emphasizes the importance of teaching grammar in context. Consequently, teachers should use passages from the class textbooks to teach students about sentence structure. For example, the teacher might begin with a short passage like the one about the colonists:

The early colonists struggled to become self-sufficient because they lacked familiarity with local conditions. Colonists who planted the wrong crops or planted them at the wrong time could not survive in the new land.

The teacher rewrites the passage, making each clause a simple sentence:

1. The early colonists struggled to become self-sufficient.

2. The early colonists lacked familiarity with local conditions.

3. Colonists could not survive in the new land.

4. They planted the wrong crops or planted them at the wrong time.

The teacher passes the list of sentences out to the students. Then the students, working in groups, decide how to combine the sentences. When they finish, the groups can write their results on the board or put them on an overhead transparency and explain the process they went through. The class could also create a composite paragraph using ideas from the groups. What is important here is for students to talk about how and why they combined sentences as they did. Students can also compare their reconstructed paragraphs with the original. In some cases, students may decide they like their version better than what the published author wrote.

To scaffold this activity, the teacher should give students practice in combining sentences using nonembedded clauses. The teacher should use examples related to the content the class is studying. The teacher might begin with two simple sentences logically related by cause and effect, such as "There was a prolonged drought in the area. Many of the plants died," and discuss different ways they could be combined. Using the previous example, students might write, "Because there was a prolonged drought, many of the plants died." They can also discuss the difference between this sentence and one that begins with the clause about plants dying, "Many of the plants died because there was a prolonged drought." The teacher should help the students understand that the order of clauses can be changed. The class can also discuss the idea that the clause that comes first is the one the writer wants the reader to focus on. One order puts the focus on the drought and the other emphasizes the effect on the plants. After students have practiced with other pairs of sentences showing cause and effect, the teacher can introduce sentences related in other ways, such as sequence.

After students understand how to combine sentences using nonembedded clauses, the teacher can introduce embedded clauses. The teacher might give students two sentences such as "The plants received adequate sun and water" and "The plants were healthy." First, students can discuss how these two sentences can be combined to show cause and effect. Then, the teacher can show them that the sentences can also be combined by putting one clause inside the other to produce "The plants that received adequate sun and water were healthy." Next, students can practice this new way of combining clauses with other sentence pairs.

After showing students the two basic ways of combining clauses, teachers can have students analyze passages in their textbooks to see how writers combine ideas into complex sentences. Students can also begin to use these kinds of sentences in their own writing. Carefully scaffolded sentence-combining exercises can help ELLs and struggling readers and writers understand and produce academic texts.

Signal Words

As students learn to combine simple sentences in different ways to produce more complex writing, they need to develop a repertoire of words and phrases to connect clauses. Many ELLs and SELs overuse a few common connectors because their vocabulary is limited. One way to help students move past this early stage is to build their vocabulary by introducing other, more precise, words to show the relationships between ideas. These transition words are often referred to as signal words because they signal to the reader how two ideas are related. Signal words may connect ideas within a sentence or across sentences. Fisher, Rothenberg, and Frey (2007) explain how a team of ninth-grade teachers worked to help their students develop vocabulary to link ideas.

The teachers examined student writing and found that their ELLs often left transitions out. The teachers found a word list that grouped signal words by function. The functions included addition, example, comparison, contrast, cause and effect, concession, and conclusion. For each function, several words were listed. For example, for addition, the list included *also, and, besides, furthermore, in addition, indeed, in fact, moreover, so,* and *too* (52).

The teachers posted this list in their rooms as a word wall. They took time on a regular basis to review the words with their students. As they read aloud to their students, they made a point of emphasizing words in the texts that were on the list. According to Fisher and his colleagues, "Over time, students started to notice the terms in their reading and began incorporating them into their writing" (51). The process the teachers used enabled the struggling SELs and ELLs in their ninth-grade classes to enrich their vocabulary by adding words that show logical connections between ideas.

Strategies to Help Students with Academic Writing

Fang (2008) describes other strategies teachers can use to help ELLs and SELs who struggle with reading to read and write academic texts. One strategy is sentence transformation. Students are given sentences with complex noun phrases in which the noun is a nominalized form of a verb or adjective. Students are asked to rewrite each sentence into everyday language, changing the noun back into a verb. For example, students might have the following sentence: "The transportation of the hazardous chemicals across the lake caused concern among the inhabitants of the region." The students would need to convert *transportation* into the verb *transport* and *concern* into *were concerned* to write a sentence like "When the chemical company wanted to transport hazardous chemicals across the lake, people in the area were concerned."

This strategy takes considerable scaffolding and should be used only with ELLs at more advanced levels. First, the students need to understand how verbs and adjectives can be turned into nouns, perhaps using the kinds of exercises Brown (2009) outlines and that we described earlier. Then, they have to begin with simpler sentences before building up to a complex sentence like the one in the example. However, sentence transformation does help students see the difference between everyday speech and academic language. If students can complete these transformations, teachers can also give them the more difficult task of changing everyday sentences into academic text with the nominalized form of the verb.

Another strategy that Fang describes is paraphrase. This strategy involves translating an informational text with academic language into everyday spoken English. For this strategy, students work in small groups to develop a radio show series they will record on tape. The teacher gives each group a short informational text. The groups rewrite the text into a three- to five-minute segment for a radio talk show. Once students write the text, they practice reading it on audiotape. They listen to the recording and compare it with the original informational text. They can also discuss the kinds of changes they made to convert the written text into speech. This is a good activity for ELLs because it helps them understand the differences between spoken and written language.

We have noticed that when students are asked to paraphrase material, they end up copying words and phrases from the source. One of our colleagues worked with a teacher who developed a good way to help students paraphrase more effectively. She had the students write down key words as they read a short passage. Then the students closed their books and, using the key words, wrote their paraphrases. They used only the key words and did not look back at their books. For example, in reading a passage about Native Americans, one ELL listed the words *Utes, dwellings, wickiups, cone-shaped, branches,* and *grasses.* Then she wrote her paraphrase: "The Utes lived in cone-shaped dwellings called wickiups. They were made with poles, branches, and grasses." This strategy helped students learn to paraphrase, and it also helped them learn the content knowledge of their textbook.

Conclusion

ELLs and SELs who struggle with reading need to develop academic language proficiency at the paragraph and sentence levels. In academic writing, paragraphs are made cohesive in various ways. Brown (2009) outlines three patterns that connect sentences within a paragraph. Teachers can help students write more cohesive paragraphs by explicitly teaching them how to connect their sentences.

Teachers can also work with students to help them develop an academic style of writing at the sentence level. Sentences in academic writing are generally complex and consist of several clauses. They are lexically dense with a high percentage of content words in each clause. Students need to understand the complex structure of academic sentences to write and eventually to read them in more sophisticated texts.

Students also need to understand how writers use signal words to connect clauses in a sentence or sentences in a paragraph. To produce academic writing, students need an expanded vocabulary of signal words they can use to show different kinds of relationships, such as sequence or cause and effect. Strategies such as sentence transformation and paraphrasing can help ELLs and struggling readers and writers better understand and produce academic texts.

Applications

1. Look back at an academic paper you have written. What cohesive devices did you use in your paper? Underline examples of reference, conjunctions, and nominalization. Bring the paper to class or your study group to share.

2. In the same paper, find the topic and the comment in the sentences in one of the paragraphs. Underline the topic and the comment of each sentence.

3. Using the same paper, determine the patterns you used to connect your sentences in one paragraph. Label each pattern as constant, derived, or chained. Find a second paragraph in your paper that uses a different pattern. Be prepared to share your analyses.

4. Read over the following paragraph from the *World Geography* (Boehm 2003) textbook. Mark the topics and the comments. Then determine what pattern of cohesion is used: constant, derived, or chained. If the pattern is chained, is it through repetition, substitution, or nominalization? Mark and label each connection. Discuss with a group.

> Several factors have limited industrial growth in Latin America. Physical geography may present obstacles. The High Andes and the dense Amazon rain forest, for example, limit access to natural resources. Ties to more developed regions also have limited growth. Foreigners have brought new technology to the region, but many have drained local resources and profits. Finally, political instability in many Latin American countries has made investors wary of investing in Latin American enterprises. (239)

5. Looking at the passage in application 4, identify all the signal words. What kind of relationship does each one signal (cause-effect, sequence, addition, conclusion, etc.)?

6. Look at the following isolated sentences. Combine them into a cohesive paragraph. Use the different cohesive devices discussed in this chapter. Label the devices you use, and be prepared to discuss how you created the paragraph.

   1. A food chain is a model.

   2. A food chain shows how matter and energy move through an ecosystem.

   3. Nutrients and energy move.

   4. They move from autotrophs to heterotrophs to decomposers.

   5. A food chain can be drawn.

   6. Arrows indicate the direction of the energy.

   7. Energy is transferred from one organism to another.

   8. Food chains have two, three, or four transfers.

9. The first transfer has the most energy.

10. The final transfer has only a small portion of the original energy.

11. Energy is given off as heat at every transfer.

12. Each transfer is a feeding step.

13. Feeding steps are called a trophic level.

6

Developing Academic Vocabulary and Writing Content and Language Objectives

ELLs face a difficult task in acquiring English vocabulary. Pinker (1994) estimates that educated adult speakers of English know about sixty thousand words. These words include both conversational and academic vocabulary. Any approach to vocabulary study for ELLs has to recognize that a great number of words must be acquired through exposure to meaningful English, since no program would enable students to learn sixty thousand words. At the same time, to help ELLs and struggling readers develop academic vocabulary, teachers must make careful choices about which words to teach and how to teach them.

In previous chapters, we discussed academic language at the text, paragraph, and sentence levels. In this chapter, we focus on the word level and offer specific ways teachers can help ELLs and struggling readers develop academic vocabulary. We first look briefly at the history of the English language to trace how academic words entered the vocabulary. Next we distinguish between two types of academic words: content-specific words and general academic words. Then, we discuss four keys that researchers have found to be essential for developing academic vocabulary. In the last section of this chapter we explain how teachers can write content and language objectives at the text, paragraph, sentence, and word levels to help ELLs and struggling readers develop academic language proficiency.

The Development of Academic English

In Chapter 2 we discussed Corson's (1997) linguistic study. He found that the vocabulary of everyday speech is quite different from that of academic texts. Even students who speak English well need to learn a great deal of new vocabulary to read and write academic texts. As Corson observes, academic texts contain many words with Latin and Greek roots while conversational language contains many more Anglo-Saxon words. A brief look at the history of English shows how these two strands of vocabulary developed.

The Celts were the original inhabitants of the British Isles, but few Celtic words can be found in current English vocabulary. Over time, different groups invaded the island, and each group contributed to current English vocabulary (Tompkins and Yaden 1986; Freeman and Freeman 2004). During the Old English period, from about 450 to 1100, the Angles, Saxons, and Jutes invaded Britain and drove the native Celts into the northern and western areas. These three groups of Germanic invaders spoke *Englisc*. Few words from Old English remain. Some of those that do are basic words such as *child, hand, foot, mother*, and *sun*, which form part of the conversational register.

Missionaries who reintroduced Christianity to Britain in 597 brought in religious Latin words like *angel, disciple, hymn*, and *priest*. In 787, the Vikings invaded from the north and ruled England for three centuries. The Vikings contributed pronouns including *they, their*, and *them* and many everyday words like *husband, low, ugly*, and *window*.

The Norman-French invasion of England in 1066 contributed much of our academic vocabulary. The Normans, who were actually other Vikings (Norsemen) who had invaded France, ruled England for three centuries. The French they spoke was a dialect of Latin that had evolved in France over a long period. About ten thousand Latinate Norman-French words were added to English during this period (McWhorter 2001).

Then, during the Renaissance, many more Greek and Latin terms were added to the English vocabulary such as *congratulate, democracy*, and *education*, along with

Anglo-Saxon	French	Latin
fear	terror	trepidation
win	succeed	triumph
kingly	royal	regal
holy	sacred	consecrated

figure 6.1 Vocabulary from Three Sources

many scientific terms, such as *atmosphere, pneumonia,* and *virus.* Educated Englishmen regarded Latin and Greek terms as more scholarly. Brook points out that because of this infusion, especially of Latin terms, "One basic meaning could be expressed by three different English words that come from three sources—Anglo-Saxon, French, and Latin" (1998, 26). Brook provides some examples, which are listed in Figure 6.1.

English has many sets of words like these. Notice that Latin- and Greek-based words seldom occur in everyday conversation, but they are typical of academic discourse.

Content-Specific and General Academic Vocabulary

In general, we can define academic vocabulary as words and phrases that occur frequently in academic texts. Most of these words are derived from Latin and Greek roots. It is useful to further divide academic vocabulary into two types of words: content-specific words and general academic words. Donley and Reppen (2001) explain that content-specific vocabulary includes technical words related to a specific academic discipline while general academic vocabulary consists of words that cut across disciplines and appear in different content areas. Examples of content-specific words are *fault* in geology, *ethnocentrism* in sociology, *protagonist* in language arts, and *radius* in math. General academic vocabulary includes words like *context, therefore, hypothesis,* and *analyze* (Freeman and Freeman 2004).

In most subject areas, content-specific vocabulary appears in the texts students read. Content-specific science words, for example, appear in biology or chemistry texts. The exception is literature. The content-specific words for literature, such as *synecdoche* or *iambic pentameter*, do not appear in literature. They are specialized words used to describe and analyze literature, and they may appear in textbooks about literature. However, students would not see these words as they read a poem or a novel. For that reason, teachers of literature need to make extra efforts to introduce, explain, and use the content-specific words of their content area.

Donley and Reppen (2001) conducted research showing that students acquire context-specific vocabulary more quickly than general academic vocabulary. They list several reasons for this finding. For one thing, readers notice content-specific words because they are strongly connected with the topic. For example, someone learning about geometric shapes would notice a word like *rhombus* because it fits into this topic. In addition, content-specific words are conceptually related to other words used to discuss a topic. A word like *rhombus* is related to *parallelogram* and *trapezoid*. Within a text, content-specific words are often typographically enhanced. They may be bolded or italicized. These words are often defined by glosses within the text or at the end of a chapter. Finally, students notice content-specific words because these are the words that often appear on tests and because teachers usually emphasize these words.

Students can acquire general academic vocabulary through extensive reading of academic texts. Since these words appear frequently across the content areas, students encounter them often enough to acquire them. Content-specific words occur less often, since they are restricted to one content area. For that reason, teachers may want to teach some of the important content-specific words directly. An effective program for increasing students' academic vocabulary should include both extensive reading and some targeted instruction of content-specific vocabulary.

Although we don't advocate the direct teaching of general academic vocabulary, teachers may find it useful to have a list of the terms that occur most frequently across the content areas. One such list, the Academic Word List, was compiled by Coxhead (2000). This list is available online at http://language.massey.ac.nz/staff /awl/. The list is drawn from a large corpus of vocabulary found in academic journal articles, book chapters, and other sources in several different academic fields. The final list includes 570 word families (a family includes the different forms of the same word, such as *analyze, analyzed, analytical,* and *analyzing*). These word families are listed in order of frequency from most frequent to least frequent. Even though this list should not be turned into a vocabulary list to teach, teachers can briefly explain important general terms as they discuss student writing. For example, teachers can discuss the difference between *summarizing* and *synthesizing*, two important general academic words. In addition, teachers can purposefully use these words during class discussions.

Keys for Developing Academic Vocabulary

Developing academic vocabulary is essential for academic success for both native English speakers and ELLs. For that reason, teachers in each of the academic content areas should address vocabulary instruction. Students in middle and secondary schools need to learn the content-specific vocabulary of the different subject areas, and the responsibility for teaching that vocabulary cannot rest solely with the English language arts teacher or the ESL teacher. An effective vocabulary program depends on all teachers using consistent, research-based methods for teaching the vocabulary of their subject areas.

In *The Vocabulary Book: Learning and Instruction,* Graves (2006) summarizes the research on vocabulary teaching and learning. Based on his review of the research, he concludes that teachers should follow four procedures to ensure effective vocabulary development:

1. provide rich and varied language experiences;

2. teach individual words;

3. teach word-learning strategies; and

4. foster word consciousness.

Provide Rich and Varied Language Experiences

Rich and varied language experiences include classroom conversations and reading. An effective vocabulary program includes both oral language and literacy development.

Academic language development through oral interactions • In earlier chapters we discussed the importance of engaging students in classroom discussions to build oral language. We suggested ways teachers could respond to students to help them extend their answers. ELLs and struggling readers often attempt to remain unnoticed during classroom discussions, but it is very important that they develop their oral language.

In his review of research on ELLs, Graves concluded that "students need to develop their oral language skills in both their native language and in English" (2006, 34). Skills developed in one language transfer to a second language (Cummins 2000). Students with a large academic vocabulary in one language can more easily build vocabulary in their second language.

Bilingual students in programs that help them build both of their languages for an extended period of time achieve higher scores on standardized tests of reading in English than students in programs in which their first language is not developed (Ramírez 1991; Thomas and Collier 1997). The report of the National Literacy Panel also concluded that "there is no indication that bilingual instruction impedes academic achievement in either the native language or English. . . . Where differences were observed, on average, they favored the students in a bilingual program" (August and Shanahan 2006, 397).

Many older ELLs have not had the benefit of long-term bilingual programs. However, teachers can help them build their academic vocabulary by encouraging them to use both their languages during classroom discussions. When teachers don't speak the first language of all their students or when ELLs speak a variety of first languages, teachers can have students work in pairs or small groups, and during this time, students can choose which language to use.

Gutiérrez (2002) conducted research in three high school mathematics classes. The teachers of these classes all had been very successful in helping their Hispanic students achieve at high levels. Gutiérrez noted that the three teachers used similar strategies. They had students work in groups often, they allowed students to work in their first languages, they supplemented the textbook materials, and they built on students' previous knowledge. Gutiérrez observed, "Given that the teachers defined themselves, for the most part, as nonfluent in Spanish, their classroom practices illustrated that at some level they were aware of the importance of allowing their students to speak in whichever language made them most comfortable" (1074–75). The teachers changed student groupings often, and students sometimes spoke English, sometimes used Spanish, and sometimes code-switched. What was important was that in these small groups, students had the opportunity for extended oral discussions of mathematics. The result, for all three teachers, was that their students achieved at high levels in math.

Academic vocabulary development through extended reading • In addition to rich classroom discussions, students need to be engaged in extended reading to develop their academic vocabulary. Since this vocabulary appears primarily in academic texts, unless students do a great deal of reading, they cannot build the vocabulary they need to succeed in school. Krashen (2004b) has summarized a great deal of the research on the benefits of free voluntary reading. He concludes that programs in which students read for extended periods of time on a regular basis improve all aspects of their language proficiency. Other studies have shown more specifically the vocabulary increase that results from extensive reading.

Nagy, Anderson, and Herman (1987) investigated the number of words students gain from reading. Their subjects were 352 students from third, fifth, and seventh grades. The students read both narrative and expository passages. Six days later, they were tested on selected words from the passages. The researchers concluded, "Our results demonstrate beyond a reasonable doubt that incidental learning of word meanings does take place during normal reading" (261). The researchers found that the probability of learning a word from reading was only 5 percent. This translates into about a one-in-twenty chance of learning a new word from reading.

Although this probability seems small, the gains in vocabulary can be large for a student who reads extensively. Anderson and Nagy (1992) report that the average fifth grader reads about twenty-five minutes a day. This translates into about one million words a year. If at least 2 percent of the words the student reads are unfamiliar, then the student is exposed to twenty thousand new words. "If one in twenty of these is learned, we have accounted for at least a thousand words a year" (46). Anderson and Nagy go on to point out that "for children who do a fair amount of independent reading, then natural learning could easily lead to the acquisition of five to ten thousand words per year" (46).

When students engage in extensive reading, they encounter new words in context. To develop a thorough understanding of new words, students need to see them in different contexts. Otherwise, they may learn a word's meaning but still use the word incorrectly. For example, one student who was given a list of vocabulary words looked each word up and wrote a definition. Then she wrote sentences for each word. When she reached the word *condolences* on her list, she wrote, "I gave the girl my condolences." The student knew that *condolences* had to do with expressing sympathy or saying you are sorry. However, in English we can *express* our condolences, *send* our condolences, or *offer* our condolences, but we can't *give* them. The only way the student could learn this would be by seeing or hearing the word in different contexts.

It is also important for students to see words in context as they read because many words in English have multiple meanings. ELLs and struggling readers often know the meaning of a word as it is used in conversational language, but they might not know the specialized meanings the word has in different content areas. For example, *table* is a content-specific academic word in several different content areas, as shown in the following sentences:

1. She consulted the periodic table.

2. She worried that the water table had dropped because of the drought.

3. She studied the population table in the book that showed the increase in ELLs.

4. She practiced her multiplication tables.

5. She tabled the motion.

Table can also serve as a general academic word, as shown in these sentences:

1. She looked through the table of contents.

2. She learned the differences among a chart, a figure, and a table.

It is only by exposure to academic vocabulary in context that students can acquire the different meanings of words. Students who read extensively more easily use their academic vocabulary as they engage in class discussions and write academic papers in the different subject areas. ELLs need rich and varied language experiences to build academic vocabulary. Without this component, no program to develop academic vocabulary can succeed.

Teach Individual Words

The second component in an effective program for building academic vocabulary is teaching individual words. It is especially important for teachers to identify the content-specific words from their subject areas to teach. These are the words that will be most useful to ELLs and struggling readers for building academic language proficiency.

A number of writers have described strategies teachers can use to help students learn individual words. In her book *Word Play: Building Vocabulary Across Texts and Disciplines, Grades 6–12,* Whitaker (2008) describes a number of word-learning strategies. For example, one strategy asks students to brainstorm synonyms for an academic word the teacher chooses and then to work in groups to rank the words from most neutral to most powerful. The class then discusses similarities and differences among the words. Neutral words would be those in conversational registers while powerful words would appear more often in academic registers. This activity can help ELLs understand the differences in meaning between everyday words like *said* and academic words such as *stated* and *declared*. Because the discussions first take place in small groups, ELLs can participate more fully in the activity.

Another strategy for learning individual words that Whitaker explains involves filling in a graphic organizer. She describes how a teacher helped students learn a content-specific word, *force*. The students were given a graphic organizer originally developed by Frayer:

> This graphic organizer is divided into four main sections to include the
> definition, characteristics, examples, and non-examples of words being

studied. Revolutionary for its time, this model requires students to both analyze words and apply word knowledge. (2008, 153)

For the word *force*, students worked in groups to fill in the four squares of the Frayer model. For their definition, they put "a push or pull." They listed several characteristics, such as "measured in Newtons." Then they wrote examples like catching or throwing a ball and nonexamples like mass and weight. As they worked together to fill in the four boxes, the students discussed what *force* meant and, in the process, refined their understanding of this key term. This simple graphic organizer scaffolds instruction for ELLs and struggling readers. The students are also supported in their learning by working in small groups. They have opportunities to discuss the meanings of words and clarify their understandings. Whitaker includes a number of such activities that teachers can use to help their students develop academic vocabulary.

Other writers have also explained useful word-learning strategies. For example, in *Inside Words: Tools for Teaching Academic Vocabulary, Grades 4–12*, Allen (2007) describes a number of strategies that would be appropriate for ELLs because they include graphic organizers in almost every case. Graphic representations help students store words in long-term memory. ELLs can visualize the relationships among words when given a graphic organizer as a scaffold. In addition, in *Word Wise and Content Rich, Grades 7–12: Five Essential Steps to Teaching Academic Vocabulary*, Fisher and Frey (2008b) include a number of excellent strategies for teaching individual words.

For a vocabulary program to be effective, teachers from each of the content areas need to help students increase their knowledge of the content-specific words found in their subject areas. For example, mathematics contains many content-specific words, such as *divisor, quotient,* and *coefficient* (Dale and Cuevas 1992). These are specialized terms that students encounter only in mathematics. In addition to individual words, mathematics employs many phrases, like *least common multiple* and *negative exponent*. Students need to understand these phrases to succeed in math.

Mathematics is also difficult because students must learn that different terms can be used to refer to the same process. Dale and Cuevas (1992) give the example of addition, which can be expressed by *add, plus, combine, and, sum,* and *increased by*. Students must recognize these different vocabulary items all indicate the same operation. At the same time, they must recognize the difference between expressions like *divided into* and *divided by*.

Thompson and Rubenstein (2000) describe how teachers have used daily journal writing to help students understand the language of math. The teachers give prompts such as "Complete the following analogy, and explain your thinking: Prism is to pyramid as cylinder is to _____" or "Square and cube have geometric meanings and are also used for second and third powers respectively. How are the geometry and powers related?" (570). This sort of daily writing helps students think through the math they are learning. As they write, they develop their understanding of important math terms.

Slavit and Ernst-Slavit (2007) provide still other strategies teachers can use to help ELLs understand and use the language of math. These include introducing vocabulary in a systematic way within the context of lessons, identifying and highlighting words with multiple meanings, previewing and reviewing each lesson so that ELLs understand the whole before being immersed in the details, and brainstorming the meaning and origin of technical terms. All of these strategies help ELLs learn content-specific math terms. Teaching individual words is important in each subject area. In addition to providing rich and varied language experiences, teachers should develop a variety of ways for teaching individual words.

An Effective Approach to Teaching Individual Words

Marzano (2004) has developed a comprehensive approach to choosing and teaching individual words. He explains how this approach can be used in any content area and how it can be modified to meet the needs of ELLs. Marzano's model has strong research support, and it has been widely implemented.

We have explained that teachers in the different content areas should choose content-specific words as the focus of their vocabulary instruction. At the same time, they should involve students in classroom discussions and extended reading to build their general academic vocabulary. To determine which content-specific words teachers should teach, Marzano and his colleagues analyzed the state and national content standards to determine key vocabulary items that occur consistently in the different content areas at various grade-level clusters. Context-area teachers can refer to these lists as they decide which words to teach. The lists are included in two books: *Building Background Knowledge for Academic Achievement: Research on What Works in Schools* (Marzano 2004) and *Building Academic Vocabulary: Teacher's Manual* (Marzano and Pickering 2005).

Once teachers decide which words to teach, they should use a consistent method of instruction. Marzano's approach involves six steps. In the following sections, we describe each step and the modifications Marzano and Pickering suggest for use with ELLs.

Step 1 • For the first step, the teacher provides a description, explanation, or example of the new term. A description is different from a dictionary definition. For example, if a teacher asked students to look up the word *hyperbole* for their language arts class, they would find a definition like "exaggerated statements or claims not meant to be taken literally." Students are not apt to understand a dictionary definition. Instead a teacher could describe the word as "saying something that people know can't be true because it is so exaggerated." The teacher can also provide an example. An example of *hyperbole* might be "His eyes were bigger than his stomach." A good example helps students remember word meanings.

Marzano and Pickering (2005) suggest that for this step, teachers should first find out if students already know the word or have an idea of what it might mean. Then teachers can build on the students' understanding. The authors stress that a teacher doesn't need to simply provide information. For example, a teacher could build on some experience the class has had to introduce the term. The teacher might tell a story that includes the term. The teacher could also have small groups or individual students investigate the term and report back to the class. Students or the teacher could find or create pictures to exemplify the term.

Marzano and Pickering offer modifications of each step for teachers working with ELLs. For this step, they comment, "Ideally, your description, explanation, or example should be given in the students' native language" (35). They point out that this allows students to make connections more easily with things they already know. If the teacher doesn't speak the first language of the ELLs, she can pair students who speak the same first language or form small groups, so that a student with more facility in English can translate the term for the others. In addition, a bilingual paraprofessional or a parent volunteer could explain the term in the students' first language.

Step 2 • In the second step, the students are asked to restate the description, explanation, or example in their own words. Marzano and Pickering (2005) comment that students shouldn't just repeat what the teacher has said but should try to rephrase it using their own words. If the teacher notices that students are having trouble restating the meaning of the word or phrase, this is a good time to go back and give additional explanations or examples. Students are also asked to record their descriptions in a vocabulary notebook. Marzano and Pickering suggest that students keep a vocabulary notebook with different labeled sections for each content area. The notebook might have space on each page for two or three words.

For the second step, ELLs can restate the description or explanation using their first language. They can also record information about cognates. Teachers can encourage ELLs to look for connections between their first-language vocabulary and words or phrases in English.

Step 3 • Students are then asked to construct a picture, symbol, or graphic representation for the term. In their notebooks, there should be space on each page to write the description and draw a picture or other nonlinguistic representation. Marzano and Pickering (2005) note that some students are reluctant to draw pictures, so it is important for the teacher to model this step many times. Teachers can also show examples of work other students have done, and they can allow students to work together at first. Figure 6.2 shows a kidspeak activity that allows students to use their own words and also jot down drawings or sketches to help them remember key terms. The first column has the word or term; the second, the teacher's definition; the third, the student's definition in kidspeak; and the final column, some clue to help the student remember the meaning.

For some vocabulary items, it may be difficult to create a pictorial or graphic representation. Marzano and Pickering suggest that teachers can do several things. They can draw the actual thing in some cases. For other words, they can draw a symbol or an example. The drawings can also dramatize the word using cartoon bubbles and

Word	Teacher Definition	Kidspeak	Clue
formula	The words, letters, and numbers we use to explain or show a procedure	How we show what we need to do	Formula for area of a square: Area $= S^2$
Bill of Rights	The first ten amendments to the U.S. Constitution, which list people's rights	Tell what people and government can and can't do legally	We can say and write what we want to. We can go to church where we want.

figure 6.2 Kidspeak Organizer

WORD	SYMBOL OR DRAWING
immigrant	
DEFINITION	**WORD OR PHRASE THAT REMINDS YOU OF THE MEANING**
A person who comes into a new country	José

figure 6.3 Four-Box Vocabulary Organizer

people's faces. In some cases, the word is better represented by a graphic. Students can also find a graphic on the Internet to copy into their notebook.

Figure 6.3 shows another activity using drawings or graphics. In this four-box activity, students write the words in the first box, draw a picture or symbol in the second, write a definition in their own words in the third, and add a clue to help them remember the meaning in the fourth. In Figure 6.3 *José* is the name of a recent immigrant.

This third step is very important for ELLs. Even though they may have difficulty explaining a term in words, they can often draw a picture, symbol, or graphic to represent the term. Since the teacher has already presented the term pictorially in step 1, it is important that ELLs create a new way to represent the term and not simply copy what the teacher has done.

The first three steps can be done on the same day. Marzano and Pickering suggest that these steps might take about fifteen minutes. The teacher can introduce the word, the students can restate it, and then they can illustrate it. Of course, this process may also be spread over more time.

Step 4 • Marzano and Pickering (2005) emphasize the importance of revisiting the terms to deepen students' understanding. For that reason, the fourth step is to engage students periodically in activities that add to their understanding of the terms. The authors suggest several ways teachers can involve students in thinking more about a term. For example, the students might highlight a prefix or suffix that will help them remember the term, identify synonyms or antonyms for the term, draw additional pictures or graphics, list related words, write notes to themselves about the term that they want to remember, or, for ELLs, translate the word into their first languages. Marzano and Pickering provide a template for a page in a student's vocabulary notebook that contains extra room for students to make these additions.

They also provide a number of other detailed activities for helping students develop a deeper understanding of the vocabulary they are learning. These include having students brainstorm words related to the term, completing sentence stems for comparing terms, using graphics, such as a Venn diagram, to compare and contrast terms, filling in a matrix with characteristics of the term, following different procedures for classifying terms, solving analogy problems using the terms, and creating metaphors for the terms. For each of these suggestions, the authors provide templates and examples. Step 4 can be done periodically using different techniques to review the terms students are learning.

For the fourth step, as they review terms, ELLs can again use their first languages. Teachers can give them an analogy in English to complete and they can fill it in with English or words from their first languages. For example, the teacher might give them a sentence such as the following to complete: "Square is to triangle as _____ is to _____."

Step 5 • In the fifth step, students discuss the terms with one another. Marzano and Pickering (2005) suggest that teachers use a think-pair-share approach for this step. First, students think about the vocabulary item and review what they have written and drawn. Then they pair with another student to compare descriptions and explain their understandings to one another. At this point they can discover any areas of disagreement or confusion. When students discuss a term together, the teacher might want to pair students who speak the same first language so that they can discuss the term in more detail. After they discuss the term, students report back to the class any new understandings they have discovered.

Step 6 • For this step, teachers involve students in different games to play with the terms. Marzano and Pickering describe a number of games teachers can use to help students review the academic vocabulary they are learning. They write, "Games are one of the most underused instructional tools in education" (2005, 30). When teachers provide time for structured games designed to review terms, students develop a much better understanding of the terms. During language games, the teacher can have ELLs work with partners or in threes to ensure that they can participate.

The authors state that teachers should monitor student work and review their notebooks from time to time. They also provide a rubric students can use to evaluate their own understanding of the terms they are using. They can record their self-evaluations in their notebook. They can also create a chart to list how well (for example, at what level on a four-point scale) they understand the different terms they are learning. This self-evaluation is an important way for students to begin to take ownership of their learning.

Instead of studying a few words each week and then forgetting them, students in classes using this approach come back to look at and think about content-specific words repeatedly. At a school that implements this model in each content class, students' understanding of the academic vocabulary of each content area deepens, and students retain this knowledge. Teaching individual words in this way can increase the academic vocabulary knowledge of ELLs and struggling readers and raise their levels of academic language proficiency.

Teach Word Learning Strategies

According to Graves (2006), a third research-based component of an effective program for building vocabulary is teaching word-learning strategies. These strategies include using context clues, using word parts, and using the dictionary. Teachers can demonstrate these strategies, and then students can use them as they read independently.

Using context clues • Graves states, "Using context clues to infer the meanings of unknown words is the first word-learning strategy I consider because it is the most important one" (2006, 94). All readers use context clues as they read. However, skilled readers make better use of context clues than struggling readers. ELLs who read well in their first language can transfer their skills, including using context clues, to a second language. However, many older ELLs do not read well in their first language or in English. For both struggling readers and ELLs, some explicit instruction in how to use context can be useful.

Graves describes a four-step method he has developed for helping students use context clues. First, the teacher introduces the idea of using context to infer word meanings. Then she teaches the four steps of the method, comparing each step to using a VCR. She puts up a poster with the steps:

1. Play and Question

2. Slow Advance

3. Stop and Rewind

4. Plan and Question

In step 1, students learn to read carefully. As they read, they ask themselves, "Does this make sense?" Step 2 occurs when students come across a word whose meaning they are unsure of. They slow down and reread the sentence, looking for meaning clues. If this doesn't work, students go on to step 3. They go back to the previous sentence and reread both sentences to find clues to meaning. In the fourth step, the students guess what the word might mean. They substitute their guess to see if it makes sense. If it does, they keep reading. If not, they go back, reread, and try another guess.

Graves explains how teachers can implement this four-step strategy. They teach each step and give students guided and independent practice in using the steps. They discuss kinds of clues to look for. With practice, students can start to use context clues more effectively as they read.

Using word parts • The second word-learning strategy that Graves lists is using word part clues to infer meanings of words. Words that make up the academic vocabulary of English often have Latin or Greek roots as well as prefixes and suffixes. Students can use these word parts to infer the meaning of words in context.

Thompson and Rubenstein (2000) describe how a math teacher used word parts to help her students understand a content-specific math term. The teacher explained, "*Perpendicular* comes from a root, *pend*, meaning *to hang*, because when a weight hangs freely on a string, it forms a perpendicular to the ground" (571). Then she connected the math term to everyday words like *pendant* and *pendulum* to help the students remember the meaning.

This teacher used the word root to explain *perpendicular*. She helped her students remember the word by connecting to other words they knew, and she showed that word histories can be interesting. Often students like to investigate these etymologies. However, in most cases, teaching non-English roots is not effective. Graves comments,

> I do not recommend teaching non-English roots for several reasons: There are a large number of non-English roots; individual roots are not used in anywhere near the number of words common prefixes are used in; they are often variously spelled and thus difficult to identify; and the relationship between the original meaning of the root and the current meaning of the English word in which it is used is often vague. (2006, 110–11)

Graves' last point is a good one. For example, the root *ject* comes from the Latin word *jacere*, meaning "to throw." This root appears in words like *eject*, *reject*, *adjective*, *conjecture*, and *inject*. Knowing the meaning of this root would probably not help most students figure out the meanings of those words.

Although teaching non-English roots is generally not effective, students can benefit from knowledge of some prefixes and suffixes. These word parts occur frequently and provide consistent clues that help students infer word meanings. In many cases, prefixes and suffixes attach to English base words that students know. If they also know the meaning of the prefix or suffix, they can infer the meaning of the whole word. For example, *implant* has the recognizable English base *plant*, so if students know that *im* means "in," they can use this knowledge to figure out the meaning of the word.

Prefixes and suffixes provide different kinds of information. Prefixes change or add to the meaning of the root or base while suffixes signal the part of speech. For example, *re* means "again" or "back," so *replace* must mean something like "to place again" or "to put back." In a word like *placement*, the suffix, *ment*, doesn't add to or change the meaning of *place*. Instead, this suffix signals that the word is a noun.

Prefixes, then, provide the most useful clues for understanding complex words. White , Sowell, and Yanagihara (1989) analyzed words taken from a word-frequency list for school texts in grades 3–9. They found that four prefixes accounted for 58 percent of the prefixes in their data: *un, re, in,* and *dis*. They recommend teaching these four prefixes first. Teachers can begin by listing these four prefixes on a chart and having students find words with the prefixes as they read and add them to the chart. Looking at the list of words, the students and teacher can discuss the meaning of each prefix. Students might notice that *in* means "not" in a word like *ineligible* and "in" for *inside*. The teacher can suggest that students try each meaning to see which one makes sense. The teacher can also add other words to the chart. For example, *implant* has a prefix that looks like *in* and means "in" but for *impassable*, the *im* prefix means "not." Students can gather other words with *im* and try to make a generalization about when the prefix is spelled *im*, not *in*. Activities like these can trigger students' interest in words.

Teaching these four most commonly occurring prefixes can give students clues to the meanings of many words. In addition, teachers can work with students to create a wall chart listing suffixes that signal that a word is a noun, verb, adjective, or adverb. As students read, they can look for words with suffixes that indicate each of these major parts of speech. Teachers can discuss how knowing that a word is a noun, verb, adjective, or adverb can help readers figure out its meaning in a sentence. Students will also see that adjectives and adverbs usually provide extra descriptive information and are not as important in understanding the meaning of a sentence as the nouns and verbs.

Teaching word part clues can be a useful word-learning strategy if used judiciously. Teachers should choose words related to their content area. They should look primarily for words with a recognizable English base that occurs in several words in their field. Then teachers can show students how prefixes modify the meaning of the base and how suffixes provide clues about the part of speech. By teaching word parts and word histories, teachers can instill an interest in words and help students develop academic language.

Using dictionaries and related reference tools • The third word-learning strategy that Graves (2006) recommends is to teach students how to use the dictionary and related reference tools. To teach students about dictionaries, a teacher needs to find dictionaries at the right level. For beginning ELLs, for example, a picture dictionary is a useful resource. For more advanced students, student dictionaries are appropriate. Many dictionaries and other reference tools are available online, and students need to learn how to access and use those. For example, many students can find information about a topic on Wikipedia. This resource can help them clarify words that are labels for the complex concepts they study in different academic fields.

Graves offers several tips for helping students use dictionaries effectively and efficiently. He suggests giving students guidelines like these:

- When reading a definition, be sure to read all of it, not just part of it.
- Remember that many words have more than one meaning.
- Be sure to check all the definitions a dictionary gives for a word, not just one of them.
- Decide which definition makes sense in the passage in which you found the word.
- Often the dictionary works best when you already have some idea of a word's meaning. This makes the dictionary particularly useful for checking on a word you want to use in your writing. (112)

These are good guidelines since students often read only the first entry in a dictionary without considering how that definition fits the word in context. Teachers could display Graves' suggestions in the classroom.

Even for older students, it is good for a teacher to take some time to introduce how a dictionary is set up, how entries are written, and what some of the commonly used symbols mean. Students benefit when the teacher models how to find words and then provides guided practice. However, this instruction should not take too much time. Teachers should remind students that using a dictionary is only one of several strategies for determining meanings of unknown words. Teachers can also introduce other tools, such as the thesaurus, that students can use as they read and write. Since many students have access to computers, they should be shown the tools available to them online. In addition, most word-processing programs include dictionaries and thesauruses.

Sometimes ELLs overuse the dictionary. They may look up many words in a bilingual dictionary to be sure they are getting the meanings right. However, in the process of looking up a word, they often lose the meaning of a sentence, and by the time they finish reading a page, they have little idea of what they have read. They may come to depend on the dictionary rather than use context clues or word part clues. Teachers should monitor to be sure that students are using the dictionary appropriately.

Word-learning strategies can help students increase their academic vocabulary. Fisher and Frey (2008a) describe a sequence for teaching reading strategies that includes the following steps: focus lessons, guided instruction, collaborative learning, and independent learning. They emphasize the importance of modeling strategy use. When they observed middle school teachers modeling word-solving strategies, they found that effective teachers consistently do three things. "First they model the use of context clues to figure out words. Second, they use word parts (prefixes, suffixes, roots, bases, and cognates) to determine word meaning. And third, when the first two fail to help, they use resources such as other people, the Internet, and dictionaries" (20). These middle school teachers included all the word-learning strategies Graves (2006) outlines for building vocabulary.

Using cognates • An additional word-learning strategy that ELLs can use to build their academic vocabulary is to draw on cognates (Freeman and Freeman 2004). Cognates are words that come from the same root, that were literally "born together." Of course, some students speak languages that are not related to English, and there are few, if any, cognates. However, many ELLs do speak languages related to English. The largest number of ELLs, nearly 80 percent, are Spanish speakers. Graves (2006) refers to studies that estimate that 20 percent to more than 30 percent of English words have Spanish cognates. Academic English words with Latin and Greek roots are often cognates with Spanish words. For example, *hypothesis* has the Spanish equivalent *hipótesis*.

Many everyday terms in Spanish are part of the academic language register in English. However, as Spanish-speaking students read or interact in classrooms, they often fail to draw on this knowledge base. Goldenberg notes, "Teachers cannot assume that transfer is automatic. Students sometimes do not realize that what they know in their first language (e.g., cognates such as *elefante* and *elephant,* or *ejemplo* and *example*; or spelling and comprehension skills) can be applied in their second" (2008, 16).

Teachers can help students access cognates by engaging them in activities that increase their awareness of similar words across languages. Williams (2001) lists several strategies teachers can use. For example, a teacher might begin by putting book pages on an overhead transparency and having students find cognates as a group. Then students can work in pairs to identify cognates. The teacher can also put a chart up in the classroom, and students can list the cognates they find on the chart. This activity can extend throughout a unit of study, and students can list as many cognates as possible related to the topic. They can find both general academic words, such as *análsis* and *analysis,* and content-specific words, such as *triángulo* and *triangle.* The students can also develop a classroom cognate dictionary, using the words from the cognate chart.

Rodríguez (2001) suggests that once students identify cognates, they can work together to categorize them, looking at patterns. This is an excellent activity to increase the important academic skill of categorization. Rodríguez's students found several ways to classify cognates. For example, some like *colonial* and *lateral* have the same spelling in English and Spanish. Others like *civilization* and *civilización* and *multiplication* and *multiplicación* have a predictable variation in spelling. The derivational suffix *tion* in English is spelled *ción* in Spanish. Other cognates like *sport* and *deporte* have the same root. Some cognates share only one of the meanings of the word. For example, the word *letter* in English can refer to a letter of the alphabet or a business letter, but in Spanish, the cognate *letra* only means a letter of the alphabet. The categorization exercise helps make students more aware of the different cognates that exist. Students can then apply their knowledge of cognates to academic English reading.

Slavit and Ernst-Slavit (2007) report on how a middle school teacher with large numbers of Mexican and Central American students helped them use cognates in his math class. He explained to the researchers:

> My Spanish-speaking students know more English than they realize. For example, they know *círculo* (circle), *lateral* (lateral; related to the side), *cuadrado* (a square or special quadrilateral), and even words like *edificio* (edifice), *casi* (quasi; resembling something), and *creciendo* (crescendo). (10)

By helping students realize they already knew many terms in English, this teacher validated their language and culture as they built their academic vocabulary.

Foster Word Consciousness

Each of the components for vocabulary development that Graves lists is crucial. Students need to engage in class discussions and to read and write extensively to build their vocabulary. Teachers need to teach some content-specific words directly. They should also provide students with strategies for learning words independently.

In addition, teachers should plan activities to help students develop word consciousness. According to Graves:

> The term *word consciousness* refers to an awareness of and interest in words and their meanings. As defined by Nagy and Anderson (1992), word consciousness involves both a cognitive and an affective stance toward words. Word consciousness integrates metacognition about words, motivation to learn words, and deep and lasting interest in words. (7)

Students are often interested in word histories. Teachers can bring up interesting words and discuss their histories with students. A good resource is Bryson's (1994) book, *Made in America: An Informal History of the English Language in the United States*. Bryson goes through U.S. history and explains when and where new words entered the language. For example, in the chapter "The Melting Pot: Immigration in America," Bryson chronicles the many words new immigrants added to English. The Dutch, for instance, contributed words like *coleslaw, boss, bedspread, cookie, waffle,* and *nitwit.* Students could look these words up and find their original meanings. Other chapters in Bryson's book discuss how the movies and advertising added new words to the English vocabulary.

In addition to discussing word histories, teachers can foster word consciousness by pointing out similarities and differences across languages. For example, English has *crocodile* and in Spanish, the word is *cocodrilo*. The class could discuss how letters sometimes get transposed as they move across languages. Since ELLs speak a language other than English, discussion of cognates and false cognates, such as *assist* (help) and *asistin* (to attend), can also spark interest in language.

Teachers can also make a point of using new words as they lecture or lead class discussions. If the teacher has come across a new word in her reading, she can ask if anyone in the class has heard the word, and she can ask them what they think it might mean. The teacher can also read the section where the word appears and think aloud about how the context gives clues to the word's meaning. It is important that students know that teachers also learn new words as they read.

Students are always interested in slang. Teachers can ask them to list some new slang terms. Students can explain what the words mean. They can also look into the history of some slang terms. How did these words develop? Teachers can share slang from the past to show students how some slang has only a short shelf life while other slang becomes an accepted part of the language. This can lead to a discussion of how people decide which words will be added to dictionaries. Students can compare dictionaries to see if they have the same words.

Teachers who show an active interest in words help their students develop word consciousness. They provide an important model showing students that words are important. When students see that their teachers are interested in words and that teachers continue to learn words, they also become more conscious of all the words they encounter each day. The goal for any program of vocabulary development should be to foster word consciousness. When ELLs and struggling readers become interested in words and become aware of the power of words, they build the academic vocabulary they need to succeed in school.

Integrating Academic Language into Planning Instruction

In this and the previous chapters, we have defined academic language and discussed the different levels of academic language. Any effective approach to helping ELLs and struggling readers develop academic language proficiency must include teaching academic language at the text, paragraph, sentence, and word levels. This teaching naturally occurs within the context of content instruction in the different subject areas. To teach both content and academic language, teachers need to plan carefully. We suggest that they use a backward planning design and include both content and language objectives.

Backward Design

Wiggins and McTighe (2005) explain that teachers should begin their planning while keeping the end in mind. For teachers with the goal of building both academic content knowledge and academic language, this means deciding what students need to know at the end of a unit and what language they will need to comprehend and express that knowledge. Wiggins and McTighe have developed what they call a backward planning model that includes these three steps:

1. Identify desired results.

2. Decide how you will determine if students have achieved those results.

3. Plan instruction and learning experiences.

These steps can be used to plan for content instruction and academic language development.

Identify desired results • Backward planning begins with identifying desired results. Standards can be a good place for teachers to start because standards state what students should understand and be able to do. For example, in teaching the section "Nutrition and Energy Flow" in a biology textbook, a first step would be to look at a related content standard. The corresponding California 9–12 science content standards under ecology require that "students know at each link in a food web some energy is stored in newly made structures but much energy is dissipated into the environment as heat. This dissipation may be represented in an energy pyramid" (California State Board of Education 1997, 45). The biology teacher sees that students need to understand the food chain, how energy is stored, and what happens to energy that is not stored. In addition, students must be able to represent that content as an energy pyramid.

Most textbooks now have teacher's editions that include these kinds of standards stated as objectives. The objectives are listed next to content standards so that teachers do not need to look them up. In the Texas Teacher Wraparound Edition of the Glencoe Science biology textbook *Biology: The Dynamics of Life* (Biggs et al. 2004), teachers are provided with objectives for each section of the text and the objectives are connected to the TEKS (Texas Essential Knowledge and Skills). In addition, the guide lists activities and ideas for engaging students in scientific processes and field and laboratory research, which are also part of the standards for Texas, California, and other states. The Texas biology textbook suggests that the objectives for the "Nutrition and Energy Flow" section that are connected to the TEKS should enable students to "trace the path of energy and matter in an ecosystem" and "analyze how matter is cycled in the abiotic and biotic parts of the biosphere" (34a).

Decide how to assess student knowledge and skills • With the desired results in mind, teachers then can move to the second step of backward planning: Decide how you will determine if students have achieved those results. Content-area teachers often rely on quizzes or other written assignments to determine whether or not students have learned the content. When teachers use these means to assess the content learning of ELLs, they may find it difficult to separate language learning from content learning. Sometimes students know or are learning the content, but because they struggle with English and reading, they do not understand questions or are unable to write clear answers.

When teachers use alternate means of assessment, they can get better measures of students' understanding of academic content. For example, teachers might conduct informal assessments. These assessments avoid having students read quiz or test questions, and they allow students to show what they know. Teachers can ask their students to read a passage from their textbook and write a summary in their own words. In addition, by observing students as they engage in this activity and by reading the summaries, a teacher can get a great deal of information about each student's understanding of the material. Follow-up assessments might include cloze procedures in which students read a passage and then use that knowledge to fill in blanks in another passage that covers the same information.

Using group work to assess what students know is useful for all struggling readers. The successful high school math teachers that Gutiérrez (2002) observed frequently had students work in groups to take tests. In groups students can read together, write joint summaries, and report back orally. Teachers can find out what bilingual students know or are learning by putting them in same-language groups, allowing them to talk about the content in their first languages, and them asking them to summarize the information in English to report back. Often, ELLs are not confident enough to show what they know or to ask questions individually but gain confidence in a group.

For the "Nutrition and Energy Flow" section in the biology text, it is probable that struggling readers will not be able to show the content they know through multiple-choice tests or long essay answers. However, a biology teacher can see if students have control of the content and key terms by asking them to draw and label a food chain or an ecological pyramid, by having them carry out a lab experiment to detect carbon dioxide and log their results, or asking them to analyze in a few sentences each part of a pictured diagram showing the carbon cycle.

Plan instruction and learning experiences • After teachers have decided what they want students to know and how they will assess students, they can plan lessons and learning experiences. As they review the standards for each subject area, teachers identify key concepts and turn them into big questions. For example, in the area of biology and the study of nutrition and energy flow, a teacher might identify concepts such as producers and consumers and the flow of energy in ecosystems to ask questions such as Why is the sun important to life on earth? What happens when food chains are interrupted? or Why is it important to understand the decreasing availability of energy in the pyramid of energy? The important thing is for teachers to familiarize themselves with the standards and then decide what concepts each standard requires. This is a process that Wiggins and McTighe (2005) refer to as *unpacking the standards*.

> *Language arts:* Students will understand the concept of tone. They will write an analysis of a section of the novel they are reading and explain the tone of that section.
>
> *Biology:* Students will demonstrate an understanding of cell characteristics and cell parts by listing characteristics and labeling parts of a cell on a diagram.
>
> *Social studies:* Students will list events that led up to women's suffrage and be able to explain the arguments for and against women's right to vote in the early 1900s.
>
> *Math:* Students will be able to solve simple algebraic equations and explain the operations they used to solve the problems using proofs.

figure 6.4 Sample Content Objectives

Once teachers have established what big questions they would like students to investigate during the content-area study, they write content objectives. These objectives should specify what students should know (declarative knowledge) and what they should be able to do to demonstrate that knowledge (procedural knowledge). A few examples of content objectives, which call for both declarative knowledge and procedural knowledge, are shown in Figure 6.4. Notice that the content objectives include verbs such as *understand, write, explain, demonstrate, list*, and *solve*. These verbs have to do with knowing the content and showing that knowledge.

Language Objectives

We have described how teachers can use a backward design to plan content instruction. To help their ELLs and struggling readers develop academic language, teachers should teach both content and language. The same three steps of backward planning should be involved in teaching language. Teachers should identify aspects of academic language students should learn, decide how to determine if students have achieved those results, and plan instruction and learning experiences to help students achieve those results.

As a result of careful planning for content instruction, teachers develop content objectives, as we have explained. Content objectives are taken from content-area standards and specify the knowledge and skills students are expected to develop in each content area. In planning for language instruction, teachers should develop language objectives. Language objectives specify the language forms and functions students should develop to comprehend and express the content they are studying. Ideally, content-area textbooks would include suggestions for teaching both content and language. Unfortunately, this is not the case.

Textbook suggestions for teaching language • Teacher's guides do not offer much help in suggesting the academic language to teach beyond bolding some key vocabulary. The section "Nutrition and Energy Flow" in *Biology: The Dynamics of Life* (Biggs et al. 2004) contains several suggested teaching activities. These activities are labeled to indicate whether they are meant for students with learning disabilities, for students of all levels, for students who are above average, or for ELLs.

One activity, titled "Using Science Terms" and marked for all students including ELLs, reads, "Call students' attention to the derivations of the terms *herbivore*, *carnivore*, and *omnivore* presented in the margins of the pages. Ask students to explain the appropriateness of each term to the feeding habits of the organisms it describes" (47). Another activity, labeled "Struggling Learners" and marked, in addition, for ELLs and students with learning disabilities, reads as follows: "Pair students who understand the concept of producer and consumer with students who are having difficulty. Make two groups of terms: *producer, plant, autotroph,* and *consumer, heterotroph, animal.* Have the pairs of students analyze the meaning in groups" (47).

Both of these suggestions focus on academic vocabulary, but the activities would not help ELLs develop academic language. One activity gets at word roots, but it is not presented as a word-learning strategy students could transfer to other contexts. For the other activity, no suggestions are given about how students should analyze the two groups of words. This textbook is the special Texas edition for a state with very large numbers of ELLs, yet the suggestions for teachers about how to help students develop the language they need to understand the reading are not consistent with the research synthesized by Graves or Marzano that we discussed earlier.

Language standards • Textbooks are not a good resource for developing language objectives. Instead, teachers can look to language standards for language objectives in the same way that they look to content standards for content objectives. TESOL (Teachers of English to Speakers of Other Languages) has developed a useful resource for educators, the *PreK–12 English Language Proficiency Standards* (Gottlieb et al. 2006). Although these standards were developed for ELLs, they are also appropriate for struggling readers.

The developers describe five stages of language acquisition: *starting, emerging, developing, expanding,* and *bridging.* The first stage represents abilities of newly arrived students with very limited English. By the final stage, *bridging,* students are almost equal in proficiency to native speakers. For each stage, the developers suggest performance indicators, "examples of observable, measurable language behaviors that English language learners can be expected to demonstrate as they engage in classroom tasks" (43). They list sample performance indicators for listening, speaking, reading, and writing in four content subject areas: language arts, mathematics, social studies, and science. The performance indicators are clustered for grade levels of preK–K, 1–3, 4–5, 6–8, and 9–12.

Figure 6.5 shows an example of a language proficiency standard for 9–12 science in the domain of speaking. It lists the topic and the activities students can do to demonstrate proficiency at each level of development. For example, a developing-level student could work with a partner and use sequence words (sequential language) to outline steps in transformations or exchanges involving chemical or physical reactions.

These sample performance indicators provide teachers with a good indication of the English language proficiency expected of ELLs at each stage of development. Like content standards, these language proficiency standards can be used to develop language objectives.

Examples of Related Content and Language Objectives

Language objectives should be connected to the content being studied. They can be written for the text level, the paragraph level, the sentence level, or the word level. For example, if the big-question for an integrated unit is What are the cycles we find in our lives, our environment, and our history? and the students are studying the water cycle, a content objective might be for students to demonstrate their understanding of the water cycle by drawing a diagram, labeling the phases, and writing a short paragraph explaining what happens during each phase of the cycle. A text-level language objective could be for students to refer to a diagram and write a science report about the water cycle. At the paragraph level, students could use chaining to connect sentences. At the word level, an objective could be for students to use signal words showing sequence, such as *first*, *next*, and *then*. Teachers would not want to assign all the language objectives at one time, but through various assignments, they could teach and assess ELLs' developing language proficiency. Figure 6.6 lists possible content and language objectives for a unit on the water cycle.

To take a second example, if the class was studying westward migration in the United States, the content objective might be for students to demonstrate their understanding of the reasons for the westward migration by listing them. Since accounts explain why certain historical events occurred, a language objective at the text level would be for students to write a historical account. A language objective at the sentence level might be to have students use complex sentences with clauses that show cause and effect as they write and talk about

Domain	Topic	Level 1: Starting	Level 2: Emerging	Level 3: Developing	Level 4: Expanding	Level 5: Bridging
Speaking	Chemical or physical change compounds	Name and describe common mixtures and compounds, and their composition from visuals, real-life examples, or symbols (e.g., H_2O)	State or predict transformations or exchanges involving chemical or physical reactions with a partner	Outline steps, using sequential language, in transformations or exchanges involving chemical or physical reactions with a partner	Report and exchange information on processes and results from chemical or physical reactions with a partner	Explain changes in matter, the nature of changes, and their real-world applications in extended discourse

figure 6.5 Sample TESOL Language Proficiency Standard for Speaking Domain (Gottleib et al. 2006, 94)

<table>
<tr><td colspan="1">

Content and Language Objectives

</td></tr>
</table>

Content and Language Objectives
Content area: science
Big-question theme: What are the cycles we find in our lives, our environment, and our history?
Content objective: Students will demonstrate their understanding of the four stages of the water cycle through labeled drawings and an explanatory paragraph.
Language objective (text level): Students will write a science report referring to their drawing.
Language objective (paragraph level): Students will use chaining to connect sentences within a paragraph.
Language objective (word level): Students will use sequence words such as *first*, *next*, and *then* in their science report.

figure 6.6 Content and Language Objectives for Water Cycle Theme

the westward migration. For example, students might write sentences such as "People living in the east moved to the west because there was open land in the west" or "Since eastern cities were crowded, people in the east moved to the west." At the word level, students could use content-specific academic vocabulary such as *pony express* or *land rush* in their writing. Figure 6.7 lists content and language objectives for a unit on westward migration.

One way to help ELLs develop metalinguistic awareness is to develop a theme around the big question In what ways are languages alike and different? During this language arts theme, students can compare and contrast different languages. A content objective for this theme might be to draw a Venn diagram comparing and contrasting a student's first language and English. A text-level language objective that would come naturally from this content objective would be to write a comparison-contrast report. At the sentence level, students can use relative clauses in sentences such as "English, which has subject-verb-object word order, differs from Japanese, which places the verb at the end." At the word level, students can use content-specific words like *syntax* and *morphology* to show comparison and contrast. Figure 6.8 shows content and language objectives for a unit on language comparison.

Teachers who plan by following the backward design model and writing both content and language objectives provide effective instruction for English language learners and struggling readers alike. This scaffolded instruction helps all their students develop academic content knowledge and academic language proficiency.

Content area: social studies

Big-question theme: What have been the causes and effects of expansion in the United States?

Content objective: Students will demonstrate their understanding of the westward migration by listing reasons for the westward migration that occurred in the United States.

Language objective (text level): Students will write a historical account of the westward migration describing why events occurred in a particular sequence.

Language objective (sentence level): Students will use complex sentences with clauses that show cause and effect as they write and talk about the westward migration.

Language objective (word level): Students will use content-specific academic words such as *pony express* and *land rush* as they write their account.

figure 6.7 Content and Language Objectives for Westward Movement Unit

Content area: language arts

Big-question theme: In what ways are languages alike and different?

Content objective: Students will demonstrate their understanding of the similarities and differences in the language structure of their first language and English by completing a Venn diagram comparing and contrasting features of the two languages.

Language objective (text level): Using the Venn diagram, students will write a comparison-contrast report describing the two languages.

Language objective (sentence level): Students will use relative clauses in sentences such as "English, which has subject-verb-object word order, differs from Japanese, which places the verb at the end."

Language objective (word level): Students will use content-specific words such as *syntax* and *morphology* to show comparison and contrast.

figure 6.8 Content and Language Objectives for Language Comparison Unit

Developing Academic Vocabulary and Writing Content and Language Objectives **151**

Conclusion

To develop academic language proficiency, ELLs and struggling readers need to build academic vocabulary. Academic vocabulary contains both content-specific words and phrases and general academic terms. A research-based approach to vocabulary building includes providing students with rich and varied language experiences, teaching individual words, teaching word-learning strategies, and fostering word consciousness. A program of study that contains these components can help students build word consciousness.

Academic language development occurs in tandem with content instruction. A good model for planning instruction is to use the backward design model. Following this model, teachers identify desired results, decide how they will determine if students have achieved those results, and plan instruction and learning experiences. This same process can be applied to planning for both content and language instruction.

Content-area teachers should develop language objectives as well as content objectives for their lessons. Language objectives specify the language students need to understand academic content and to demonstrate that understanding. Language objectives are particularly important for ELLs; however, when all teachers attend to language as well as content, every student benefits.

Applications

1. In the next week, look at a cookbook, a popular magazine, a newspaper, and an academic book. Make a list of words you think come from Anglo-Saxon, or Greek, or Latin roots. Look the words up in a good dictionary that gives derivations to see if you were correct.

2. Look at a textbook in one of the content areas. It can be a literature anthology, a science textbook, a social studies textbook, or another content book. List words that the textbook writers have identified that students should know. Are these content-specific words or general academic words?

3. Go over the strategies suggested in this chapter for teaching vocabulary. Choose at least two of these strategies and use them during the week to teach vocabulary to your students. What were the results? Share with your class or study group.

4. Look at a text you are teaching in the following week. Write down at least twenty words that have prefixes or suffixes. Identify the base or root of each

word. Do prefixes or suffixes and roots and bases help define those words? What language objective could you develop to help students use word parts to understand these words?

5. Wiggins and McTighe (2005) suggest three steps in backward planning:

   1. Identify desired results.

   2. Decide how you will determine if students have achieved those results

   3. Plan instruction and learning experiences.

   Does your school plan like this? How do teachers plan in your school?

6. Choose a topic you are going to teach soon. What is a big question you could use? Write both content and language objectives for at least two lessons in this big-question integrated unit of study.

7

Teaching Academic Language and Subject-Area Content

A Border Example

Recently, at our university, the School of Education faculty had a series of meetings to decide what to do to improve the quality of our graduate education programs. The faculty brainstormed and prioritized various concerns. The top item on the list was academic writing. Also, included among the first five items was the ability to read, understand, and synthesize academic texts and articles. Our university is on the border between Mexico and the United States, our population is largely Hispanic, and many of our students, including those at the graduate level, were ELLs and struggled academically during their early schooling. In fact, during those early schooling years, the students fit several of the general characteristics for ELLs in the United States as listed by García, Kleifgen, and Falchi (2008):

- Most are Spanish-speaking Latinos (75 to 79 percent).
- Most are poor (75 percent).
- Most live in households where only the younger generation speaks English.
- Half live with parents who have not completed eight years of schooling.
- Half were born in the United States.

In our local school district, 90 percent of the students receive free lunch. Of the nearly 49,000 students in the district, 94.4 percent are listed as economically disadvantaged and 42.4 percent are classified as LEP (Brownsville Independent School District 2008).

When one considers that the majority of the students at our university are from the local area, it is perhaps not surprising that our faculty chose the priorities they did. Students, especially those for whom English is not the first language, can arrive at the university level and even the graduate levels and still struggle with academic English. In addition, a large number of our students were not considered English language learners in school and just got by, but they arrived at the university as SELs who never developed the academic English they needed for higher education. Since the university is committed to an open-door admission policy, many of our students arrive ill prepared for the academic challenges that face them.

In this chapter, we first review test results that confirm that many ELLs do not develop academic language proficiency. We then consider several factors that contribute to their poor performance. We provide a number of suggestions for improving the academic performance of ELLs and struggling readers, giving examples from teachers who have worked successfully with these students.

Test Results for ELLs

Both ELLs and SELs struggle in school. Scores on national tests show that many ELLs in middle and secondary schools have not developed academic language proficiency. The results of the NAEP (National Assessment of Educational Progress) tests are especially telling. A review of the 2005 NAEP eighth-grade scores for four states found that only 4 percent of the LEP students and 19 percent of the students formerly identified as LEP scored at the proficient level in reading, and 5 percent of the LEP students and 19 percent of the former LEP students scored at the proficient level in math (Batalova, Fix, and Murray 2007). These figures show that ELLs now mainstreamed as well as those still classified as ELLs have not developed adequate levels of academic language or content-area knowledge.

Students who score low on the NAEP find it difficult to pass high-stakes tests, including graduation exams. The *2000 Elementary and Secondary School Civil Rights Compliance Report* included a survey that asked schools to report the performance of students on a district- or state-required test that students needed to pass or that was used as a significant factor in deciding graduation. The results showed that 62.4 percent of all high school students who were tested passed, but only 33.1 percent of the LEP students passed. In contrast, about 24 percent of the general population who were tested failed while nearly 50 percent of the LEP population failed. These numbers include students who were given accommodations. The remaining students were not tested or took alternative tests (Hopstock and Stephenson 2003).

Test results are seldom helpful for planning instruction. Alvarez and Corn (2008) examined one district's required reading assessment for ELLs, including newcomers and LTELs, at the fourth- and fifth-grade levels. They concluded that the tests "were designed for purposes of accountability and record keeping, allowing administrators to track the progress of a whole school or a large subgroup of students" (363). They pointed out the tests not only did not help teachers assess individual students' needs but "with the high-stakes attached to them, [the tests] encouraged a style of teaching that benefited predominantly our more high-achieving, English proficient students" (364). After looking closely at the students in their classrooms, Alvarez and Corn concluded, "Rather than compliantly implementing agendas dictated by policymakers, good teachers must be supported in their learning—about students' needs and how to meet them; about language, literacy and second language acquisition—in order to better meet the challenges they face" (364). When large numbers of ELLs cannot pass high-stakes tests or graduate, all those involved in their education need to consider the factors that contribute to their poor performance.

Inadequate First-Language Support and Development

Theory and research on second-language acquisition can inform educators as they try to determine why students who speak a language other than English are not prepared to do the academic work of school and why so many drop out. One reason many researchers cite is the failure to support the development of students' first languages. Goldenberg points out that five separate meta-analyses have reached the same conclusion:

learning to read in the home language promotes reading achievement in the second language. Readers should understand how unusual it is to have five meta-analyses on the same issue conducted by five independent researchers or groups of researchers with diverse perspectives. The fact that they all reached essentially the same conclusion is worth noting. No other area in educational research with which I am familiar can claim five independent meta-analyses based on experimental studies— much less five that converge on the same basic finding. (2008, 15)

The five meta-analyses are Greene (1998); Rolstad, Mahoney, and Glass (2005); Slavin and Cheung (2004); Willig (1985); and August and Shanahan (2006). Although the research clearly confirms that newcomers should be educated in their native language while they are learning English, "there is a growing dissonance between *research* on the education of emerging bilinguals and policy enacted to educate them" (García, Kleifgen, and Falchi 2008, 6).

With mandates in California, Arizona, and Massachusetts that all instruction be given in English, and a general mood across the country opposing bilingual education, fewer and fewer students are given the first-language support that research shows they need (Ramírez 1991; Greene 1998; Krashen 1999; Cummins 2001; Crawford 2004; Rolstad, Mahoney, and Glass 2005; Cummins 2008). Although the ELL population in grades K–12 grew by 72 percent between 1992 and 2002, the percentage of students enrolled in bilingual programs declined from 37 percent to 17 percent (Zehler et al. 2003). Before the passage of the English-only laws, 29.1 percent of the ELLs in California and 31.2 percent in Arizona were enrolled in bilingual education, but by the 2001–2 school year, only 9.7 percent and 9 percent, respectively, of ELLs were in bilingual classrooms (Crawford 2007).

In their 2003 study, Zehler and her colleagues report the amount of first-language instructional support ELLs received across the country: "In terms of language use, 59.6 percent were taught *all English*, 20.1 percent with *some native language use* (2% to 24%), and 20.4% with *significant native language use* (at least 25%)" (38). Given the research supporting the importance of significant use of native language instruction for ELLs, a large percentage of English learners are not receiving the first-language support that would help them succeed academically.

In a second descriptive study conducted to determine services to LEP students, researchers found that 6.7 percent of schools provided no services at all to ELLs, 24.7 percent provided some all-English support, 23.2 percent provided extensive all-English support, and 17 percent gave support with "significant native language" (Hopstock and Stephenson 2003). Clearly, schools are not providing students with the first-language support that could help them develop the academic language they need.

Inadequate Instructional Support

Zehler and her coauthors (2003) describe the types and duration of support service ELLs do receive. They report that the three most common types of instruction include (1) specific ESL instruction, (2) extra help from aides, and (3) extra support from Title I resource teachers. Students are not helped for long. It takes from 5 to 7 years to acquire enough English to achieve academically at grade level (Cummins 2008). Yet, Zehler and her colleagues (2003) found that students received some kind of LEP services for an average of 3.5 years. Their study showed that elementary-age students received services for 3.71 years. Middle and high school students got even less, averaging 3.10 and 3.24 years, respectively.

In another report focused on the concerns for developing academic literacy among California's secondary English learners, Maxwell-Jolly, Gándara, and Benavídez explain that the reason students are not succeeding "has been the overly simplistic perspective that improving their limited English will automatically lead to educational success" (2007, 4). Simply providing some type of language support for immigrants, regardless of the amount and time, is not enough. Students need to "learn the appropriate rules of conduct for adolescents in their new social environment" (4). They also need academic language and content-area knowledge.

The best support that immigrant students can receive is content instruction in their first languages while they are acquiring English. Students who are mainstreamed into regular classes and receive English-only instruction often fall behind in social studies, science, math, language arts, and other subject areas. They pick up conversational English but miss much of the content instruction because they have to learn English and content at the same time. They usually start school with less academic background than native English-speaking classmates and fall further behind them in the process of learning English. Betances described this phenomenon well when he reflected on his own English-only education as a child: "I was learning English at the expense of my education" (1986, 15).

Even when students are provided with some type of support, such as specialized ESL instruction, many ELLs receive an education that is unequal. While they are learning English, ELLs, especially those in middle and high schools, "are tracked into courses that do not provide them with challenging content" (García, Kleifgen, and Falchi 2008, 39). In her two-year study of twelve- and thirteen-year-olds, Valdés (2001) found that that ELLs were not being given the kind of work that would prepare them to compete with native English speakers. She concluded that students were engaged in seatwork focused on learning vocabulary or copying sentences. Little went on in the classroom that could prepare them to develop the kinds of proficiencies they would need to succeed in other classes. Teachers' goals and objectives involved following the textbook, teaching English-language forms, and sometimes merely keeping the children quiet. (147)

Reports on services for ELLs show that school leaders and teachers must be better prepared to understand how to work with the growing ELL population. When LEP coordinators were interviewed about services to ELLs, 30 percent admitted that support for these students depended "a great deal" on the availability of qualified teachers, and another 30.9 percent reported that appropriate instruction depended "to some extent" on the availability of qualified personnel (Hopstock and Stephenson 2003). Together, that means 60 percent of the teachers working with second-language learners needed more background on effective ways to meet student needs. The reality is that schools with high numbers of ELLs tend to have administrators and teachers with less experience and fewer educational qualifications in general than schools where the majority of the students are native English speakers (Capps et al. 2005).

In addition to problems with the lack of rigorous curriculum and qualified educators, both the García, Kleifgen, and Falchi (2008) report and the Valdés (2001) study point out that there are inadequate resources and facilities for ELLs. Perhaps one of the most important findings is that ELLs are almost completely separated from other mainstream students. Often immigrant students attend schools where there are many other students like them and few students who succeed academically and go on to college. Valdés explains that the ESL students she interviewed were "completely isolated from English-speaking same-age peers" (147). This is a general trend for ELLs and extends beyond the ESL classroom. Capps and his colleagues found that "most LEP children live in linguistically isolated families and attend linguistically segregated schools" (2005, 36).

In this book we are focusing on older struggling students who lack academic language. Given the findings of the reports we have discussed, it is not surprising that many of the graduate students at our university, described at the opening of this chapter, struggle with reading and writing academic texts. Many of them have made it to the graduate level despite the obstacles they faced. Unfortunately, because of the factors we have outlined, many of the students who were their classmates in their early years were not able to develop the academic language proficiency they needed to continue their education.

Francisco: An Example of an ELL High School Student

Francisco came to the United States at age fourteen from El Salvador with his twelve-year-old brother. Francisco's mother had come to the United States when he was six, leaving her sons with their grandmother. She worked in the fields in the Central Valley of California to save enough money to pay a lawyer to help the boys come legally into the country to stay.

When asked about his first years in high school, Francisco commented, "I don't remember learning anything." Like Betances (1986) Francisco was "learning English at the expense of his education" (15). The high school he attended had more than three thousand students, and it was easy for a newcomer like Francisco to go unnoticed. Since he had not studied English before coming to the United States, he was put into ESL classes along with basic math and shop.

His ESL teacher was very traditional. Francisco recalled filling out worksheets and studying lists of vocabulary but seldom speaking English. In the few content classes he attended, he remembered praying, "Please don't let the teacher call on me." Even if he knew the answer, he was certain he would have trouble saying the words in English. He worried that other students would laugh at him.

Francisco made friends with some of his classmates, who were also learning English, as well as with boys on the soccer team. Outside of class, Francisco spoke Spanish to his friends, mostly Mexican immigrant students. At times, he thought that he was picking up more Mexican Spanish than English. Francisco seldom had the opportunity to interact with native English speakers, who tended to ignore new immigrants (Valdés 2001).

Francisco's mother insisted that he work hard in school. Fortunately, when he started school in the United States, he was at grade level in Spanish in literacy development and in content-area knowledge. The knowledge he had developed in his first language provided a base for the subjects he studied in English. Francisco was able to graduate in four years. At that time, the high school did not have an exit exam, and he earned enough credits for graduation.

Because he was a star soccer player, he received a scholarship from a small, local private university. However, the classes he had taken in high school did not prepare him for college. He had done only limited reading and writing in English, and he felt lost both academically and socially in the first year of college. Francisco simply did not have the academic language he needed for college and struggled in all of his classes.

Francisco was put on probation and would have dropped out of the university had he not been encouraged by the soccer coach, who went to Francisco's home and talked to his mother about the importance of not giving up. The university did not really know how to help the few second-language students who were enrolled, mostly other soccer players. Francisco was assigned to a developmental reading course and was required to study in the library during specific hours. One of his most vivid memories is sitting in the library and staring at his books and writing assignments, knowing that he was not prepared to do the work that was expected. What his professors did not understand at that time was that Francisco lacked academic English. He spoke English quite well, so when he struggled on essays and tests, his professors assumed that Francisco had not studied hard enough. Francisco blamed himself for his poor grades and tried to study more, but his confidence was low. He often spent hours studying the wrong things or trying to memorize information for an exam, but none of this helped him become more proficient in reading and writing in English.

There are many students like Francisco. As a result, researchers and policy makers have begun to try to find ways to help students who do not have the academic language they need. In the past few years, research articles and reports from several agencies have not only identified the problems we have discussed but begun to make specific suggestions for helping students.

Recommendations for Success

Several sources provide specific guidance for educators working with older struggling students. We draw upon those resources and our own work to provide specific suggestions for helping students develop academic language. We first list suggestions from a major report that synthesizes current research. Then we suggest what we believe is the best approach for supporting the development of academic language: teaching language and content through integrated units of study based on big questions. It is important to teach both language and content themes for ELLs and SELs. An extended example will show how one teacher teaches academic language to newcomers, long-term English learners, and struggling native English speakers.

Success Despite Double the Work

Short and Fitzsimmons point out that "English language learners must perform *double the work* of native English speakers in the country's middle and high schools" (2007, 1). These students face the struggle of learning English at the same time they are learning academic content. Unfortunately, many ELLs and struggling readers do not get the challenging curriculum they need in order to develop academic language and literacy. Short and Fitzsimmons emphasize that the academic literacy students need is "a complex endeavor that involves reading, writing, listening, and speaking for multiple school-related purposes using a variety of texts and demanding a variety of products" (4).

It is important to point out that many ELLs develop functional literacy in English. These students are often responsible for reading, translating, and writing many kinds of documents that their parents are unable to read or write. These English learners are language brokers for their families. That is, they interpret when their non-English-speaking parents need to carry out business such as banking, paying the bills, visiting the doctor, or filling out government documents such as immigration papers or even tax forms.

Being language brokers involves a great deal of reading and writing in English. ELLs often take these responsibilities seriously and understand that their family members rely on them. However, in school, teachers seldom appreciate language brokering nor are they aware that many academically struggling English learners frequently carry out complex tasks outside of school (Jiménez 2000, 2005). As a result, teachers may miss opportunities to build school-based tasks on the literacies students bring to school.

Identity, Engagement, and Motivation with Culturally Relevant Texts

Short and Fitzsimmons (2007) list three factors as being key for literacy development for all adolescents: identity, engagement, and motivation. Older second-language learners like Francisco often struggle with identity. They come to a new country where, often, they are invisible or, worse yet, their backgrounds and knowledge are not recognized or valued. Francisco could read and write at grade level in Spanish, but his teachers were not aware of this skill and did not try to build on this knowledge base. Francisco did find Mexican friends, but his identity was with El Salvador. His identity got lost in his interactions not only in English but also in Spanish. Most teachers and other students thought Francisco was Mexican. Cummins (2001) has explained that school is a place where students negotiate identities. When schools take an assimilationist approach and ignore students' cultures and languages, students may lose a sense of who they are. Students like Francisco need to be acknowledged for who they are, and instruction should build on their backgrounds.

One way teachers can connect the curriculum to students' lives is to provide ELLs with texts that are interesting to them and validate their identities. The use of culturally relevant books helps motivate students and engage them in reading. The last year Francisco was at the university, he was assigned to read Villaseñor's

(1991) epic immigrant novel *Rain of Gold* for a sociology course. When he first saw that the book was 562 pages long, he was overwhelmed. However, once he began reading the novel, he could not put it down. He identified with the experiences, the characters, and the theme of the book because it was so much like his own story. He admitted to us that *Rain of Gold* was the first novel in English he had ever read from cover to cover.

After this reading experience, Francisco looked for other books like *Rain of Gold* and found several about his native country, El Salvador. He read three by Benítez: *A Place Where the Sea Remembers* (1993), *Bitter Grounds* (1997), and *The Weight of All Things* (2002). Through these novels, he learned some of the history of his country. He began to understand the problems his country had faced with the civil war and why his mother had wanted to get both of her sons out of El Salvador to avoid conscription into one of the two armies. These books converted Francisco into an engaged reader.

If Francisco's teachers had provided him with culturally relevant books in high school, he would have been better prepared for college. For example, when English teachers expose adolescents who are from migrant families or whose parents work in agriculture to books like *The Circuit* (Jiménez 1997) and *Breaking Through* (Jiménez 2001), inner-city Hispanics to *Parrot in the Oven: Mi vida* (Martinez 1996) or *Buried Onions* (Soto 1997), or immigrant Asians to *Hey, Hmong Girl, Whassup?* (Rempel 2004) or *The Gangster We Are All Looking For* (Thúy 2003), students are more likely to become engaged. Students identify with the characters in the books because they have experienced many of the same things they read about. Because they have background knowledge, students comprehend culturally relevant books. Goldenberg explains that "when ELLs read texts with more familiar material, for example, stories with themes and content from the students' cultures, their comprehension improves" (2008, 18). When students connect personally to culturally relevant books, they are motivated to read, and, at the same time, they can learn about key elements of literature such as character, plot, setting, and theme.

Regular English and ESL teachers we have worked with include many culturally relevant texts among the books they read to and with their students. In order to choose and evaluate books for their students, teachers can use the Culturally Relevant Texts Rubric developed by Ann Freeman (Freeman 2000; Y. Freeman, A. Freeman, and D. Freeman 2003). This rubric is shown in Figure 7.1. This rubric can be used in various ways. Older students can use the rubric after reading the book. They can answer the questions or use the questions as a guide for a book report. Students can also use the rubric as a guide during small-group literature discussions. Individual students or small groups can rate books using the rubric,

1. Are the characters in the story like you and your family?

Just like us .... Not at all

    4   3   2   1

2. Have you lived in or visited places like those in the story?

Yes .... No

    4   3   2   1

3. Could this story take place this year?

Yes .... No

    4   3   2   1

4. How close do you think the main characters are to you in age?

Very close .... Not close at all

    4   3   2   1

5. Are there main characters in the story who are boys [for boys] or girls [for girls]?

Yes .... No

    4   3   2   1

6. Do the characters talk like you and your family do?

Yes .... No

    4   3   2   1

7. How often do you read stories like these?

Often .... Never

    4   3   2   1

8. Have you ever had an experience like one described in this story?

Yes .... No

    4   3   2   1

figure 7.1 Cultural Relevance Texts Rubric

and other students can use these ratings in choosing books. Teachers can survey the whole class using the questions and then use individual questions during class discussion. In addition, teachers can use the rubric during reading conferences with individual students.

When teachers use culturally relevant books, they draw on the three factors mentioned by Short and Fitzsimmons (2007). Students can identify with culturally relevant texts. Culturally relevant books engage them. And students are motivated to read texts that connect to their lives and experiences. Figure 7.2 lists a few culturally relevant books for middle school and high school learners that might help

Hispanic

Abraham, S. G., and D. G. Abraham. 2004. *Cecilia's Year*. El Paso, TX: Cinco Puntos.

Ada, A. F. 2002. *I Love Saturdays and Domingos*. New York: Atheneum Books.

Anzaldúa, G. 1993. *Friends from the Other Side*. San Francisco: Children's Book Press.

Atkin, S. B. 1993. *Voices from the Fields: Children of Migrant Farmworkers Tell Their Stories*. Boston: Little, Brown.

Benítez, S. 1993. *A Place Where the Sea Remembers*. New York: Scribner.

———. 1997. *Bitter Grounds*. New York: Picador USA.

———. 2002. *The Weight of All Things*. New York: Hyperion.

Bunting, E. 1998. *Going Home*. New York: HarperTrophy.

Byrd, L. 2003. *The Treasure on Gold Street: El tesoro en la calle oro*. El Paso, TX: Cinco Puntos.

Cisneros, S. 1991. *Woman Hollering Creek*. New York: Vintage.

Cohn, D. 2002. *¡Sí se puede! Yes, We Can! Janitor Strike in L.A.* El Paso, TX: Cinco Puntos.

Crosthwaite, L. H., J. W. Byrd, and B. Byrd, eds. 2003. *Puro Border: Dispatches, Snapshots, and Graffiti from La Frontera*. El Paso, TX: Cinco Puntos.

Elya, S. M. 2002. *Home at Last*. New York: Lee and Low Books.

García, A., and A. C. García. 2004. *Our Journey*. Barrington, IL: Rigby.

Garza, C. L. 1990. *Family Pictures: Cuadros de familia*. San Francisco: Children's Book Press.

———. 1996. *In My Family: En mi familia*. San Francisco: Children's Book Press.

Griswold del Castillo, R. de 2002. *César Chávez: The Struggle for Justice/César Chávez: La lucha por justicia*. Houston: Piñata Books.

Hayes, J. 2001. *El cucuy: A Bogeyman Cuento in English and Spanish*. El Paso, TX: Cinco Puntos.

———. 2003. *La llorona: The Weeping Woman*. El Paso, TX: Cinco Puntos.

Herrera, J. F. 2007. *Reasons Mexicanos Can't Cross the Border*. San Francisco: City Lights.

Jiménez, F. 1997. *The Circuit: Stories from the Life of a Migrant Child*. Albuquerque: University of New Mexico Press.

———. 2001. *Breaking Through*. Boston: Houghton Mifflin.

Malín, A. 2007. *Estrella's Quinceañera*. New York: Simon Pulse.

Martinez, V. 1996. *Parrot in the Oven: Me vida*. New York: HarperCollins.

figure 7.2 Selection of Culturally Relevant Books

Mora, P. 2000. *My Own True Name: New and Selected Poems for Young Adults.* Houston: Piñata Books, Arte Público.

———. 2007. *Yum! ¡MmMm! ¡Qué rico! America's Sproutings: Haiku by Pat Mora.* New York: Lee and Low Books.

Rice, D. 2001. *Crazy Loco.* New York: Dial Books.

Rodríguez, L. 1997. *América Is Her Name.* Willimantic, CT: Curbstone.

———. 2002. *The Republic of East L.A.* New York: HarperCollins.

Romo, D. D. 2005. *Ringside Seat to a Revolution: An Underground Cultural History of El Paso and Juárez: 1893–1923.* El Paso, TX: Cinco Puntos.

Ryan, P. M. 2000. *Esperanza Rising.* New York: Scholastic.

Saldana, R. 2001. *The Jumping Tree.* New York: Delacorte.

Saliñas, B. 1998. *The Three Pigs: Los tres cerdos, Nacho, Tito, and Miguel.* Oakland, CA: Piñata.

———. 2001. *Cinderella Latina.* New York: Scholastic.

Soto, G. 1997. *Buried Onions.* San Diego: Harcourt Brace.

Multicultural

Atkin, B. 1996. *Voices from the Streets.* New York: Little, Brown.

Knight, M. B. 1993. *Who Belongs Here? An American Story.* Gardiner, ME: Tilbury House.

Nikola-Lisa, W. 1997. *America: My Land, Your Land, Our Land.* New York: Lee and Low Books.

Rosa-Casanova, S. 1997. *Mama Provi and the Pot of Rice.* New York: Atheneum Books.

Wing, N. 1996. *Jalapeño Bagels.* New York: Atheneum Books.

Chinese/Japanese

Cheng, A. 2000. *Grandfather Counts.* New York: Lee and Low Books.

Lee, G. 1991. *China Boy.* New York: Penguin.

Levine, E. 1989. *I Hate English.* New York: Scholastic.

Say, A. 1993. *Grandfather's Journey.* Boston: Houghton Mifflin.

———. 1999a. *El Chino.* Boston: Houghton Mifflin.

———. 1999b. *Tea with Milk.* Boston: Houghton Mifflin.

figure 7.2 *continued*

Soentpiet, Y., and C. Soentpiet. 2001. *Coolies*. New York: Philomel.

Yee, L. 2003. *Millicent Min: Girl Genius*. New York: Scholastic.

Hmong

Brown, J. 2004. *Little Cricket*. New York: Hyperion Books.

Cha, D. 1996. *Dia's Story Cloth: The Hmong People's Journey of Freedom*. New York: Lee and Low Books.

Coburn, J. 1996. *Jouanah: A Hmong Cinderella*. Arcadia, CA: Shen's Books.

Rempel, L. 2004. *Hey, Hmong Girl, Whassup?* Saint Paul, MN: Hamline University Press.

Shea, P. D. 1995. *The Whispering Cloth*. Honesdale, PA: Boyds Mills.

———. 2003. *Tangled Threads: A Hmong Girl's Story*. New York: Clarion.

Korean

Choi, Y. 2001. *The Name Jar*. New York: Knopf.

Park, L. S. 2006. *A Single Shard*. London: Oxford University Press.

Shin, S. Y. 2004. *Cooper's Lesson*. San Francisco: Children's Book Press.

Middle Eastern

Ellis, D. 2002. *The Breadwinner*. Toronto: Groundwood Books.

Halaby, L. 2003. *West of Jordan*. Boston: Beacon.

Heide, F., and J. Gilliland. 1990. *The Day of Ahmed's Secret*. New York: Scholastic.

Khedairi, B. 2002. *A Sky So Close*. New York: Pantheon Books.

Laird, E. 2006. *A Little Piece of Ground*. Chicago: Haymarket Books.

Nawwab, N. I. 2004. *The Unfurling Poems*. Vista, CA: Selwa.

Shea, P. D. 2003. *The Carpet Boy's Gift*. Gardiner, ME: Tilbury House.

Shihab-Nye, N. 1994. *Sitt's Secrets*. New York: Aladdin.

———. 1997. *Habibi*. New York: Simon and Schuster.

———. 2002. *19 Varieties of Gazelle*. New York: HarperCollins.

Native American

Bruchac, J. 1992. *Thirteen Moons on Turtle's Back: A Native American Year of Moons*. New York: Putnam and Grosset.

———. 1996. *Between Earth and Sky*. San Diego: Harcourt Brace.

figure 7.2 *continued*

————. 2004. *Growing Up Abenake*. Barrington, IL: Rigby.

Tingle, T. 2003. *Walking the Choctaw Road*. El Paso, TX: Cinco Puntos.

————. 2006. *Crossing Bok Chitto: A Choctaw Tale of Friendship and Freedom*. El Paso, TX: Cinco Puntos.

Vietnamese

Gilson, J. 1966. *Hello, My Name Is Scrambled Eggs*. New York: Pocket Books.

Thúy, L. 2003. *The Gangster We Are Looking For*. New York: Knopf.

Whelan, G. 1992. *Goodbye Vietnam*. New York: Random House Children's Books.

figure 7.2 *continued*

teachers begin to look for more books relevant to their students. The bibliography is not meant to be exhaustive. The texts are at varied levels of difficulty so that students with different reading abilities can access them.

Teaching with a culturally relevant text: *The Circuit* • Mary teaches English to tenth graders in a large high school where more than 95 percent of the students are Hispanic. Because many of her students are from migrant families or have relatives who work in agriculture, Mary decided to have the students read and respond to *The Circuit* (Jiménez 1997), a book based on the life of a migrant boy. Mary wanted to use this book to teach some key concepts called for in the standards, including finding textual evidence to support opinions, using reference materials, and using reading strategies. She also planned to teach literary terms listed in the standards, including *tone, allusion, flashback, symbol,* and *foreshadowing*.

Preview, view, review • To introduce the book, Mary used the *preview, view, review* strategy. This strategy allows teachers and students to make use of students' first languages to access content and enhance comprehension. While teachers might hesitate to use students' first languages in their content classes, Gutiérrez (2002) showed the importance of allowing students to use their primary language, Spanish, in high school math classes. She interviewed students who were allowed to use Spanish during class time. The students explained that they felt more comfortable in discussing the content when allowed to use their first language. One student said, "You know, we're all calm about [the math] that way. We all speak Spanish and we are comfortable" (1075). The teachers in the study were not fluent Spanish speakers and often did not understand their students, but they all agreed that allowing students to use Spanish was important. At the same time, the teachers "were keenly aware of the importance for students to negotiate the mathematics in English as well" (1076). The teachers in the Gutiérrez study encouraged the use of Spanish as a way for students to negotiate meaning about the content but did not have a specific organization for when to use the language.

We suggest the preview, view, review strategy to provide this organization. In his report of the research, Goldenberg writes, "Another way to use the primary language but keep the focus on English instruction is to introduce new concepts in the primary language prior to the lesson in English, then afterward review the new content, again in the primary language" (2008, 19).

Mary's lesson provides an example. Since she speaks Spanish, Mary gave a brief summary of *The Circuit* in Spanish and then asked the students what they knew about migrant students or coming to live and work in a new country. During this discussion students were allowed to use Spanish, their first language, if they wished. These supports provided all the students with some background before reading the story in English.

If Mary had not been able to speak Spanish, or if she had had students from other language backgrounds, she would have used a bilingual student in the class, a paraprofessional, or a parent volunteer to give a brief preview of the novel. If no one was available, Mary would have asked the students what they knew about migrant workers, then allowed them to work in pairs or small groups using their first languages, and then report back in English.

Following the preview, Mary taught several lessons using English. She avoided concurrent translation. She knew that concurrent translation, simply translating words and phrases, is an ineffective way to teach language to students. At the end of each lesson, Mary allowed students to again use Spanish to summarize the main ideas. The students worked in small groups to discuss what they had learned and then reported back to Mary in English. Figure 7.3 shows the steps of preview, view, review.

Supporting the reading of *The Circuit* • During the view part of her lesson, Mary first gave the students a sheet titled "What are some strategies for reading?" Students used the handout to take notes as Mary lectured on strategies they could use before and during reading to figure out words they didn't know. As she lectured, Mary wrote the key ideas down on an overhead and the students copied them. These strategies included using context clues, dictionaries, glossaries, and prefixes, roots, and suffixes, some of the same key strategies discussed in Chapter 6. A sample from Emma is shown in Figure 7.4.

Preview
first language
The teacher gives an overview of the lesson or activity in the students' first language (e.g., the teacher offers an oral summary, reads a book, shows a film, asks key questions).
View
second or target language (English)
The teacher teaches the lesson or directs the activity in the students' second language.
Review
first language
The teacher or the students summarize key ideas and raise questions about the lesson in their first language.

figure 7.3 Preview, View, Review Strategy

These strategies helped Mary's students build academic vocabulary as they read. Mary also focused on some words, teaching them directly. She involved the students in different activities. They made posters that illustrated words and included their own definitions. They also made posters that listed synonyms and antonyms for words they were studying as well as examples. One student made a colorful poster as he worked on the word *renege*, first giving the definition in his own words, "to go back on a promise; to go back on one's word." For the opposite, he wrote, "agree, stand firm." When he gave an example, he wrote, "I reneged on my promise when I did not help my dad," and under the category of "What is the word similar to?" he wrote "break one's word." He did all of this on bright blue paper, and the sections filled in with the content looked like bubbles floating up in the air.

On another day, Mary gave her students a sheet about the important skill of summarizing. Again, as Mary lectured and wrote on the overhead, students took notes on the definitions of *summary* and *gist* with examples of each from the text they were reading and discussing. These lecture activities reinforced important skills the students needed to be able to both access academic texts and write about what they were reading.

To reinforce literary terms such as *tone, setting, story elements, characters, allusion, flashback, symbol, foreshadowing,* and *theme,* Mary worked with her students in the large group, discussing examples from *The Circuit.* Then she had students

What are some strategies for reading?

<u>Before you read</u>

* Read tittle.
* look at Pictures.
* remember what you know.

<u>As you read</u>

* what is the tone?
* How is the selling important?
* How would I Summarize?
* keep track of story elements?

* Graphic Organizer.

<u>Understanding word strategies</u>

* Dictionary
* look for clues - other words give you the ~~and~~ word's meaning.

<u>Using context</u>

* Use the imformation you understand to help with word's /phrases you don't understand.

<u>Using prefixes, roots, suffixes</u>

Prefixes = beginning of a word
root = the foundation which carries meaning.
Suffix = end of word.

<u>Using glossaries and dictionaries</u>

Many words have multiple meanings —use context to determine correct definition.

figure 7.4 Emma's Notes on Reading Strategies

work in pairs. She gave them photocopied sections of the text and asked them to find examples of the different terms, such as allusions to famous Mexican heroes and flashbacks to earlier childhood experiences. When they found an example, the students cut it out and pasted it on a large sheet of butcher paper that they shared with the entire group.

They also practiced finding textual evidence to support key ideas in the chapters. Mary and the students talked about what some key concepts were, including how migrant laborers work extremely hard for low wages, how they experience prejudice, and how schooling can provide a way out of poverty. Once key ideas were identified, students again worked in pairs. They listed the key ideas on a piece of butcher paper and located supporting evidence from the different chapters. They cut out passages or sentences that provided evidence for each idea from photocopied book pages. They pasted the information they had located on the sheets of butcher paper next to the ideas. Then each group shared its evidence. This activity helped students understand how to go through a text to find key ideas and then find supporting evidence. Students also worked in groups to summarize one chapter from the book and then shared their summaries. Class discussion helped the students see if the information they included was important to the summary.

After completing these activities, Mary put students into groups to review what they had learned. Students could use their first language to talk to each other, but they reported back to the class in English. During the discussions in their first language, students could clarify key ideas and deepen their understanding of the content. When they reported to the class, they used the content-specific and general academic English they were learning. As a final project, students worked in groups to prepare a short PowerPoint presentation showing the setting, the characters, and the theme. They also showed examples of allusion, flashback, symbol, and foreshadowing that they had found in the text.

Mary's goal is for all her students to become proficient readers and writers of English. To accomplish this goal, she involves students in activities to build their academic language. Mary knows that her students do not use academic language in their everyday conversations, but in order to succeed in school, they need to use content-specific vocabulary, such as *tone, voice, problem, solution,* and *textual evidence,* and they need to be able to explain these concepts in writing. Mary's lessons scaffolded academic vocabulary and guided her students toward the academic writing they needed to do. We will return to Mary's classroom and this unit on *The Circuit* to describe other specific ways that Mary develops academic language with her students later in the chapter.

Research-Based Effective Practices to Support Academic Literacy

Based on their review of the research and their observations of model programs for struggling adolescent ELL readers and writers, Short and Fitzsimmons list nine effective instructional practices (2007, 34–38). A review of Mary's lesson shows that she incorporated all of these.

1. *Integrate all four language skills—reading, writing, speaking and listening—into instruction from the beginning.* Mary's students were involved in all four of the skills throughout her lessons. They read, they wrote, they presented, and they listened to their teacher and to one another during lectures, discussions, and sharing sessions.

2. *Teach the components and processes of reading and writing.* Since most of her students had developed basic decoding skills, Mary showed them how to preview their reading, make predictions, paraphrase, and infer. She also taught them the processes of writing, including brainstorming, drafting, and editing.

3. *Teach reading comprehension strategies.* Mary lectured on reading strategies and the students took notes. As they read, the students practiced these strategies and then used terms such as *context* and *strategy* as they discussed the book.

4. *Focus on vocabulary development.* Mary continually worked with the students on vocabulary. She taught them to use suffixes and prefixes. She always kept the vocabulary instruction in a context, often involving the students in art, as evidenced by the vocabulary posters the students worked on. Later we will explain how Mary used academic vocabulary cards, cognates, and various kinds of student-made dictionaries.

5. *Build and activate background knowledge.* The choice of a culturally relevant book was key in activating background knowledge. Mary had students brainstorm what they knew about migrants and farmwork before they read the text. In this way, she helped them activate background knowledge.

6. *Teach language through content and themes.* Mary used *The Circuit* and the struggles of migrant life as her theme, and through that integrated unit of study, she taught her students the literary content required by the standards, including finding textual evidence and using different resources.

7. *Use native language strategically.* Through the preview, view, review strategy, Mary used the students' first language, Spanish, but separated the languages and avoided concurrent translation. She also helped her students build vocabulary by drawing on cognates.

8. *Pair technology with existing interventions.* Mary used interventions suggested by Short and Fitzsimmons, including project-based instruction and heterogeneous student grouping. For one of their projects, Mary's students investigated migrant life and the benefits of schooling to escape poverty using the Internet as one of their sources. They also learned how to make a PowerPoint slide show to present their ideas to others.

9. *Motivate ELLs through choice.* Mary included different elements of choice throughout her teaching. Students usually could choose their partners for their projects. When they made vocabulary posters, they chose the academic words they wanted to include and decided how to use art to illustrate their words.

Teaching Both Language and Content

All nine practices that Short and Fitzsimmons (2007) list as potential solutions to meet the challenge of helping ELLs develop academic literacy are extremely important. When teachers like Mary incorporate these practices in their lessons, students develop the academic language registers of school. Although all nine practices are important, from our perspective the most crucial is that teachers should teach language and content organized around thematic units of study.

Teaching both language and content has been a topic of interest for researchers and educators alike in recent years, especially for those in the fields of second-language acquisition and bilingual education. Barwell provides a broad general definition of language and content integration:

> Language and content integration concerns the teaching and learning of both language and subject areas (e.g. science, mathematics, etc.) in the same classroom, at the same time. (2005, 143)

Traditionally, language was taught in isolation from content, and second-language learners studied English as a subject. However, Barwell explains that more recently linguists have seen "language as a resource for participation in human activity" (144). Barwell outlines a framework to consider in teaching language and content. This framework has four dimensions:

1. *The policy and curriculum dimension*: Educators always consider how to organize instruction and choose materials to support teaching ELLs language and content. In addition, policy for placement of ELLs in appropriate settings is part of this dimension.

2. *The institutional dimension*: At the school level, decisions about staff and resources are considered. For example, each department might decide to have specific teachers and materials to teach language and content. However, those teachers need to be professionally prepared to teach the content to students whose first language is not English. Some schools may decide to partner content teachers with ESL teachers to meet the needs of their ELLs (Carrier 2005).

3. *The classroom interactional dimension*: Students and teachers interact at the classroom level, and the success of learning both language and content at the same time is constantly evaluated. In addition, at this level the complexity of classroom communities becomes important. Classroom interactions define relations of power and help define ethnic, social, and gendered identities.

4. *The theoretical-methodological dimension*: This dimension is important because the theories and models that teachers and their administrators hold about both content and language learning affect how instruction is organized and carried out for ELLs.

As educators working with LFS students, LTELs, and SELs who are struggling readers organize curriculum, they should consider these dimensions at the school and classroom levels. When content and language teaching experts collaborate in designing and implementing curriculum, ELLs benefit. One such collaboration has been between science teachers and ELL teachers and researchers. The result is a book published by the National Science Teachers Association, *Science for English Language Learners: K–12 Classroom Strategies* (Fathman and Crowther 2006). This book is a very useful resource for mainstream teachers who teach science in classes with ELLs. The editors write:

> Input from both science and language teachers in creating lessons can ensure that components are included that encourage science inquiry while at the same time building background, providing practice, emphasizing vocabulary, reviewing, and providing assessment for learners at all proficiency levels. (7)

Science for English Language Learners includes important information about teaching science and teaching and assessing ELLs in science. It contains a number of sample science lessons from teachers at different grade levels. The teachers who contributed these lessons show how they modified instruction to meet the needs of ELLs. Included are lessons written by science experts with comments by language teaching experts. It is this sort of collaboration that results in the most effective lessons for all students. Teachers interested in teaching both language and content would find that this book provides useful and practical models of how to keep a dual focus on academic content and academic language development.

Reasons to Teach Language and Content

We have stressed the importance of teaching both academic language and academic content together. There are four reasons that teaching both language and content is important for ELLs and for many struggling readers.

Students learn both language and content • When working with older struggling readers and writers, teachers often feel a sense of urgency. Students have a great deal to learn and not many years to learn it. Although it might appear to be the solution, teaching students academic vocabulary and grammar first and then teaching content is not beneficial. In fact, Krashen (1998, 2000, 2004a, 2004b) claims that the best way to teach both language and content is through meaningful reading and enterprises or project-based lessons. Students can learn their new language as teachers teach social studies, science, math, and literature, using strategies to make the content comprehensible. In addition to extensive reading, students also need some direct instruction in academic language at the text, paragraph, sentence, and word levels.

Even if one could effectively teach language and then teach content, there is no time to teach language first and content later. In the same way that children growing up in a bilingual environment can develop two languages simultaneously, ELLs can acquire language structures and forms as they study the content of the various subjects in school. They learn academic English as they learn the academic content. Developing high levels of academic English and academic content proficiency takes time, so it is important that ELLs learn English and subject matter knowledge from the start.

Language is kept in the natural context • A second reason for teaching language and content is that this approach keeps language in its natural context. It is natural to talk about the hypotenuse of a triangle if you are studying geometry. Math is the natural context for this word. As they learn this word, students understand how it is related to other words such as *triangle* and *angle*. It is easier to learn words in context than in isolation or as part of a list of unrelated words.

Key words for different subject areas are best understood as part of a network of related terms needed to understand some aspect of a subject. In the area of literature, for example, it is easier to learn a term like *rising action* in the process of talking about the development of plot. The student comes to understand *rising action* as one phase of plot development that is related to other words, such as *climax* or *falling action*. Content-based language teaching naturally lends itself to presenting vocabulary in context.

In the same way, the natural context for learning how to write reports is in a history or science class. After students have studied a subject, they can write a history or science report. Students can also learn how to connect sentences and write cohesive paragraphs in the process of writing different kinds of papers in the content areas. With careful planning, teachers can ensure that students are learning both language and content in each lesson.

Students have reasons to use the language • A third reason for teaching language and content together is that students have reasons to use the language they are learning. They are not just memorizing words for a test, words they will forget very quickly. Instead, they need to use the words as they listen to lectures, talk with classmates, read textbooks, work on projects, and write reports.

Use of academic vocabulary leads to deeper learning and greater retention. An ELL studying geometry will develop a better understanding of *hypotenuse* as she listens to the teacher explain the parts of a triangle, reads proofs in her textbook, and then engages in problem-solving activities. An ELL studying literature will come to understand *rising action* as he writes an analysis of the plot development in a novel. In each case, the students are motivated to learn the academic language they need to talk, read, and write about academic content.

Students learn the academic vocabulary of the content areas • A final reason for teaching language and content together is that students learn the academic vocabulary of the different content areas. As the previous examples show, students learn key words like *hypotenuse* and *rising action* in the process of listening, reading, talking, and writing about academic subjects. Students also come to understand that in different contexts, the same word can take on different meanings. In literature a character might attend a social *function*, but in math, *function* takes on a very different meaning.

Organizing Curriculum Around Integrated Units of Study Based on Big Questions

The only way that ELLs can develop the academic language they need for school success is to be immersed in that language as they study the different content areas. Connecting these content areas through integrated units of study makes the instruction even more effective (Freeman and Freeman 2007). This approach is beneficial for all students; however, it is especially important for ELLs and struggling readers. Teachers can develop units based on big questions taken from the content standards. Wiggins and McTighe (2005) argue that curriculum must deal with big ideas or questions worth investigating. These are questions that do not have a simple answer.

During an integrated unit of study such as What are the political, economic, and sociological effects of global warming? students would access different texts, including literature and informational texts from the different content areas, to build their understanding of weather patterns, the rate of changes in weather patterns, the effects of industrialization on different societies, the depletion of the rain forest, the response of nations to calls for environmental responsibility, and individual responses to global warming. Students could gather information from different content areas as they explored these related topics. Organizing around big questions leads to an inquiry approach to education (Short, Harste, and Burke 1996).

Teachers can connect curriculum to state and federal standards. A unit on global warming connects naturally to science standards. For example, the Texas high school science standards include global warming under the section "Environmental Systems":

> TEKS 112.44, b (1): Students study a variety of topics that include: biotic and abiotic factors in habitats; ecosystems and biomes; interrelationships among resources and an environmental system; sources and flow of energy through an environmental system; relationship between carrying capacity and changes in populations and ecosystems; and changes in environments. (TEA 1998, C10)

The science standard also states that "students should understand that certain types of questions can be answered by investigations" (TEKS 112.44 b (4); TEA 1998, C10). This same big question on global warming also fits into social studies in the world geography standard 113.34, which states that students are expected to

> analyze the effects of physical and human geographic patterns and processes on events in the past and describe their effects on present conditions, including significant physical features and environmental conditions that influenced migration patterns in the past and shaped the distribution of culture groups today. (TEKS 113.34 c (1) (A); TEA 1998, C22)

The big question for both of these standards could also be How does where we live influence how we live? Students can begin by studying the local community and then look at other communities that are different from theirs because of differences in the physical environment. Secondary students then need to know how geographic contexts and processes of spatial exchange influenced events in the past and helped shape the present.

Teachers can often include literacy and math standards within questions based on social studies and science standards. It is important to spend time focusing on literacy and math skills, but they are best learned in the context of language arts, social studies, and science. For example, students can read a novel or an expository text about weather and climate change during the unit on How does where we live influence how we live? They can record the high and low temperatures daily, measure wind speed and rainfall, study weather movement, and then graph the results. Both literacy and math skills can be developed as students read and write about this big question.

Basing big questions on standards makes good sense in a time when accountability is being stressed in schools. This approach also is logical because textbooks and supplementary materials available at each grade level reflect the standards. At the secondary level, teachers from different subject areas can meet to form interdisciplinary teams. Teachers at each grade level might meet to plan curriculum together, deciding on the big questions and the materials and methods they will use to engage students in inquiry of these questions. This sort of horizontal planning is useful because each teacher can use her expertise and interests to teach a section of the theme.

At one large middle school, interdisciplinary teams were made up of a language arts teacher, a social studies teacher, a science teacher, and a math teacher. Students rotated in teams through these teachers' classes. This model resulted in great improvement in the academic performance of the ELLs at the school (Freeman and Freeman 2001). Some high schools have also organized their curriculum around big questions that draw on the different subject areas (García 2002). Organizing interdisciplinary units at the secondary level is complex, but the results have been consistently positive. In schools that do not take this approach, individual teachers can either organize their own curriculum around integrated units of study or pair up with a teacher from another content area to study a big question together. For example, the language arts teacher might coordinate with the social studies teacher.

Teaching language and content organized around integrated units of study is beneficial for ELLs and struggling readers for several reasons. Through thematic units, teachers can connect curriculum to students' lives. As students study global warming, for example, they can look for the effects of global warming in the paper or in TV reports. Studying the same big question across content areas ensures that certain concepts and vocabulary are repeated naturally. Teachers can differentiate instruction to match the proficiency levels of different students as they study the same theme. Students can read easier or harder books on the same topic and then contribute what they have learned to a general class discussion. As they investigate big questions that interest them, students become more engaged and experience more success.

Identity, Engagement, and Motivation with *The Circuit*

Short and Fitzsimmons (2007) list identity, engagement, and motivation as three important factors in improving adolescent literacy for both ELLs and native English speakers. Earlier, we discussed these three factors and applied them to our analysis of Francisco. We also described Mary's class and explained how many of the activities she uses help her students develop academic language. Her approach is consistent with the nine promising practices that Short and Fitzsimmons outline.

We conclude this chapter on teaching academic language and subject matter content organized around integrated units of study by describing additional activities Mary used to help her mostly Latino students develop the academic registers of school during her unit on *The Circuit* (Jiménez 1997). Mary has taught this book several times in different settings. Each time she adds and changes activities. Earlier we described activities she carried out with tenth graders. Mary has also used this book with students in regular ninth-grade English, second-year ESL students, and high school newcomers. In each setting, Mary's goal has been to differentiate her instruction and to motivate and engage her students as they read about characters they can identify with. For each group, she planned activities to increase their content-specific academic vocabulary and their ability to read grade-appropriate literature.

Using Graphic Organizers to Scaffold Instruction

To help all her students understand what they were reading and to build key literary concepts, Mary used different scaffolding activities for each chapter of *The Circuit*. She used the same activities but carried out the activities differently depending on her students' language proficiency. One of the first scaffolds that Mary used was a map of California, the setting for the novel. For her newcomers, Mary drew the route, the circuit, the characters in the book took as a migrant family and talked about the map with them. Her other students who were more proficient worked on their own maps as she described where the family traveled. The students referred to this map as the characters moved around the circuit in the different chapters. Figure 7.5 shows the map with the circuit drawn in.

As Mary read aloud the first chapter of *The Circuit*, her students followed along. When a new character or event was mentioned, Mary asked students to write down the name of the character and some of the words that described what

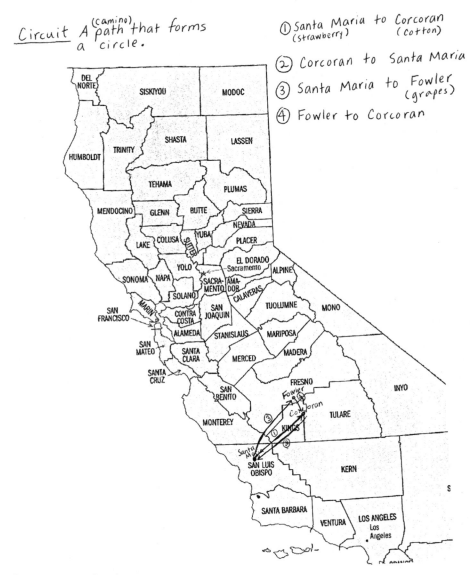

figure 7.5 Map for *The Circuit*

was happening. For her newcomers, Mary put the graphic organizer shown in Figure 7.6 on the overhead projector. The students told Mary the names of key characters, which she wrote in the center boxes. Together, Mary and the students came up with vocabulary to explain the key events. She wrote these in the clouds and then listed supporting details in the boxes connecting to the clouds. As they talked, the students filled in their own graphics using the information from the class graphic on the overhead. For this and the other chapters, Mary used graphics she found on the Internet. She simply googled "free printable graphic organizers." That took her to a page with numerous sites for free downloads of different graphics. She then chose graphics that fit with each chapter.

This Chapter 1 activity helped provide Mary's English learners with the important information they needed to understand this chapter. Students in her other classes read the chapter alone or in pairs and then filled out the same graphic organizer in groups or on their own. This activity gave all of Mary's students the opportunity to develop the literacy concepts of main idea and supporting details.

For Chapter 2, Mary worked on note-taking skills with the students by teaching them how to use Cornell notes as they read. First, Mary gave students a form to take notes on. For her newcomers, she dictated questions that were key to the chapter, and students wrote the questions in the left-hand column. Mary explained that readers can better understand a text by asking themselves questions and then reading to find answers. Mary read the first question. Then she read aloud the first part of the chapter. Once she had finished the section telling how Francisco spent his mornings, she directed students to look at the overhead again. They reread the first question and then worked together to find answers, which Mary wrote on the right side of the form. She followed this procedure through the rest of the chapter.

For other classes in which her students had higher levels of English proficiency Mary explained the form and gave them some sample questions. Then students worked in groups or individually to read the chapter and answer the questions. Mary circulated through the room to give the students extra support. It is important to note that Mary intentionally included general academic vocabulary, such as *outcome*, in activities like these. Figure 7.7 shows the form Mary and the newcomers filled out as they read the second chapter.

In Chapter 3, the main character remembers his first days in school in the new country, how lost and lonely he felt, and how he represented this experience by drawing a butterfly hatching. Again using the overhead projector, Mary wrote down topics from the chapter that she and her newcomer students identified in the branches of a tree graphic, and together they filled in details, as shown in Figure 7.8. For her other classes, students worked in pairs and completed their own trees,

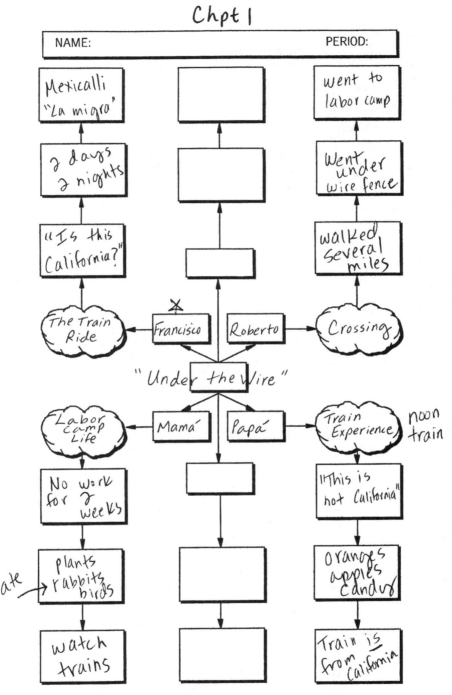

figure 7.6 Graphic Organizer for Chapter 1 of *The Circuit*

Name _____   Date _____

Donna High School AVID Subject_____   Period _____

"Soledad"

How did Francisco spend his mornings?	Mom, dad, and Roberto pick cotton.
	Francisco stays in the car with Trampita (6 months)
	Francisco feels sad.
What did the family do at lunch time?	Ate tacos
	Ate on an army blanket
What idea does Francisco have?	Learn to pick cotton.
	3¢ per pound
	Puts dirt inside
What is the outcome?	Mom mad because of Trampita.
	Dad mad because of dirt.
	Goes to Roberto for comfort.
Summary	

figure 7.7 Cornell Notes Organizer

looking through the chapter. After they completed this activity, the students used their graphics to summarize the chapter orally to each other in small groups. They talked about whether they had chosen the same key events and supporting details and together decided which events and details were most important.

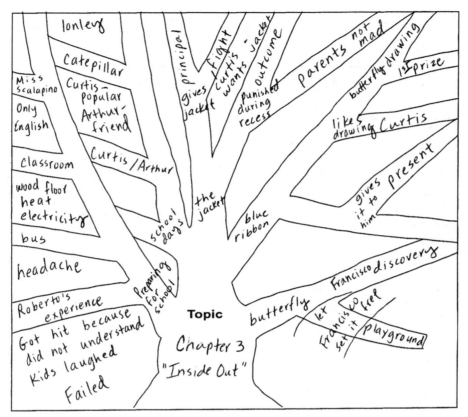

figure 7.8 Tree Graphic Organizer

In the next chapter, the main character in the book watches a goldfish and compares his life to that of the goldfish he is watching. Mary gave her students the compare-and-contrast map found in Figure 7.9. After Mary read the chapter to them, she and her newcomers filled in the graphic together. As with the other activities, the students filled in their own compare-and-contrast maps as Mary wrote. Using this same graphic organizer, the students in her other classes worked in pairs to list ways the character's life was similar to and different from the goldfish's.

Mary gave her students a different graphic organizer for Chapter 5, "The Christmas Gift." The students filled in the events from the chapter, numbering their occurrence in order. Figure 7.10 shows how Mary and her newcomers had so much information to include as she wrote down their ideas that Mary had to divide some of the boxes to create more spaces to write in.

Figure 7.11 shows how Mary helped the students work on character development. In the sixth chapter, the character Torito becomes very sick, and it appears that he might die. In this activity, students filled in a character wheel graphic,

Topic: "El angel de oro"
Name: _____ Date: _____

COMPARE AND CONTRAST MAP

Francisco	Goldfish

Different	Same	Different
• Family played games and told stories • Miguelito and Francisco good friends • Miguelito gone	Alone!	• Fish swimming back + forth alone • Fish has a friend

figure 7.9 Compare-and-Contrast Map

recording key points made in the reading such as "name and physical description," "feelings," "attempted cures," "sickness," and "actions of the family." This assignment, as well as others for the remaining chapters, helped all the students understand the content, scaffolded their writing, and supported the development of vocabulary. As with the other activities, students needing more support worked with Mary or in groups. Students who could work alone completed their own character wheels and then reported back to the whole class. Figure 7.11 shows the graphic for Torito that Mary and her newcomer English learners did together.

Identity Connections with Favorite Quotes

Once students had read the entire book, Mary gave further assignments to help the students make text-to-self connections. For example, in the "Favorite Quote" activity, she asked the students to go back into the text and find a favorite part and copy that section out as a favorite quote. Her assignment included the following steps:

1. Look through the chapters and pick a favorite part.

2. Copy a sentence or several sentences from that part of the story.

① Got food from the trash
— fruits
— vegetables

② Woman is pregnant
Couple needs money
"we're broke"

③ Man offers the handkerchief for 10¢ ⑦

④ Franciso wants a ball for Christmas

⑤ Live in a tent

Mama was wrapping gifts + crying

⑥ The kids got candy
— sad

Papa gives Mama the handkercheif

"The Christmas Gift"

figure 7.10 Events Sequence Graphic Organizer

3. Paraphrase: Write what it is about in your own words.

4. Why was this quote your favorite?

5. Compare this part of the story to something in your own life.

6. Make a drawing or symbol to represent this part of the story.

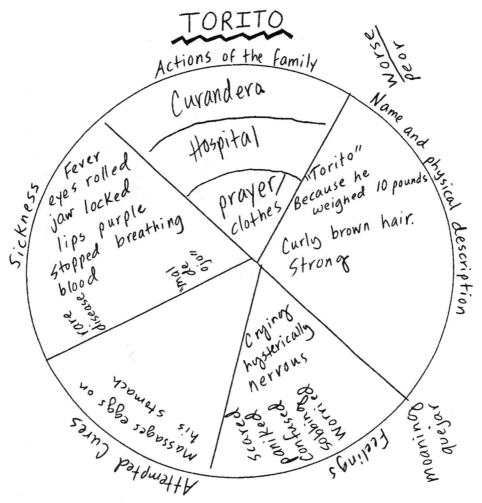

figure 7.11 Character Wheel Graphic

Figure 7.12 shows how much of a personal connection a student can make with an assignment like this one. Julia, a second-year English learner, wrote, "I liked this part because sometimes I feel the same." Looking at the drawing, we can see that Julia often felt alone when she was little.

Identity Connections with "Best/Worst" Activity

Drawing on the chapter summaries and "Favorite Quote" activity, all the students then created their own individual summaries of the book using a unique activity

"Once lost sight of them, I felt pain in my chest, that the same pain I always felt whenever they left Trampita and me alone."

This part of the story was when Francisco's parents and his brother went to work and Francisco and Trampita stayed alone in his Carcachita.

I liked this part because sometimes I feel the same.

figure 7.12 Julia's "Favorite Quote" Poster

figure 7.12 *continued*

that required them to synthesize and evaluate key events in the novel. Depending on their English proficiency, students were able to write more or less in English. However, all students had understood enough of the book to complete the activity.

First, students wrote paragraph summaries of each chapter they had read, including one or two quotes from each chapter. Through this activity, Mary again had students go back into the text to read and review. For each chapter summary, students chose a key experience of the main character, Francisco. Then, using a graph format, the students rated how good or how bad that experience was.

Figure 7.13 shows Julia's graph, the work of the same student who made the "Favorite Quote" poster in Figure 7.12. Note that the horizontal line is the list of chapter numbers for the first six chapters. Then, above the line are Francisco's best experiences from the chapters, rated on a scale of +1 to the very best, +8. For example, Julia wrote, "He get a blue ribbon" at the +8 level for a best experience. Below the line, Mary's students listed the worst experiences from most of the chapters. They also rated these on an eight-point scale. Julia rated "Kids laughed when he talk English" as a –8 experience. Obviously, this was very negative in her mind. As

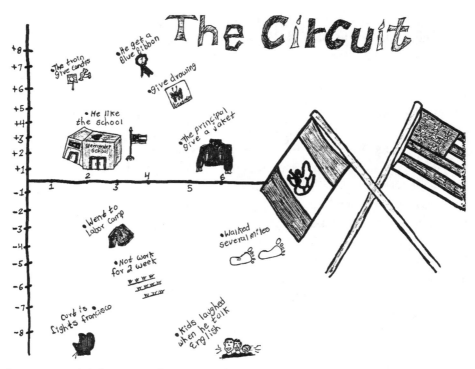

figure 7.13 Julia's "Best/Worst" Picture Graph

students examined Francisco's experiences, they were identifying his experiences with their own experiences and feelings.

Identity, Engagement, and Motivation Through Drama

Mary is an English and drama teacher, and she drew on her background and interest to design a dramatic writing activity for her classes. She asked students to work in groups and choose one of their favorite parts of the book. Once they had chosen the section they liked, they changed the narrative into a dramatic script. To do this, they identified the characters, the scenes, and the dialogue that would convey this section of the book.

One newcomer group, for example, chose a section of the chapter titled "La mariposa" ("The Butterfly"). In this chapter, the main character goes to school for the first time. He does not speak English and does not understand how schools work in this country. As so often happens, a student who does speak English picks on him and makes his life miserable. Following a model that Mary had given them, the students rewrote this chapter in the form of a play. The first page of their drama, written down by José, which is shown in Figure 7.14, sets the stage for the action that will follow. The principal gives Francisco a jacket from the lost and found. Unfortunately, the jacket belongs to Curtis, the bully who has been picking on Francisco. Francisco tells a sympathetic friend, "Look, Arturo, the principal gave me a beautiful green jacket." However, Arturo realizes the problem right away. "That's nice, but I think that this jacket belongs to Curtis."

The group of students who wrote, and eventually acted out, this drama for their peers, connected well with the experiences they had read about despite the fact that their English was at a beginning level. Students in other classes also chose chapters or chapter sections that connected to their lives in specific ways. *The Circuit* included many details that Mary's Latino students could identify with because the characters in the book had experiences like many of their own.

Through this drama activity and the other assignments, Mary's students learned key literary concepts and vocabulary terms in English that they needed to succeed academically. Using differentiated activities like the ones described here, Mary engaged all the students, motivated them, and validated their identities to help them build academic language proficiency.

Conclusion

Both ELLs and struggling readers need to develop academic language to meet the demands of content-area instruction. As students move up through the grades and into the university, success is increasingly measured by the ability to read and write academic texts. Test results indicate that many ELLs fail to develop academic language proficiency. This failure may be attributed in part to inadequate primary-language support and inadequate instructional support.

Although many ELLs show low levels of academic achievement, with the right instruction they can develop the academic language and content-area knowledge necessary for school success. Short and Fitzsimmons (2007) point out that ELLs face double the work of native English speakers. They have to develop both English and academic knowledge. Many struggling readers and writers face a similar challenge. They may speak English, but they lack the academic registers of English. ELLs and struggling readers succeed when teachers plan lessons to build engagement, motivation, and identity.

Two ways that teachers can engage and motivate students while affirming their identities is to use culturally relevant texts and to follow a preview, view, review format for lessons. Mary used preview, view, review as she engaged her students in reading *The Circuit*, a culturally relevant book. Her teaching reflected all nine of

Great scene!
I like all
*   of the dialogue you*
*   use.*

Scene I (in the school)
Characters: (Francisco, Principal, Curtis, Arturo)

Principal: Francisco, Today its a Cool day
Right?

Francisco: Yeah, its very cool.

Principal: Well, letme give ᵧₒᵤ something.

Francisco: Something?

Principal: Yeah, I give ᵧₒᵤ a Jacket

Francisco: a Jacket, oh my good. ᴳᵒᵈ

Principal: take it, its from ᵗʰᵉ de lost things that
~~forgot~~ the Students. forget

Scene II (in the Patio)

Francisco: look Arturo the Principal give ~~to~~ ᵍᵃᵛᵉ
me a beautiful Green Jacket.

Arturo: thats nice, but I think so
That this Jacket i$ belongs to Curtis

figure 7.14 Student Play Based on Part of *The Circuit*

the effective practices that Short and Fitzsimmons (2007) identified as being critical for school success for ELLs.

As she taught *The Circuit*, Mary focused on both academic language and academic content instruction in the area of language arts. When teachers teach language and content organized around integrated units of study based on big questions, their students benefit because they get both language and content, the language is kept in its natural context, students have real purposes for using the language, and students learn the content-specific academic vocabulary of the content area.

Early in this book, we introduced Dolores. We analyzed her essay to show what she had learned during her years in high school and what she still needed to learn. We then explained the different dimensions of the academic registers of schooling. Students like Dolores must gain proficiency in these registers to succeed in school. We ended with the example of Mary, a teacher who provides her students with the kind of instruction they need to develop academic language proficiency. Although ELLs face double the work of other students, they can succeed when teachers implement effective instructional strategies and teach both language and content to all their students.

Applications

1. In the first part of this chapter we discussed the kinds of instruction available to ELLs, how long extra supports are usually provided, the availability of qualified teachers and resources, and the isolation of ELLs. Look carefully at a school or district you know. Considering each of these factors, write a profile of the education of ELLs either at your school or in the district.

2. Consider the ELL population at your school. Choose four or five books that you consider to be culturally relevant for that population. Bring the books to your class or study group to share. Be prepared to explain how the books fit the culturally relevant rubric (see Figure 7.1).

3. Short and Fitzsimmons (2007) make nine suggestions for effective instructional practices with adolescent ELLs. Which of these do you or a teacher you observe regularly use? Which of the practices would you like to try?

4. We describe four reasons it is important to teach language and content. Evaluate a content unit you have recently taught (or one you plan to teach). Explain how students benefited from this unit, referring to each of the four reasons. Show

how you used each (for example, how students got both language and content). If you didn't use them all, how might you revise your unit next time to do so?

5. List the subject or subjects you teach and also list the integrated units of study that you are teaching or have taught recently for each subject. What are the big questions? How do your ELLs and SELs benefit from the use of integrated thematic units? Be specific, giving details from your unit. If you haven't been teaching thematically, how might you organize your teaching around big questions in the future?

6. Review the activities that Mary used during the reading of *The Circuit*. In what specific ways did Mary help her students develop identity and become more engaged? How did the activities motivate her students?

7. With a group, list specific ways that teachers can support the development of academic language for ELLs and SELs. Draw on the entire book. Make a composite list in your class or study group.

References

Allen, J. 2007. *Inside Words: Tools for Teaching Academic Vocabulary, Grades 4–12*. Portland, ME: Stenhouse.

Alvarez, L., and J. Corn. 2008. "Exchanging Assessment for Accountability: The Implications of High-Stakes Reading Assessments for English Language Learners." *Language Arts* 85 (5): 354–65.

Anderson, R., and W. Nagy. 1992. "The Vocabulary Conundrum." *American Educator* Winter: 14–18, 44–47.

August, D., and T. Shanahan, eds. 2006. *Developing Literacy in Second-Language Learners: Report of the National Literacy Panel on Language Minority Children and Youth*. Mahwah, NJ: Lawrence Erlbaum.

Baker, C. 2006. *Foundations of Bilingual Education and Bilingualism, 4th Edition*. Clevedon, England: Multilingual Matters.

Balfanz, R., and N. Legters. 2004. *Locating the Dropout Crisis: Which High Schools Produce the Nation's Dropouts? Where Are They Located? Who Attends Them?* Baltimore, MD: Johns Hopkins University. www.jhu.edu/news_info/news/home04/jun04/promote.html.

Barwell, R. 2005. "Critical Issues for Language and Content in Mainstream Classrooms: Introduction." *Linguistics and Education* 16 (2): 143–50.

Batalova, J., M. Fix, and J. Murray. 2007. *Measures of Change: The Demography and Literacy of Adolescent English Learners*. Washington, DC: Migration Policy Institute. www.migrationpolicy.org/pubs/Measures_of_Change.pdf.

Beers, K. 2003. *When Kids Can't Read—What Teachers Can Do*. Portsmouth, NH: Heinemann.

Benítez, S. 1993. *A Place Where the Sea Remembers*. New York: Scribner.

———. 1997. *Bitter Grounds*. New York: Picador USA.

———. 2002. *The Weight of All Things*. New York: Hyperion.

Betances, S. 1986. "My People Made It Without Bilingual Education: What's Wrong with Your People?" *California School Boards Journal* 44:15–16.

Biber, D. 1986. "Spoken and Written Textual Dimensions in English: Resolving the Contradictory Findings." *Language* 62 (2): 384–414.

Biggs, A., C. Whitney, K. Cris, L. Lundgren, P. Rillero, K. Tallman, and D. Zile. 2004. *Biology: The Dynamics of Life*. New York: McGraw Hill.

Boehm, R. G. 2003. *World Geography*. New York: Glencoe McGraw-Hill.

Brook, D. 1998. *The Journey of English*. New York: Clarion Books.

Brown, D. 2009. *In Other Words: Grammar Lessons for Code-Switching, Composition, and Language Study*. Portsmouth, NH: Heinemann.

Brown, H., and B. Cambourne. 1987. *Read and Retell*. Portsmouth, NH: Heinemann Educational Books.

Brownsville Independent School District (BISD). 2008. *Facts and Statistics*. www.BISD.US/.

Brozo, W., G. Shiel, and K. Topping. 2007–2008. "Engagement in Reading: Lessons Learned from Three PISA Countries." *Journal of Adolescent and Adult Literacy* 51 (4): 304–17.

Bryson, B.1994. *Made in America: An Informal History of the English Language in the United States*. New York: HarperCollins.

California State Board of Education. 1997. *Content Standards and Frameworks*. Sacramento: California Department of Education.

Capps, R., M. Fix, J. Murray, J. Ost, J. Passel, and S. Herwantoro. 2005. *The New Demography of America's Schools: Immigration and the No Child Left Behind Act*, 1–41. Washington, DC: Urban Institute.

Carrier, K. 2005. "Key Issues for Teaching English Language Learners in Academic Classrooms." *Middle School Journal* 37 (2): 4–9.

Cazden, C. 2001. *Classroom Discourse: The Language of Teaching and Learning*. Portsmouth, NH: Heinemann.

Cohen, C., N. Deterding, and B. Clewell. 2005. *Who's Left Behind? Immigrant Children in High and Low LEP Schools*, 1–19. Washington, DC: Urban Institute.

Collier, V. 1989. "How Long? A Synthesis of Research on Academic Achievement in a Second Language." *TESOL Quarterly* 23 (3): 509–32.

Corson, D. 1997. "The Learning and Use of Academic English Words." *Language Learning* 47: 671–718.

Coxhead, A. 2000. "A New Academic Word List." *TESOL Quarterly* 34 (2): 213–38.

Crawford, J. 2004. *Educating English Learners*. Los Angeles: Bilingual Education Services.

———. 2007. *The Decline of Bilingual Education: How to Reverse a Troubling Trend?* http://ourworld.compuserve.com/homepages/JWCrawford/.

Cummins, J. 1981. "The Role of Primary Language Development in Promoting Educational Success for Language Minority Students." In *Schooling and Language Minority Students: A Theoretical Framework*, 3–49. Los Angeles: Evaluation, Dissemination and Assessment Center, California State University, Los Angeles.

———. 1984. *Bilingualism and Special Education: Issues in Assessment and Pedagogy*. Clevedon, England: Multilingual Matters.

———. 1994. "The Acquisition of English as a Second Language." In *Kids Come in All Languages: Reading Instruction for ESL Students*, ed. K. Spangenberg-Urbschat and R. Pritchard, 36–62. Newark, DE: International Reading Association.

———. 2000. *Language, Power and Pedagogy: Bilingual Children in the Crossfire*. Tonawanda, NY: Multilingual Matters.

———. 2001. *Negotiating Identities: Education for Empowerment in a Diverse Society*. 2d ed. Ontario: California Association of Bilingual Education.

———. 2008. "BICS and CALP: Empirical and Theoretical Status of the Distinction." In *Encyclopedia of Language and Education*, vol. 2, ed. N. Hornberger, 71–84. New York: Springer Science and Business Media.

Dale, T., and G. Cuevas. 1992. "Integrating Mathematics and Language Learning." In *The Multicultural Classroom: Readings for Content-Area Teachers*, ed. P. Richard-Amato and M. Snow, 330–48. White Plains, NY: Longman.

Daniels, H., and S. Zemelman. 2004. *Subjects Matter: Every Teacher's Guide to Content-Area Reading*. Portsmouth, NH: Heinemann.

Donley, K., and R. Reppen. 2001. "Using Corpus Tools to Highlight Academic Vocabulary in SCLT." *TESOL Journal* (Autumn): 7–12.

Dooling, D., and R. Lachman. 1971. "The Effects of Comprehension on Retention of Prose." *Journal of Experimental Psychology* 88 (2): 216–22.

Duke, N. 2003. "Informational Text? The Research Says, 'Yes!'" In *Exploring Informational Texts: From Theory to Practice*, ed. L. Hoyt, M. Mooney, and B. Parkes, 2–7. Portsmouth, NH: Heinemann.

Duke, N., V. Purcell-Gates, L. Hall, and C. Tower. 2007. "Authentic Literacy Activities for Developing Comprehension and Writing." *The Reading Teacher* 60 (4): 344–55.

Fang, Z. 2008. "Going Beyond the Fab Five: Helping Students Cope with the Unique Linguistic Challenges of Expository Reading in the Middle Grades." *Journal of Adolescent and Adult Literacy* 51 (6): 476–87.

Fathman, A., and D. Crowther, eds. 2006. *Science for English Language Learners: K–12 Classroom Strategies*. Arlington, VA: National Science Teachers Association Press.

Fisher, D., and N. Frey. 2008a. "What Does It Take to Create Skilled Readers? Facilitating the Transfer and Application of Literacy Strategies." *Voices from the Middle* 15 (4): 16–22.

———. 2008b. *Word Wise and Content Rich, Grades 7–12: Five Essential Steps to Teaching Academic Vocabulary*. Portsmouth, NH: Heinemann.

Fisher, D., N. Frey, and D. Lapp. 2008. "Shared Readings: Modeling Comprehension, Vocabulary, Text Structures, and Text Features for Older Readers." *The Reading Teacher* 61 (7): 548–56.

Fisher, D., C. Rothenberg, and N. Frey. 2007. *Language Learners in the English Classroom*. Urbana, IL: National Council of Teachers of English.

Fix, M., and R. Capps. 2005. *Immigrant Children, Urban Schools, and the No Child Left Behind Act*. Washington, DC: Migration Information Source.

Fleming, M. 2004. *César Chávez: The Farm Workers' Friend*. Barrington, IL: Rigby.

Freeman, A. 2000. Selection of Culturally Relevant Text. Unpublished manuscript. Tucson: University of Arizona.

Freeman, D., and Y. Freeman. 2001. *Between Worlds: Access to Second Language Acquisition*. 2d ed. Portsmouth, NH: Heinemann.

———. 2004. *Essential Linguistics: What You Need to Know to Teach Reading, ESL, Spelling, Phonics, and Grammar*. Portsmouth, NH: Heinemann.

———. 2007. *English Language Learners: The Essential Guide*. New York: Scholastic.

———. 2008. *Closing the Achievement Gap for English Language Learners*. Worthington, OH: Reading Recovery Council of America.

Freeman, Y., A. Freeman, and D. Freeman. 2003. "Home Run Books: Connecting Students to Culturally Relevant Texts." *NABE News* 26 (3): 5–8, 11–12.

Freeman, Y., and D. Freeman. 2002. *Closing the Achievement Gap: How to Reach Limited Formal Schooling and Long-Term English Learners*. Portsmouth, NH: Heinemann.

García, E. 2002. *Student Cultural Diversity: Understanding and Meeting the Challenge*. 3d ed. Boston: Houghton Mifflin.

García, G. 2000. *Lessons from Research: What Is the Length of Time It Takes Limited English Proficient Students to Acquire English and Succeed in an All-English Classroom?* Washington, DC: National Clearinghouse for Bilingual Education.

García, O., J. Kleifgen, and L. Falchi. 2008. *From English Language Learners to Emergent Bilinguals*. New York: Teachers College.

Gee, J. 1988. "Count Dracula, the Vampire Lestat, and TESOL." *TESOL Quarterly* 22 (2): 201–25.

———. 2008. *Social Linguistics and Literacies: Ideology in Discourses*. New York: Routledge.

Gibbons, P. 2002. *Scaffolding Language, Scaffolding Learning: Teaching Second Language Learners in the Mainstream Classroom*. Portsmouth, NH: Heinemann.

Goldenberg, C. 2008. "Teaching English Language Learners: What the Research Does—and Does Not—Say." *American Educator* (Summer): 8–44.

Gottlieb, M., L. Carnuccio, G. Ernst-Slavit, and A. Katz. 2006. *PreK–12 English Language Proficiency Standards*. Alexandria, VA: Teachers of English to Speakers of Other Languages (TESOL).

Graves, M. 2006. *The Vocabulary Book: Learning and Instruction*. New York: Teachers College Press.

Greene, J. 1998. *A Meta-Analysis of the Effectiveness of Bilingual Education*. Claremont, CA: Tomas Rivera Policy Institute.

Griswold del Castillo, R. 2002. *César Chávez: The Struggle for Justice/César Chávez: La lucha por justicia*. Houston: Piñata Books.

Guthrie, J. 2004. "Teaching for Literacy Engagement." *Journal of Literacy Research* 36 (1): 1–29.

Guthrie, J., and M. Davis. 2003. "Motivating Struggling Readers in Middle School Through an Engagement Model of Classroom Practice." *Reading and Writing Quarterly* 9: 59–85.

Gutiérrez, R. 2002. "Beyond Essentialism: The Complexity of Language in Teaching Mathematics to Latina/o Students." *American Educational Research Journal* 39 (4): 1047–88.

Hakuta, K., Y. Butler, D. Witt, et al. 2000. *How Long Does It Take English Learners to Attain Proficiency?* Santa Barbara: Linguistic Minority Research Institute, University of California.

Halliday, M., and R. Hassan. 1989. *Language, Context, and Text: Aspects of Language in a Socialsemiotic Perspective*. Oxford, England: Oxford University Press.

Harklau, L. 2003. *Generation 1.5 Students and College Writing*. ERIC Clearinghouse on Languages and Linguistics. Washington, DC: ERIC Digest. EDO-FL-03-05.

Heath, S. 1983. *Ways with Words: Language, Life, and Work in Communities and Classrooms*. Cambridge, England: Cambridge University Press.

Hopstock, P. and T. Stephenson. 2003. *Descriptive Study of Services to LEP Students and LEP Students with Disabilities: Special Topic Report 2*. Washington, DC: Office of English Language Acquisition (OELA).

Hymes, D. 1970. "On Communicative Competence." In *Directions in Sociolinguistics*, ed. J. Gumperz and D. Hymes, 35–71. New York: Holt, Rinehart and Winston.

Ivey, G., and K. Broaddus. 2007. "A Formative Experiment Investigating Literacy

Engagement Among Adolescent Latina/o Students Just Beginning to Read, Write, and Speak English." *Reading Research Quarterly* 42 (4): 512–45.

Jiménez, F. 1997. *The Circuit: Stories from the Life of a Migrant Child*. Albuquerque: University of New Mexico Press.

———. 2001. *Breaking Through*. Boston: Houghton Mifflin.

Jiménez, R. 2000. "Literacy and the Identity Development of Latina/o Students." *American Educational Research Journal* 37 (4): 971–1000.

———. 2005. *Moving Beyond the Obvious: Examining Our Thinking About Linguistically Diverse Students*. Naperville, IL: North Central Regional Educational Laboratory.

Jiménez, R., L. Handsfield, and D. Fisher. 2008. "Rethinking Cognitive Strategy Instruction and Multilingual Students: A Review and Critique." In *Studies in First and Second Language Reading Strategies*, ed. K. Moktari and R. Sheorey, 113–30. Norwood, MA: Christopher-Gordon.

Kilgallon, D., and J. Kilgallon. 2007. *Grammar for High School: A Sentence-Composing Approach*. Portsmouth, NH: Heinemann.

Krashen, S. 1998. "Teaching Grammar: Why Bother?" *California English* 3 (3): 8.

———. 1999. *Condemned Without a Trial: Bogus Arguments Against Bilingual Education*. Portsmouth, NH: Heinemann.

———. 2000. "What Does It Take to Acquire Language?" *ESL Magazine* 3 (3): 22–23.

———. 2001. "What Really Happened in California: Dropping Bilingual Education Did Not Increase Test Scores." Letter to the editor, *Portland Oregonian*, April 16, B2.

———. 2004a. *The Acquisition of Academic English by Children in Two-Way Programs: What Does the Research Say?* Albuquerque: National Association of Bilingual Education (NABE).

———. 2004b. *The Power of Reading: Insights from the Research*. Portsmouth, NH: Heinemann.

———. 2004–2005. "Proposition 227 and Skyrocketing Test Scores: An Urban Legend from California." *Educational Leadership* 62 (4): 37–39.

Krull, K. 2003. *Harvesting Hope: The Story of César Chávez*. San Diego: Harcourt.

Lee, O., and S. Fradd. 1998. "Science for All, Including Students from Non-English Backgrounds." *Educational Researcher* 27 (4): 12–21.

Lemke, J. 1990. *Talking Science: Language, Learning, and Values*. Norwood, NJ: Ablex/JAI.

Los Angeles Unified School District. 2002. *Academic English Mastery Program for Standard English Learner*. Los Angeles: LAUSD. www.learnmedia.com/aemp /AEMPBROCHURE.pdf.

Martinez, V. 1996. *Parrot in the Oven: Mi vida*. New York: HarperCollins.

Marzano, R. 2004. *Building Background Knowledge for Academic Achievement: Research on What Works in Schools*. Alexandria, VA: Association for Supervision and Curriculum Development.

Marzano, R., and D. Pickering. 2005. *Building Academic Vocabulary: Teacher's Manual*. Alexandria, VA: Association for Supervision and Curriculum Development.

Maxwell-Jolly, J., P. Gándara, and L. Benavídez. 2007. *Promoting Academic Literacy Among Secondary English Language Learners: A Synthesis of Research and Practice*. Davis: University of California Linguistic Minority Research Institute.

McLaughlin, C., M. Thompson, and D. Zike. 2002. *Integrated Physics and Chemistry*. Columbus, OH: Glencoe/McGraw-Hill.

McNeil, L., E. Coppola, and J. Radigan. 2008. "Avoidable Losses: High-Stakes Accountability and the Dropout Crisis." *Education Policy Analysis Archives* 16 (3): 1–45.

McWhorter, J. 2001. *The Power of Babel: A Natural History of Language*. New York: Times Books.

Meltzer, J., and E. Hamann. 2004. *Meeting the Literacy Development Needs of Adolescent English Language Learners Through Content Area Learning. Part 1: Focus on Motivation and Engagement*. Providence, RI: Education Alliance at Brown University. www.alliance.brown.edu/pubs/adlit/adell_litdv1.pdf.

———. 2005. *Meeting the Literacy Development Needs of Adolescent English Language Learners Through Content Area Learning. Part 2: Focus on Classroom Teaching and Learning Strategies*. Providence, RI: Education Alliance at Brown University. www.alliance.brown.edu/pubs/adlit/adell_litdv2.pdf.

Mohr, K., and E. Mohr. 2007. "Extending English-Language Learners' Classroom Interactions Using the Response Protocol." *The Reading Teacher* 60 (5): 440–50.

Morris, C. 1994. *César Chávez: Líder laboral*. Cleveland, OH: Modern Curriculum.

Murray, D. 1985. *A Writer Teaches Writing*. Boston: Houghton Mifflin.

Nagy, W., R. Anderson, and P. Herman. 1987. "Learning Word Meanings from Context During Normal Reading." *American Educational Research Journal* 24 (2): 237–70.

Noboa, J. 2006. *Leaving Latinos Out of History: Teaching U.S. History in Texas*. New York: Routledge.

Ogbu, J. 1991. "Immigrant and Involuntary Minorities in Comparative Perspective." In *Minority Status and Schooling: A Comparative Study of Immigrant and Involuntary Minorities*, ed. M. Gibson and J. Ogbu, 3–33. New York: Garland.

Ogbu, J., and M. Matute-Bianchi. 1986. "Understanding Sociocultural Factors: Knowledge, Identity and School Adjustment." In *Beyond Language: Social and Cultural Factors in Schooling Language Minority Students*, ed. D. Holt, 73–142. Los Angeles: Evaluation, Dissemination and Assessment Center, California State University, Los Angeles.

Pinker, S. 1994. *The Language Instinct: How the Mind Creates Language*. New York: William Morrow.

Public Education Information Management System (PEIMS). 2006. Disaggregation Reports for Region, Districts, and Campuses by School Year. Edinburg, TX: Region One Education Service Center.

Purcell-Gates, V., N. Duke, and J. Martineau. 2007. "Learning to Read and Write Genre-Specific Text: Roles of Authentic Experience and Explicit Teaching." *Reading Research Quarterly* 42 (1): 8–45.

Ramírez, J. 1991. *Final Report: Longitudinal Study of Structured English Immersion Strategy, Early-Exit and Late-Exit Bilingual Education Programs*. Washington, DC: U.S. Department of Education.

Rempel, L. 2004. *Hey, Hmong Girl, Whassup?* Saint Paul, MN: Hamline University Press.

Rodríguez, T. 2001. "From the Known to the Unknown: Using Cognates to Teach English to Spanish-Speaking Literates." *The Reading Teacher* 54 (8): 744–46.

Rolstad, K., K. Mahoney, and G. Glass. 2005. "A Meta-Analysis of Program Effectiveness Research on English Language Learners." *Educational Policy* 19 (4): 572–94.

Scarcella, R. 2003. *Accelerating Academic English: A Focus on the English Learner*. Irvine: University of California, Irvine.

Schleppergrell, M. 2004. *The Language of Schooling: A Functional Linguistics Perspective*. Mahwah, NJ: Lawrence Erlbaum.

Schleppegrell, M., and M. Achugar. 2003. "Learning Language and Learning History: A Functional Linguistics Approach." *TESOL Journal* 12 (2): 21–27.

Schleppegrell, M., and L. Oliveira. 2006. "An Integrated Language and Content Approach for History Teachers." *Journal of English for Academic Purposes* 5: 254–68.

Schlosser, E. 2001. *Fast Food Nation: The Dark Side of the All-American Meal*. New York: HarperCollins.

Short, D., and S. Fitzsimmons. 2007. *Double the Work: Challenges and Solutions to Acquiring Language and Academic Literacy for Adolescent English Language Learners—A Report to Carnegie Corporation of New York*. Washington, DC: Alliance for Excellent Education.

Short, K., J. Harste, and C. Burke. 1996. *Creating Classrooms for Authors and Inquirers*. Portsmouth, NH: Heinemann.

Skutnabb-Kangas, T. 1979. *Language in the Process of Cultural Assimilation and Structural Incorporation of Linguistic Minorities*. Washington, DC: National Clearinghouse for Bilingual Education.

Skutnabb-Kangas, T., and P. Toukomaa. 1976. *Teaching Migrant Children's Mother Tongue and Learning the Language of the Host Country in the Context of the Socio-*

cultural Situation of the Migrant Family. Helsinki: The Finnish National Commission for UNESCO.

Slavin, R., and A. Cheung. 2004. "Effective Reading Programs for English Language Learners: A Best-Evidence Synthesis." Report No. 66. Baltimore: Center for Research on the Education of Students Placed at Risk (CRESPAR)/Johns Hopkins University. http://www.csos.jhu.edu/crespar/techReports/Report66.pdf.

Slavit, D., and G. Ernst-Slavit. 2007. "Teaching Mathematics and English to English Language Learners Simultaneously." *Middle School Journal* 39 (2): 4–11.

Smith, F. 1983. *Essays into Literacy: Selected Papers and Some Afterthoughts.* Portsmouth, NH: Heinemann.

Snow, C., and M. Hoefnagel-Hohle. 1978. "The Critical Period for Language Acquisition: Evidence from Second Language Learning." *Child Development* 49 (4): 1114–28.

Soto, G. 1997. *Buried Onions.* San Diego: Harcourt Brace.

Swales, J. 2005. "Academically Speaking." *Language Magazine* 4 (8): 30–34.

Texas Education Agency (TEA). 1998. *Texas Essential Knowledge and Skills for Science.* Austin, TX: TEA.

Thomas, W., and V. Collier. 1997. *School Effectiveness for Language Minority Students.* Washington, DC: National Clearinghouse of Bilingual Education.

Thompson, D., and R. Rubenstein. 2000. "Learning Mathematics Vocabulary: Potential Pitfalls and Instructional Strategies." *Mathematics Teacher* 93 (7): 568–74.

Thúy, L. 2003. *The Gangster We Are All Looking For.* New York: Knopf.

Tompkins, G., and D. Yaden. 1986. *Answering Students' Questions About Words.* Urbana, IL: National Council of Teachers of English.

U.S. Congress. 2002. *No Child Left Behind Act of 2001.* Public Law 107–110. 107th Congress (January 8). *U.S. Statutes at Large* 115: 1425.

Valdés, G. 2001. *Learning and Not Learning English: Latino Students in American Schools.* New York: Teachers College Press.

Villaseñor, V. 1991. *Rain of Gold.* New York: Dell.

Vygotsky, L. 1962. *Thought and Language.* Cambridge, MA: MIT Press.

Weaver, C. 1996. *Teaching Grammar in Context.* Portsmouth, NH: Boynton/Cook.

———. 2002. *Reading Process and Practice.* Portsmouth, NH: Heinemann.

———. 2008. *Grammar to Enrich and Enhance Writing.* Portsmouth, NH: Heinemann.

Wells, G., and G. Chang-Wells. 1992. *Constructing Knowledge Together.* Portsmouth, NH: Heinemann.

Whitaker, S. 2008. *Word Play: Building Vocabulary Across Texts and Disciplines, Grades 6–12.* Portsmouth, NH: Heinemann.

White, T., J. Sowell, and A. Yanagihara. 1989. "Teaching Elementary Students to Use Word-Part Clues." *The Reading Teacher* 42 (4): 302–308.

Wiggins, G., and J. McTighe. 2005. *Understanding by Design*. Alexandria, VA: Association for Supervision and Curriculum Development.

Williams, J. 2001. "Classroom Conversations: Opportunities to Learn for ESL Students in Mainstream Classrooms." *The Reading Teacher* 54 (8): 750–57.

Willig, A. 1985. "A Meta-Analysis of Selected Studies on the Effectiveness of Bilingual Education." *Review of Educational Research* 55: 269–317.

Wong-Fillmore, L., and C. Snow. 1999. *What Educators—Especially Teachers—Need to Know About Language: The Bare Minimum*. Santa Barbara, CA: Language Minority Research Institute.

Zehler, A., H. Fleischman, P. Hopstock, T. Stephenson, M. Pendizick, and S. Sapru. 2003. *Descriptive Study of Services to LEP Students and LEP Students with Disabilities. Volume I: Research Report*. Washington, DC: Office of English Language Acquisition (OELA).

Zuckerbrod, N. 2007. "1 in 10 Schools Are 'Dropout Factories.'" Associated Press, October 30.

Index